From *Mankind* to Marlowe

From *Mankind* to Marlowe

GROWTH OF STRUCTURE IN THE
POPULAR DRAMA OF TUDOR ENGLAND

DAVID M. BEVINGTON

HARVARD UNIVERSITY PRESS
CAMBRIDGE, MASSACHUSETTS

Publication of this book has been aided
by a grant from the Ford Foundation.

Library of Congress Catalog Card Number 62–9424
Printed in the United States of America

For my wife, Peggy

Acknowledgments

Perhaps a scholar can claim only a remote and pallid kinship with the "mankind" hero of the morality play. Even so, I must, like Mankind or Everyman, give thanks for all those counselors who have compassionately watched my struggle toward an academic state of grace. Among my many teachers I am especially indebted to Professors Alfred Harbage and Bartlett Jere Whiting of Harvard University. Whatever I now know of late medieval and Renaissance drama I owe to their instruction and example. Many attitudes and conclusions contained in my study are properly theirs to an extent that can never be indicated by citation. In a different manner, but certainly to no less degree, I am grateful to my parents, both Professors of English at Duke University, who have read and reread this study with an eye to style and accuracy, and who have shared with me their faith in the vocation of teaching. Professors Gerald Bentley of Princeton University and Jonas Barish of the University of California at Berkeley read the manuscript as it neared completion, and rescued me from many errors of fact and judgment. I wish also to thank Professors Fredson Bowers and Lester Beaurline of the University of Virginia, Miss Kathleen Ahern and other editors of the Harvard University Press, and the library staffs at Harvard, Duke, and the University of Virginia. Most of all I must acknowledge the help of my wife, herself a teacher and loving taskmistress of English usage. Hers has been a service beyond the call of any duty, marital or otherwise. She has read and discussed with me all of the Tudor popular drama, and has painstakingly ameliorated the style of virtually every sentence in this book. Notwithstanding all this guidance, the ultimate assault on truth had to be mine; and I must finally confess, with Mankind, that any failures are plainly attributable to my own weak merit and not to a lack of merciful warning.

Two important studies of the Tudor stage have been published since I began this present investigation four years ago: T. W. Craik, *The Tudor Interlude* (Leicester, 1958) and Glynne Wickham, *Early English Stages 1300 to 1660,* Vol. 1 (London, 1959). I have endeavored in revising this study to incorporate their findings when applicable, to abbreviate or excise those parts of my work which they have discussed fully, and to acknowledge their research where it has anticipated my own conclusions. The overlapping has in fact been slight, for both studies deal with the stage whereas my concern is primarily with the popular drama and the evolution of its structure.

Charlottesville, Virginia
January 15, 1962

D. M. B.

Contents

I Introduction: From *Mankind* to Marlowe

Critical bias against the medieval heritage in Elizabethan drama dies slowly. Despite universal interest in the dramatic literature of Marlowe's and Shakespeare's day, scholarship has only belatedly recognized the validity of treating that drama as popular and national, deriving its themes and forms of expression to a considerable extent from its own native tradition. This pointed neglect has until recently been especially marked in appraising the Tudor morality play, in its function as inheritor and transmitter of the medieval heritage. J. A. Symonds' verdict, for example, is that the morality "can hardly be said to lie in the direct line of evolution between the Miracle and the legitimate Drama, but rather to be an abortive side-effort, which was destined to bear barren fruit." [1] Tucker Brooke speaks of the morality as the "moribund" carrier of an anemic stage convention, tedious, rambling, overly homiletic, out of contact with any semblance of a fashionable audience, and especially in its late phase abandoned to the talentless efforts of "unprogressive, leisurely poetasters," largely clerics. These were the symptoms of decay in late medieval drama, a process "of fatty degeneration which accompanied the loss of sinew and vitality." [2]

Distaste for this popular theater has led too frequently to overemphasis of classical rediscovery as the main line of development in English Renaissance drama: the humanist experiments of Medwall, Rastell, and Heywood, the early "regular" comedies of the schools and universities, and the erudite plays of the Inns of Court. The preconceived standard of classical scholarship, with its preference for intellect, philosophical probing, and the correspondences of the Aristotelian unities, measures literary progress in the sixteenth century only by the degree to which sophisticated learning freed English drama from the fetters of ignorance and bad taste. This literary preference leads to error when it confuses dramatic "cor-

rectness" with historical influence. Zealous claims for Nicholas
Udall endorse him as "the most representative" of English playwrights between John Heywood and the authors of *Gorboduc*.[3]
The anthology entitled *Representative English Comedies* contains
no example of indigenous moral drama before Kyd and Marlowe.[4]
In such usage the term "representative" loses all connotation of the
truly universal. It ignores the sole type of drama in Tudor England
that played to an entire nation rather than to a select group.

Despite recent efforts to dispel the fable that late medieval and
Tudor popular drama was the sterile product of "Monkish Dark-
ness,"[5] labels of crudity and ignorance still persist in the prevalent
attitude toward its structure. Even if this drama is granted to have
had comic vitality and color, its contributions to dramatic form are
still generally dismissed as nonexistent or as a distinct liability.
Popular and indigenous form has been made to appear "primitive"
in the worst sense — plotless, fragmented, and stereotyped. The
form of the morality has not been analyzed because it has not been
recognized as artistically significant. It is considered something that
merely happened, artless in the basic sense of containing no thought-
ful organizing principle of its own purpose. Hence it could provide
no sane alternative to the ancient Greek concept of form, transmitted
to the Renaissance by way of the Roman drama, which found a
unifying principle of relating all the parts of an artistic entity to its
whole. In particular, Senecan tragedy provided for the Renaissance
the new form, the new "regularity of structure — which, from all
appearances, it would have taken centuries for the mediaeval drama
to attain without the stimulus and authority of classical example."[6]
This contempt for a native principle of dramatic structure is most
evident in the frequently belabored quest for five-act structure in
late Elizabethan plays of the popular theater.[7]

Although it would be folly to deny the supreme accomplishment
of classical form and its influence upon the Renaissance, it is
necessary to guard against the obverse assumption that English
popular drama before it received classical guidance lacked a structure
of its own.[8] On the contrary, it is critically naive to assume that any
representation of experience abstracted by the human mind can exist
without organizing principle. Tudor popular dramatists had their
preconceptions of form, never fully stated or analyzed because theirs
was an unselfconscious art. Their method of construction was con-

ditioned by a mode of perception so unlike that of earlier or later civilizations that "classical" criteria cannot ordinarily be applied without distortion. The fallacy of enforcing classical precept upon late medieval structure is not so much the invidious comparison of greater and lesser as it is confusion of incommensurate qualities. One cannot account for these plays by aesthetic laws of unity, correspondence, subordination, and the like, because they were not composed with such ideas in mind. If some contemporary had had occasion to speak for the critically inarticulate authors of these plays, and had extracted a pattern or series of patterns from their work, he might have spoken quite differently of repetitive effect, multiplicity, episode, progressive theme. Since critical spokesmen of the Renaissance — Sidney, Gosson, Jonson — were largely hostile to the native tradition, the absence of any explanatory theory must be supplied by an examination of the plays themselves.

As Madeleine Doran has shown, a primary concept of medieval design was copiousness of detail; and the relationship of parts was a "multiple unity" wherein each member was to some extent self-sustaining and co-equal with the other members.[9] Subordination of one part to another was far less active a principle of perception than coordination. In drama as well as in graphic and plastic arts, the simultaneous presentation of separate scenes led to a panoramic, narrative, and sequential view of art rather than a dramatically concise and heightened climax of sudden revelation. The multiple staging of late medieval drama could find a direct corollary in paintings that united the beginning, progress, and end of man's spiritual history in a single panoramic continuum.

Circumscribed by these conditions, late medieval drama, including the Tudor morality play, had its own structural aims, problems, and potential solutions that bore no relation to "classical" principles. Chief among the problems was one of emphasis in a field of vision that provided little perspective or foreshortening. In its handling of plot, how was the drama to discover meaningful statement from a linear, episodic, and progressive sequence? The inherent danger was unselective choice of episode, allowing the individual members a chaotic freedom in seeking to exploit an entertaining routine for its purely risible or melodramatic effect. Medieval drama often was led astray by this temptation; nevertheless, progressive sequence was not in itself incapable of coherent effect. The ideal was organic totality in which each freely existing member contributed to the final design without surrendering its own sovereignty, and in which the connecting bond was an unfolding theme deriving its richness and variety from the contribution of each part. How successful were Tudor popular dramatists in achieving this ideal through the medium of practical theater?

Late medieval drama faced another structural problem in its tendency toward repetition of episode. The hazard was monotonous elaboration, but the potential reward was a mounting persuasiveness through varied restatement of basic truths. A third and related danger was that of creating a bizarre juxtaposition of comic and serious treatment in such a way that the comic "relief" would be no more than a digression. Again, the inclusive medieval point of view saw no virtue in eliminating one element or the other, and structural success must be measured not by the movement toward classical "purity" but by the integration of obverse and alternating textures into a single and yet multiform art.

The manner and extent to which the Tudor popular moralities inherited these problems from fifteenth-century drama, evolved pragmatic solutions, and transmitted their solutions to the later Renaissance theater are the subjects of this study. The employment of this medieval heritage in that later drama is too vast a topic for exhaustive analysis, but will be sampled with some care in Marlowe's plays written for the public theater.

The morality play, inasmuch as it was the dominant mode of popular dramatic expression for about a century, inevitably developed various forms to suit its perpetually changing environment. This study will endeavor to correct the common misapprehension that popular dramatic structure was a simple, constant entity, to which one might refer statically as "the Morality pattern." [10] It is erroneous, for example, to suppose that a single convention could account for Marlowe's indebtedness to the popular theater. The morality ingredient discernible in Marlowe's episodic plays leads to dissimilar results in the martial daring of Tamburlaine, the diablerie of Barabas, the political duel in *Edward II,* the spiritual conflict of Doctor Faustus. Other traditions found in Marlowe's reading were of course partly responsible for these differences. Nonetheless, the morality could provide more than one model for construction.

Because Renaissance critical theory ignored popular modes of dramatic construction, the method of this investigation must attempt to reconstruct the problem as it appeared to the dramatists, encompassing the practical materials with which they had to build and the limitations which they could not escape. Here, despite the lack of other information, the plays offer plentiful evidence of a structural dilemma peculiar to themselves. Tudor popular drama differed from other contemporary dramatic traditions not only in its widely national audience but in its severely limited number of professional itinerant players. The troupes, ordinarily containing from four to eight players, carried their entertainments to all parts of the kingdom, and the plays in their repertory had to be adapted carefully to limited resources in staging and casting. Often the players performed numerous roles. In *Cambises,* for example, six men and two boys performed thirty-eight roles. Clearly, such an arrangement required the author to write with his troupe continually in mind, to a degree that playwrights of other stages and in different times have been spared.[11] The Tudor popular dramatist was under constant pressure to prevent the meeting of characters whose parts were to be taken by a single actor; the introduction of new characters repeatedly necessitated the suppressing of old ones. The various methods by which the writers met this perplexing challenge unavoidably influenced the structure of all plays written for small troupes.

The primary documents in an investigation of popular structure are a group of approximately twenty plays, dating from the 1530's through the 1570's, which are "offered for acting," [12] that is, printed with casting lists to indicate how many actors are required to perform the play. Usually such casting lists demonstrate how the various parts are to be divided among the members.[13] *Cambises* again offers the best-known example of this phenomenon. Its title page indicates "the division of the parts" for eight players, assigning six parts each to players one and two, seven parts to player three, and so on. These lists were published primarily as doubling charts for the guidance of troupes wishing to produce the plays. Since the troupes tended to be of approximately the same size, the publisher could offer a play for acting to a large number of potential customers. The playwright thus wrote for a type of organization having a particular number and composition of talent, rather than for four to eight specific individuals.

As we shall see, these plays offered for acting constitute a considerable portion of the corpus of popular drama from *Mankind* to *Cambises*. Casting lists became a staple in plays published for use by the troupes, and the abundance of these lists is in itself an indication of the practical importance of casting and doubling in the creation of a native commercial theater. Fortunately, one can approach a large percentage of the plays in this period with a specific indication of the way in which the parts were doubled. This method, together with a consideration of the medieval ideal of panoramic inclusiveness that dictated the dramatists' concept of form, allows detailed observation of the playwright at work with a fundamental structural problem. The casting lists themselves are printed in the Appendix.

Such an approach calls first for the establishment of an accurate canon of the truly popular repertory. Most well-known plays of the Tudor era have been assigned to a particular stage tradition: *Gammer Gurton's Needle* to the universities, *Gorboduc* to the Inns of Court, *Endymion* to the boys' companies, and so on. In contrast to this reliable pattern, the identification of a listing for the popular stage is vague. *Mankind* is recognized as unquestionably popular, and *Cambises*—some eighty-five or more years later—is clearly an important link in the native tradition. But what of the interim? Which of the various plays not claimed by another tradition can safely be added to the canon of a genuinely national, popular, commercial drama?

Once a workable popular canon has been adduced, with a discussion of its vital differences in conditions of performance from those of the other dramatic traditions of the Tudor era, we will use the popular plays with casting lists to investigate in detail the composition of the troupes involved in producing these plays: the numbers of men and boys, methods of doubling, functions of the leading player, and the like. With this information as background it will then be possible to measure the effect of troupe structure upon the creation and development of a popular dramatic structure. Both the troupes and their plays will be followed in this manner through the period of Marlowe's dramatic activity, in order that the parallel connection in structure between his company and his plays may be observed in the historical context of the earlier popular dramatists. Such is the logic of beginning a study of dramatic structure with an investigation of the popular canon and the organization of personnel in the popular troupes.

II Criteria for a Popular Repertory

> Discuss unto me; art thou officer?
> Or art thou base, common, and popular?
> ——*Henry V*, IV, i.

In order to assemble a canon of popular professional drama, we must first define the criteria for selection. Our search is for a drama that strove through commercial presentation to win the favor of a genuinely national audience in England. Its members were professional in that they earned their regular livelihood, or a part of it, as players. The criterion of professionalism excludes popular drama of amateur auspices: the mysteries which lingered on sporadically into the sixteenth and seventeenth centuries, and the ageless folk "mummings" still extant in Thomas Hardy's Wessex. Neither played any influential part in the creation of the Renaissance theater.[1] The criterion of national audience, on the other hand, differentiates this commercial popular drama from the various others that played solely or primarily to courtly and sophisticated audiences.[2] The popular theater must be one that played to country as well as to town, to lower and middle classes as well as to the gentry, developing thereby a drama for many tastes and for a wide range of opinion on ethical, religious, and political questions. Such distinctions are needed if we are to find the professional precursors of Marlowe and Shakespeare. Their theater was a truly national one and might be expected to owe much to its own history as an institution.

One distinction invites others. The terms "interlude" and "morality" are frequently used in the nomenclature of pre-Shakespearean drama, especially popular drama. Historians have attempted with little success to make a clear division between the two labels. According to one view the moralities were those plays, exemplified by *Everyman,* which aimed at moral edification through the medium of allegory, whereas the interludes were the lively and realistic farces, exemplified by John Heywood's *Four PP,* which had freed themselves from allegorical abstraction and didactic aim.[3]

This suggested usage of "interlude" has not gained general acceptance, chiefly because it is manifestly at odds with late medieval and Tudor practices. Chambers and Gayley, for example, have shown that the term was applied without discrimination to every sort of drama known to the Middle Ages: to anecdotal farce (*Interludium de Clerico et Puella*) perhaps as early as 1300, to miracle plays in the fourteenth century, later to the most orthodox of moralities, and even to Plautine "regular" comedy.[4] Etymologically it is usually explained as a presentation between courses of a banquet or some such larger entertainment. Yet "interludes" were often presented under much more varied circumstances than those of a banquet, and Chambers conjectures that "an *interludium* is not a *ludus* in the intervals of something else, but a *ludus* carried on between (*inter*) two or more performers; in fact, a *ludus* in dialogue. The term would then apply primarily to any kind of dramatic performance whatever."[5] Chambers' derivation has not been universally accepted, but his emphasis on the widespread use of the term cannot be challenged. In such a context all of the plays considered in this study are certainly interludes, as indeed many of them declare on their title pages. The term so employed is intended to suggest nothing more specific than any sort of Tudor stage presentation; in short, a play.[6]

The term "morality" appears only seldom in Renaissance usage, but the phrases "moral play" and "moral interlude" are common in the plays themselves.[7] Such phrases signify a distinct genre of dramatic literature in the tradition of *The Castle of Perseverance* and *Mankind,* flourishing notably in the later fifteenth century and continuing strong into the early and middle years of the sixteenth century. The genre was characterized primarily by the use of allegory to convey a moral lesson about religious or civil conduct, presented through the medium of abstractions or representative social characters.[8] The most common plot of these moralities, retold in play after play, was that of an allegorical contest for the spiritual welfare of the mankind hero. Mankind's chief tempter, commonly called the Vice, attempted to turn him from good to evil. Other personages assisted the Vice in his task of perversion, or conversely defended the mankind hero against his spiritual enemies. This story of spiritual conflict, named the "Psychomachia" after an allegorical work of the fourth century by Prudentius, was the basis of nearly every morality play in the English drama. Its emphasis became increasingly secular in the mid-sixteenth century, preaching lessons of civil rather than religious conduct; in the later moralities, representative social types often outnumbered the more abstract personifications (such as Gluttony or God's Grace) of the earlier moralities. Nevertheless, the story remained one of allegorical conflict.

A late and transformed product of the moral tradition comprises a group of plays known as "hybrid moralities" or "hybrid plays," [9] not properly belonging to the canon of the orthodox morality because they deal with historical or romantic material and present as main characters specific personalities rather than types or abstractions. Exemplified by *Cambises,* these hybrids set abstractions and concrete figures side by side in the same play, and are of considerable importance to the development of the popular theater in its transition from the medieval drama of allegory to the later Renaissance drama of secular concern.

It is only because these moralities and hybrid moralities were generally the property of the popular stage, however, that they become material to the present discussion. The correspondence between the morality drama and the popular stage is striking. As will be shown, almost all pre-Marlovian plays of the sixteenth century which bear convincing evidence of popular commercial production are in fact moralities or hybrids. Nevertheless, the converse does not follow as a matter of course. It is misleading to describe the two traditions as mutually self-limiting. The vogue of the morality extended into other stage traditions such as the humanist drama or the boys' courtly drama. To deal historically with all the moralities is to ignore the advantages of a homogeneous stage tradition and its development as an institution. The morality is central to our purposes as the prevailing vehicle of expression in popular drama, but its own history outside such a drama has limited relevance here.

We are concerned with the origins not of the morality,[10] but of the professional theater. As background to a discussion of the popular repertory, the origins of the troupes may be summarized as follows. The first historical records of the profession in England date from the early fifteenth century. In 1427 "Interluders" appeared before Henry VI. At first the troupes seem to have been known primarily by the name of their leading actor or in association with certain communities, such as *"Jakke Travail et ses compaignons"* or the *"jeweis de Abyndon."* Many others took the name of noblemen or royalty, whose endorsement afforded them protection as they traveled: Richard Duke of Gloucester (later Richard III), the Earls of Essex, Oxford, Derby, Shrewsbury, and Lord Arundel.[11] Henry VII sponsored a troupe, "The Players of King's Interludes," who were entirely independent of the adult choristers in the royal chapel. These professional players were appointed for life, and were free to travel when not in demand at court festivities.[12] The number of such troupes grew so rapidly that by the beginning of the sixteenth century they had become a familiar sight and a primary means of public entertainment throughout the nation.

In their early composition these troupes were similar to the minstrel bands that they appear to have superseded in the public esteem.[13] There is little indication that the minstrels themselves turned to acting; on the contrary, they seem to have been hostile to their new competitors. Although the two sorts of bands remained distinct, the players evidently imitated the organization of the older group. Minstrels had found a place in royal and noble households by the time of Edward I. These bands consisted usually of three or four members performing upon the rebec, tabor, and lute. They traveled much of the time, for their household obligations occupied them only intermittently. When on the road they received protection from their patrons' letters of recommendation. Of course not all itinerant minstrels enjoyed this aristocratic patronage.

The minstrel repertory might consist of tumbling, sleight of hand, conjuring, marionette shows, animal imitations or actual display of performing animals, sword fights, parades, and the recitations of a poet, in addition to the staple fare of music.[14] It seems probable that they also performed dramatic farce. The remarkable *Interludium de Clerico et Puella* dates from the late thirteenth or early fourteenth century, and in its similarity to the English fabliau *Dame Siriz* may point to a lost tradition of burlesque theater which could have flourished in the heyday of the minstrels. A Wyclifite sermon, in contrasting the "pleyinge of myraclis" with the "pleyinge of other japis," suggests the existence of a nonreligious medieval drama.[15] Thus the minstrels were purveyors of two quite different kinds of entertainment: musical accompaniment for the singing and dancing festivities of their masters, and presentation of spectacle and mimetic performance before their masters or public audiences. Once these two kinds of entertainment became recognizably separate, the disintegration of these household entertainers into distinct groups of musicians and players was inevitable. This separation became a fact in the fifteenth century. By 1500 "minstrels" in the account roles had come to signify musicians. In referring to strolling players, on the other hand, the word "minstrels" gave way to *histriones* at Shrewsbury around 1480, and to *interludentes* at Winchester in 1466.[16]

Like the minstrels, the players traveled at first in groups of four or less, on foot, with packs or packhorses, and perhaps a wagon for the more prosperous. Later, the leading troupes could afford mounts. Whereas common or unlicensed players were accounted vagabonds and so handled,[17] those who wore noble livery enjoyed the prestige of such endorsement without lengthy commitments to their master's service. By the late fifteenth century the best of these players were sufficiently well-to-do to provoke comment upon the splendor of their dress.[18] Besides the occasional performance for their lord, they visited other patrician banqueting-halls, and performed in towns within the municipal buildings and on village greens. Often they presented the first show in a town before the mayor or bailiff and members of the council. Visits to London during the winter season became increasingly common in the sixteenth century, for participation in the court revels and performances in the inn-yards of the city. Even the provincial churches and churchyards were not excluded as impromptu theaters for the ubiquitous players, with the proceeds from the selling of ale going to church benefit.[19] At first the actors usually performed on a stage of trestles and barrels with a hanging backdrop for exits and entrances. Their scene was fluid and open, without stage properties to indicate setting.[20] Their playing area was a single *locus,* and they operated almost entirely without stage machinery. Such rigorous economy was necessary not only for mobility, but for keeping operating costs at a minimum. Payment came in the form of wages or local collections, out of which the players had to meet their own staging costs —unlike the purveyors of disguisings or pageants at court, who were fully subsidized for their elaborate decorations.[21]

These troupes may have included some disaffected minstrels, but they drew their players chiefly from the artisan class, many of them unemployed or displaced during the troubled years of the Wars of the Roses. Even the King's men included at various times a merchant tailor, a tailor, and a glazier.[22] Thus the association of tradesmen with the acting "quality," exemplified later by Marlowe, Shakespeare, James Burbage, Jonson, and others, was a tradition of long standing.

What dramas did these players perform? The historical documents that plentifully record their movements across the English countryside rarely mention the titles of their presentations, a fact which accounts for the difficulty in establishing a reliable canon for the popular stage. The type of play in which they excelled, however, was incontestably the morality or the Biblical redaction containing elements of moral allegory.[23] For example, the players who accompanied Princess Margaret to Scotland for the royal marriage in 1503 performed "a Moralite" after dinner.[24] The nature of such moralities, and their popularity with the English people, has been documented by one R. Willis, who late in life (1639) recalled a performance which he had seen as a boy in the 1560's or early 1570's. This passage from *Mount Tabor* evokes the response of a provincial audience to the brand of popular entertainment then in vogue:

In the City of *Gloucester* the manner is (as I think it is in other like corporations) that when Players of Enterludes come to towne, they first attend the Mayor to enforme him what noble-mans servants they are, and so to get license for their publike playing; and if the Mayor like the Actors, or would shew respect to their Lord and Master, he appoints them to play their first play before himselfe and the Aldermen and Common Counsell of the city; and that is called the Mayors play, where every one that will comes in without money, the Mayor giving the players a reward as hee thinks fit to shew respect unto them. At such a play, my father tooke me with him and made mee stand betweene his leggs, as he sate upon one of the benches where wee saw and heard very well. The play was called (the Cradle of security,) wherin 'was personated a King or some great Prince with his Courtiers of severall kinds, amongst which three Ladies were in speciall grace with him; and they keeping him in delights and pleasures, drew him from his graver Counsellors, hearing of Sermons, and listning to good counsell, and admonitions, that in the end they got him to lye downe in a cradle upon the stage, where these three Ladies joyning in a sweet song rocked him asleepe, that he snorted againe, and in the meane time closely conveyed under the cloaths where withall he was covered, a vizard like a swines snout upon his face, with three wire chaines fastned thereunto, the other end whereof being holden severally by those three Ladies, who fall to singing againe, and then discovered his face, that the spectators might see how they had transformed him, going on with their singing, whilst all this was acting, there came forth of another doore at the farthest end of the stage, two old men, the one in blew with a Serjeant at Armes; his mace on his shoulder, the other in red with a drawn sword in his hand, and leaning with the other hand upon the others shoulder, and so they two went along in a soft pace round about by the skirt of the Stage, till at last they came to the Cradle, when all the court was in greatest jollity, and then the foremost old man with his Mace stroke a fearfull blow upon the Cradle; whereat all the Courtiers with the three Ladies and the vizard all vanished; and the desolate Prince starting up bare faced, and finding himselfe thus sent for to judgement, made a lamentable complaint of his miserable case, and so was carried away by wicked spirits. This Prince did personate in the morall, the wicked of the world; the three Ladies, Pride, Covetousnesse, and Luxury, the two old men, the end of the world, and the last judgement. This sight tooke such impression in me, that when I came towards mans estate, it was as fresh in my memory, as if I had seen it newly acted.[25]

Here is a play performed by traveling interluders before the magistrates of Gloucester and any of its citizens who wished to attend. The players are "noble-mans servants," yet acting before a popular and diversified audience, performing for a fee from the Mayor and in earnest of a license for subsequent public demonstrations of their art. The staging area is simple, requiring only a raised platform and doors for access. Properties are also elementary, and yet handled with dramatic flair: a cradle, chains, a vizard "closely conveyed" under the cradle clothes. Willis especially notes the "sweet song" rendered with professional skill and the colorfully differentiated costumes. The substance of the drama is at once an edifying commentary on moral conduct and an entertaining action full of violence and "greatest jollity." The play is unfortunately lost, but Willis' account amply illustrates the reasons for its popular success.

Judging from internal evidence, the canon of this sort of drama begins with *Mankind,* written some time around 1471.[26] It is the first morality to bear unmistakable marks of commercial production. Halfway through the drama, Tityvillus, the Vice and chief attraction, entices the audience with some offstage shouts and explosions of powder, and then withholds his coveted appearance until his fellows in vice take up a collection. They make a plea for sizable donations from the "worschypfull souerence," but also indicate their willingness to accept smaller coins from the needy:

> *Now-a-days.* He [Tityvillus] louyth no grotes nor pens or to-pens,
>   Gyf ws rede reyallys yf ye wyll se hys abhomynabull presens.
> *New Gyse.* Not so! Ye that mow not pay the ton, pay the tother.
> [ll. 457–459] [27]

Once the collection is completed, Now-a-days calls in the fearful master of villainy and the play proceeds.

The audience plays a large part in the performance. Mercy addresses his prologue to "ye souerens that sytt, & ye brothern that stonde ryghte wppe [*sic*]" (l. 29), to those who pay for seats and the less well-to-do groundlings. References to a tapster and a hostler (ll. 722–725) and to "the goode-man of this house" (l. 460) point to the use of an inn-yard. The dialect of the play is that of the Eastern counties, and numerous local references in the text suggest Cambridge and Norfolk: for example, Bury, Walsingham, and Trumpington. This device may well have been a deliberate attempt to appeal to local interests, for the play appears to have traveled through this area. In fact, the distribution of place names in the text suggests that the players had two distinct districts, one centered about Cambridge and the other about King's Lynn, between which they may have toured by boat on the navigable waterways of Cam and Ouse.[28]

The close contact between players and audience is never relaxed. The Vice and his cohorts make jokes at the expense of their auditors, and exit with farewells to them. The epilogue is addressed to the "Wyrschep[f]yll sofereyns." [29] The actors shoulder their way through the spectators in making their entrances:

> Make rom, sers, for we haue be longe!   [l. 324]

They ask the audience at one point to join them in a "Crystemes songe":

> Now I prey all the yemandry that ys here
> To synge with ws with a mery chere.   [ll. 326–327]

The stage direction indicates that all sing, and the resulting chorus is one of the most remarkable passages of scatology ever printed. Throughout, the element of song is an important part of the dramatic impression, together with instrumental music and dance:

> Ande how, mynstrellys! pley the comyn trace.
> Ley on with thi bowys [bellows] tyll his bely breste.
>
> · · · · · · · · · · · · · · · · ·
>
> *Her thei daunce.*   [ll. 72–81]

The obscenity too is a staple of the comic appeal in *Mankind,* allied with routines of burlesque farce. Yet its colorful language is not extreme or degenerate, intended as it was for rural or village audiences who accepted frankness about natural processes, and who heard even in their sermons a vigorous and earthy manner of speech that would seem immodest today.[30] The plot is a moral one, presenting the original innocence of Mankind and his instruction by Mercy, then his temptation and fall into the wiles of Tityvillus, Now-a-days, New Gyse, and Nought, and his eventual recovery to spiritual grace. The emphasis in the action is on the comic degeneracy of his tempters and their plots to undo him. Tityvillus puts a board under Mankind's shovel to hinder his digging, steals the seed which he is preparing to plant, and when Mankind looks for his seed Tityvillus removes the shovel as well. Later Tityvillus and his fellows shorten Mankind's coat by degrees on the pretext of making it more fashionable, until the coat has almost disappeared. The scenes of Mankind's fall from grace are rife with humorous allusions to taverns, robbing of churches, the wiles of lascivious women, and jokes about hanging.

Yet the intention of the drama is basically serious. The comic depravity is presented in satiric terms,[31] and the recovery of Mankind to virtue is as necessary as it is inevitable. The drama appeals to sound moral instincts through comedy as well as through the didacticism of Mercy. The play was probably intended as a Shrovetide presentation, and the theme is appropriately that of a Lenten victory over licentiousness. The humor is the *exemplum* properly illustrating the allegorical content of Mercy's homilies, teaching Mankind through experience what Mercy has delivered to him in abstractions.[32] Clearly the play combines the attractions not only of the serious side of medieval drama but of its lighter side as found in the comedy of *The Second Shepherds' Play* or the amusing predicaments of Noah and his wife. The comedy stems, too, from the captivating stage spectacle of the minstrels and mimes, with their magical tricks, songs and dances, puppet-shows, and animal imitations. *Mankind* is a culmination of the most popular elements in the late medieval English stage. As such it appears to be more representative than the restrained *Everyman,* with its less typical plot of the coming of Death, its absence of burlesque comedy, and its textual affinity to continental drama.

The action of *Mankind* requires only a simple platform stage or playing arena with means of access, and an area, presumably backstage, from which noises such as Tityvillus' roars may be heard "within." Properties other than costumes are nearly nonexistent; the entire production is eminently transportable. Most important of all, it demands only six players. The size of the cast is severely limited, perhaps even cut, to conform with the size of the troupe.[33] Of the seven characters, Mercy and Tityvillus are so employed that they never meet. Presumably the leading player would have doubled in these two roles, thereby playing his own opposite in the struggle for Mankind's soul. That the doubling actually took place cannot be proved, but it has been generally assumed.[34] Doubling was common enough in later popular drama, and the Croxton *Play of the Sacrament* (usually dated shortly after 1461) offered twelve roles for nine actors during the period when *Mankind* was written.

The author of *Mankind* is unknown, but certain facts about him can be deduced from the text.[35] He was evidently acquainted with the manners and predilections of country folk in and around Cambridgeshire. He had some knowledge of Latin, and of legal terminology and court procedure. Indifferent to theology as a system, he still maintained a passionate and occasionally satiric attitude toward the Church, and combined with this satire a tendency to coarse humor. Although his sources are unknown, he was versed in the folk elements of the mumming play,[36] and was perhaps acquainted with such indigenous literary works as "Merci Passeth Rightwisnes" and *Piers Plowman.*[37] If he knew any classical literature he omitted any references to it in his play. From such a composite picture emerges the impression of a clergyman of modest training invested with a rural living near Cambridge.

Mankind thus epitomizes all the elements of popular drama for which we are seeking. It has a feasible cast for a strolling troupe, it probably employed doubling, it makes few demands of its easily improvised stage, and it uses only portable properties. It maintains a close and vigorous contact between player and spectator.[38] It is anonymous, but its author was a man of some small learning and ecclesiastical connection. Finally, it offered entertainment and instruction for financial reward to a diversified national audience who had learned to appreciate earthy humor and spectacle of song, dance, and slapstick violence in the context of a moral tale. Wherever all of these qualities, or a preponderance of them, are united in a single play, that play may be added to the canon of the popular theater from *Mankind* to *Cambises.*

Along with R. Willis' *Mount Tabor,* another important document of external evidence concerning the repertory of the popular players, and their mode of presentation, is to be found in the anonymous play *The Book of Sir Thomas More,* written around 1590. It contains a play within a play, enacted before More and his family on the occasion of a state supper given for "the Maior of London, and some Aldermen, / his Lady, and their wiues" (ll. 911–912). The actors, who are to provide entertainment before the banquet, are "My Lord Cardinalls players," and consist of four men and a boy. They are commissioned to play *The Marriage of Wit and Wisdom*:

Moore. how manie are ye?
Player. ffoure men and a boy Sir.
Moore. But one boy? then I see,
    ther's but fewe women in the play.
Player. Three my Lord: dame Science, Lady vanitie,
    and wisedome she her selfe
Moore. And one boy play them all? bir Lady, hees loden.

[ll. 931–937]

Here the players are few in number, itinerant, nobly sponsored, and dependent on doubling in order to perform more roles than they have personnel to fill singly. They perform for money, and manage their simple costume changes largely by means of exchangeable beards. The lack of a beard, in fact, precipitates a crisis that brings the witty More himself into the play as an impromptu performer. The impression is one of a playwright in the 1590's looking back on his professional ancestors with a certain amount of humorous condescension, portraying an average troupe of the early or middle century.

The dramatic repertory of these "Lord Cardinalls players" concerns us here. Although offered in this instance to an intellectual household, their repertory differs not a whit from the stock of available entertainments with which the same troupe would have toured the provinces:

> Moore. I pre thee tell me, what playes haue ye?
> Player. diuers my Lord: the Cradle of Securitie,
> hit nayle o'th head, impacient pouertie,
> the play of foure Pees, diues and Lazarus,
> Lustie Iuuentus, and the mariage of witt and wisedome.
> [ll. 918–922]

Here are seven plays which in the 1590's were evidently considered to be representative of the earlier popular canon. *The Cradle of Security* is lost, but Willis' account proves its moral and popular nature. Lost too are *Hit the Nail o' the Head,* surviving even as a title only in this reference, and *Dives and Lazarus,* which is mentioned also in Greene's *Groatsworth of Wit* and in the play *Histrio-mastix* (ca. 1599).[39] The proverbial title of the one and the Biblical title of the other suggest that they were not unlike many popular plays of their era, such as *The Tide Tarrieth No Man* and *The Life and Repentance of Mary Magdalen.*

Of the four surviving plays, one—*Four PP*—is the work of a humanist writer and a member by marriage of More's own family, John Heywood. The place in this repertory of the *Four PP* will be discussed shortly in connection with other works of the humanist school. The interesting fact that my Lord Cardinal's players are presenting a work by a member of the More circle before Thomas More himself may be coincidental, since it is unlikely that More's relations with Rastell and Heywood were widely known in the 1590's. The remaining three titles belong to a group of plays having the profoundest interest for this study: plays that are offered for acting to a specific size of professional troupe. All three contain on their title pages an indication of the number of players needed for performance. *Impatient Poverty* promises that "Foure men may well and easelye playe thys Interlude," and *Lusty Juventus* is likewise offered for four. *The Marriage of Wit and Wisdom* specifies "the deuision of the partes for six to playe this interlude." Of the three, only *Juventus* fails to elaborate on the exact method by which the parts are to be assigned among the various actors (see the Appendix for a reprint of these casting lists).

Since these plays are proffered as representative of the repertory of the popular troupes, a descriptive analysis of their characteristics may be added to that of *Mankind* to exemplify and broaden our definition of the type, and the criteria by which we may identify additional members of the canon. In *Impatient Poverty* (published in 1560, written perhaps in the 1540's or 1550's), the players refer to a "hall" as the place of entertainment ("Ioye and solace be in this hall," l. 242), which suggests either the kind of presentation found in *Sir Thomas More* or the burgess' hall of *The Cradle of Security*. The epilogue of the play addresses "soueraynes" and "thys noble audyence" (ll. 1070, 1077); on the other hand the Summoner enters with the customary and imperative "Rowme syrs auoydaunce" (l. 990), indicating a mixed audience such as would be found in the banqueting-halls of the great (with servingmen in attendance) or in *Mankind*'s inn-yard. "Soueraynes" and "noble" might be used to flatter the local dignitaries of a town as well as the truly aristocratic, just as Mercy in *Mankind* had addressed "ye souerens that sytt." The setting demands no more than a playing area with exits and a place for Misrule to sing "without comminge in" (l. 607), as in the case of Tityvillus. Costume changes take place before our eyes (ll. 218f, 685f, and 1056f), indicating the simplicity of such arrangements. The division of eight roles for four actors is eminently feasible. The play was published seemingly for the actors' market.

In substance, the play's appeal is broadly national. Its story of spiritual conflict subjects the protagonist, Impatient Poverty, to the familiar pattern of struggle between Peace and Conscience on the one hand and Envy, Abundance, and Misrule on the other. Edifying lectures are interspersed with scenes of comic degradation which run the gamut of burlesque: abusive language, profanity and scurrility, threats of hanging, fights on stage ("Here they fyght & ronne all out of the place," l. 861), references to cards, women, taverns, rioting, usury, bribery, the French, and the inevitable use of song and dance (1. 694). The play lacks division into acts and scenes, an invariable concomitant of the dramatic characteristics in which we are interested.

Lusty Juventus (1547–1553) addresses itself simply to the "people which be here present" (p. 99) and to the "good Christian audience" (p. 54), indicating general auspices for presentation. The actors feel free to jest with their audience: Juventus asks in his first soliloquy, "Is there any man here that will go to game? . . . Who knoweth where is e'er a minstrel?" (p. 47). Staging and costuming are elementary, and the title page offers nine roles for four actors, "taking such partes as they thinke best: so that any one take of those partes that be not in place at once." Although the doubling is not specified, the sound advice inculcated as to the principle of doubling has an unmistakable ring of common sense. Furthermore, the scheme of the play works easily for four players as promised. A telling note of professionalism is that all four actors are required to sing part-music (pp. 88–89). The songs are quite charming, and an important feature of the spectacle.

The offering combines entertainment and sober sermonizing. Good Counsel and Knowledge of God's Verity compete with Hypocrisy, Fellowship, and Abominable Living for our attention and for the moral welfare of Juventus. The humorous scenes capitalize on the comic consequences of Papistry, whoredom, villainous quarrels, and every aspect of abandoned virtue. Typical indecency is Hypocrisy's chortling commentary on Juventus' assignation with the slut called Abominable Living:

What a hurly-burly is here!
Smick smack, and all this gear!
You will to tick-tack, I fear,
If you had time:
Well, wanton, well;
I-wis, I can tell,
That such smock-smell
Will set your nose out of tune.   [p. 85]

It is broad enough, but the vice is never presented as anything but grotesque and damnable. Even in its amusing scenes the play is offering serious morality to a widespread audience.

The last of the three plays mentioned in *Sir Thomas More*, the manuscript *Marriage of Wit and Wisdom* (bearing the date 1570 or 1579),[40] is evidently a redaction of the "Wit and Science" theme which has survived in three sixteenth-century dramatic versions. The opportunity of comparing the three is a fortunate one, for it will make possible a contrast between popular and sophisticated versions of a similar plot and so provide a definition of some of the differences between the traditions. Probably the earliest (ca. 1530–1548) and best-known version is John Redford's *Wit and Science*, perhaps written for the boys of St. Paul's when Redford was Master there. Redford, an accomplished musician and playwright, followed a career not unlike that of John Heywood, with whom he may have been professionally associated.[41] Such a connection with the new humanist theater of the court and London suggests a refined purpose in the composition of this sprightly drama. Whether for St. Paul's or not, the play's text bears the unmistakable imprint of boy actors. Eight players appear on stage simultaneously at one point (ll. 935–968), and at the conclusion a sizable choir makes its appearance in addition to the actors who are still present:

> Heere cumth in fowre wyth violes and syng, "Remembre me," and at the last quere all make cur[t]sye, and so goe forth syngyng.

A mustering of such numbers was beyond the capacity of the early popular troupes.

The humor is lively and even buffoonish at times, but genteel when compared to *Mankind* and *Juventus*. The wit appeals primarily to the intellect, and the schoolboy touch is evident in the hilariously unsuccessful attempt to catechize Ignorance in the pronunciation of his own name. Although treated facetiously, the characterization of Experience as the parent of Science (Knowledge) indicates an affinity with the new learning in serious humanist drama.[42] The songs and dances, to the accompaniment of viols (see, for example, ll. 332f), are more graceful and masklike than are those of *Mankind*. The staging calls for a *domus* in the representation of the den of Tediousness, and of "That mowntayne before which they must assaye / . . . cald in Laten *Mons Pernassus*" (ll. 894–895). The presence of structural *loca* immediately renders the play unsuitable for a strolling troupe. There is no rubbing of shoulders with the audience. The epilogue merely wishes long life and the customary compliment "To our most noble Kyng and Quene in especiall, / To ther honorable Cowncell, and then to all the rest" (ll. 1049–1050).

The refining tendency of childrens' theater is even more marked in the printed *Marriage of Wit and Science,* composed some time before 1570. The cast calls for an inordinately high percentage of feminine or juvenile roles, such as could never be handled by an adult troupe. Recreation appears in "The Players' Names" with "three other women singers." Wit is referred to in the first scene as a "tender child, unripe and green for age" (p. 325), and Will informs Science that he is "Between eleven and twelve, madam, more or less" (p. 344). Some of the humor depends for its point on the youth of the speakers. Many of the characters are identified as women: Science, the heroine, Experience, her mother, Dame Nature, Recreation, and Idleness. All in all, in a cast of seventeen personages, only three—Reason, Tediousness, and Shame—are adult males. Accordingly, the play is delicate and elegant in tone throughout. It excels in repartee, and employs such figures of speech as stichomythia (see p. 344) and oxymoron:

I see her come, her sorrow and my joy,
My salve and yet my sore, my comfort and my care. [p. 358]

The principal piece of stage housing appears to be an elaborate and functional castle. From such evidence it seems likely that this play was the *Wit and Will* acted at court in 1567–1568.[43] The five-act structure and continental scene divisions are indicated in Latin, and the characters' names are grouped at the head of each scene. Stage directions are sparse. J. P. Collier bestows great praise on this play, and is especially pleased with the fact that "it is regularly divided into five acts, and each of the scenes is also marked."[44]

The manuscript *Marriage of Wit and Wisdom* is probably the work of a little-known writer named Francis Merbury. It is divided into ten scenes demarcated by a clear stage, but the rubric "The Second Act" placed at "The iiii. scena" scarcely constitutes a serious attempt to reconstruct classical form.[45] Perhaps the most fascinating inference to be drawn from this play is that the dramatist apparently felt it necessary to rewrite the "Wit and Science" plot for the conventions of the popular stage. Humanist programs of educational reform in the earlier version yield in the redaction to purely comic entertainment. The play is unquestionably broader than the other versions, a factor that has led MacKenzie to declare it "as bad a play as the other two are good. The first two are skillful allegories, dignified and pure in tone; the third, though it employs the same motive, is disconnected, and is varied with low comedy scenes of a grossness uncommon even in a Morality." [46]

The popular author has added some scenes of his own to the earlier plot, and these contain the most unrestrained elements in the new version. For example, when Idleness has duped Wit and stolen his purse, Idleness is himself beset by two thieves, Snatch and Catch. After much abusive obscenity they discover the purse. "Heere after thay haue scambled [*sic*] for the mony, they shall spet in the purse and giue it him againe." Lest their victim escape to report the theft, they debate whether it were best to "pull him vp by a rope" or to "rune his arse against the wall." Instead, they blindfold him with a sheet, and charge him to inform all strangers who may approach that he is going a-mumming. "Here thay rune one to one cornor of the stage, and the other to the other, and spake like cuntrymen, to begild him." Idleness falls into their trap, and calls out on the supposed rustics to help him against the robbers. Having proved him false to his instructions, Snatch and Catch beat Idleness mercilessly, warn him once more, and leave him to bemoan his fate (pp. 24–30).[47] Characteristic of the scene are its graphic stage directions and its attention to practical details of production; the manuscript reads like a prompt-copy for theatrical performance.[48] The song of the two thieves, also, contrasts in its earthiness with the refined lyrics of the boys' plays:

> We liue by spoyle, by spoyle, we moyle and toyle;
> Thus Snach and Catch doth keepe a coyle!
> And thus liue we, and thus liue we,
> By snatchin a catchin thus liue we.   [p. 25]

Yet the rude language and the boisterous humor both have their place in the moral statement of this mixed drama, as the author insists in his epilogue:

> For though the stile be rough,
>   And phryses found vnfit,
> Yet may you say vpon the hed
>   The very naile is hit!   [p. 63]

That the play is indisputably intended for actual performance by an adult troupe may be adduced from its casting list. It offers nineteen roles for six players, and a close examination of the play reveals that the plan works without a flaw. Such a feat must have required of the author a continual awareness of the practical limitations presented by the nature of his troupe. Stage properties, although numerous, are carefully selected to be readily obtainable or transportable: "a mirror, a sheet, a chair or two, a porridge pot, a table, a bauble, a purse, coins, a club, a stick, chains, a grated window (to denote a prison), a sword ('Perseuerance'), 'a peece of paper,' a letter, a rope, a basin of water, a mask or visor (to convert Irksomeness into a 'monstor'), a stilt (for Idleness), and 'a cloth vpon a stafe, like a rat catcher.' " [49] The play, then, is an adaptation of a boys' drama for a professional adult troupe. Both content and structure are altered accordingly. The spectators are referred to simply as "good audience" (p. 63), "my masters," or "this company," and as in other popular plays the actors joke freely with their countrymen:

IDLENESS [alone on stage]

A! sirra, my masters,
  How fare you at this blessed day?
What, I wen, all this compony
  Are come to se a play!
What lackest the, good fellow,
  Didest the nere se man before?
Here is a gasing!   [p. 12]

III Auspices for the Élite Drama

Before compiling a detailed list of popular professional dramas, we must pursue the comparative study begun with the three versions of "Wit and Science." To what extent may the characteristics of popular drama be determined by contrasting them with the staging methods and audiences of other Renaissance theatrical traditions, the school and university plays, boys' courtly drama, the humanist school, and Inns of Court drama? Is the distinction between "popular" and "élite" drama valid in tracing the history of this dramatic tradition?

The distinction should not be urged too far. "My Lord Cardinalls players" in *Sir Thomas More* were, after all, commissioned to perform popular moralities before a genteel audience. One of the good fortunes of Renaissance dramatic history is that the élite never lost contact with the native stage. Plays that toured the countryside appeared also at court. There was no "war of the theaters" in the earlier years of the sixteenth century. Nor did the writers of school or courtly plays reject the humor and freedom of indigenous drama, as seen in the rollicking audacity of *Gammer Gurton's Needle* or the deviations from classical precept noted by Sir Philip Sidney in *Gorboduc*. English drama was thereby less susceptible to the ingrown artificiality which afflicted the comparatively arid and imitative neoclassic theaters of France and Italy.[1] England's glory came ultimately from the fact that its courtly drama could borrow life and vitality from its humble brother, while the popular drama, never excluded from the indulgent and even affectionate attention of the court, grew into maturity instead of withering into impotence.

These factors notwithstanding, a distinction clearly did exist throughout the sixteenth century between a drama that appealed to the entire nation and a drama designed primarily for the intelligentsia and the well-to-do. The latter was inevitably more exclusive in its audience. Schoolboys performed as amateurs during the seasons of revels at their institutions. Chapel boys never traveled unless with the court, nor were the Gentlemen of the Chapel free to tour the realm as were their professional counterparts. The Inns of Court were deliberately selective in their audience. The humanist school usually, although not always, limited itself to an experimental, small-theater drama in London.

This tendency toward the separation of popular and élite was already apparent by the beginning of the sixteenth century. Following the pattern established in Henry VII's later years, Henry VIII seldom viewed the performance of entertainers not attached to his own household. During William Cornish's mastership of the Chapel children (1509–1523), for example, no outside actors appeared before the King.[2] Nor was the distinction a new one in the Tudor era. Wickham traces the tradition of an indoor coterie theater to the end of the fourteenth century, originating in the impulse toward social recreation for a small, patrician audience rather than the more universal theme of worship in the public mystery plays.[3] From such elements as the tournament, royal entry, minstrel diversion, folk mumming, and amateur singing and dancing, arose an elaborate and costly medium of indoor entertainment unsuited in theme and staging for a national, popular drama. Highly decorative stage housing, machinery, and scenic effects manifested themselves in the coterie theater much earlier than has been supposed until recently. As long as the commercial players remained itinerant and popularly supported, the use of lath-and-canvas houses, street scenes in perspective, richly instrumented music, and the like, was destined to remain the exclusive privilege of court and noble household, college and Inns of Court.[4]

The two examples of boys' courtly drama already discussed, *Wit and Science* and *The Marriage of Wit and Science*, illustrate the fallacy of assigning the morality to any single stage tradition. Despite the usual tendency to ascribe all moral plays to the native theater, numerous sixteenth-century moralities are distinctly non-popular, and must be examined to determine the nature of their unsuitability for the popular stage. One such morality is *Respublica*, acted at the Christmas season in 1553. Its title celebrates "the first yeare of the moost prosperous Reigne of our moste gracious

Soverainge, Quene Marye the first," and the play presents in allegorical guise the Catholic view of England's religious struggle. The
Prologue speaks in behalf of "we children" who are to perform to
"youe olde folke"; he also refers to the auditory as "all this noble
presence heare." It is a boys' play at court, written for a special
occasion, in all probability by Nicholas Udall, who was a special
favorite of the Queen and was given a free hand to purvey splendid
entertainments for her entourage.[5]

Like *The Marriage of Wit and Science, Respublica* offers a
correct five-act structure and continental scene divisions indicated
in Latin. The plot is based on the Psychomachia, the theme of
spiritual conflict found in *Mankind*, but offers little stage action or
humor. The ideological combats are verbal. Horseplay and scatology
are conspicuously absent. The stage directions, in Latin, are sparse
and describe almost no movement; the most vivid is an *"exeant
currentes"* (l. 950). The play depends little on stage business for
its effect. Contemporary documents of Mary's household budget
suggest that the costuming would have been highly elaborate.[6]

In casting, *Respublica* reveals a fundamental divergence from
popular method. All of its eleven characters, excepting only the
Prologue, appear on stage simultaneously in the final scene, and
sing as a choir as they exit. Five of these eleven are female roles,
including the title figure: Respublica, Mercy, Truth, Justice, and
Peace. In addition, "Nymphes" are called for in unspecified numbers as extras (l. 1483), and used perhaps to swell the singing
choir. The total number, and the high percentage of female parts,
are far more than the adult troupes could have handled without
opportunity for doubling.[7] The significance of the lack of doubling
in these courtly moralities will become obvious in later chapters
that discuss the important effect of the doubling pattern upon the
structure of popular drama. Moralities like *Respublica* obviously
have no place in the development of such a structure.

The size of the companies inherent in each of the various stage
traditions, then, is a central factor in determining the auspices of
these early plays. In 1526 the membership of the royal chapel was
fixed by Henry VIII at twelve children;[8] also, for court performances the Gentlemen of the Chapel were at hand, twenty-four to
thirty-eight in number. The gentlemen were often paid for playing
in the season of revels, and at times some of them evidently ap-

peared in the childrens' plays.[9] They were accomplished musicians
— probably all could play the organ — and may well have provided
musical accompaniment for the boys even when they did not act
in the boys' interludes.[10] St. Paul's choir had ten boys, and their
number could be supplemented by probationers or by the grammar
school. On one occasion, in November 1527, Master John Right-
wise was able to muster approximately forty boys for his Latin
morality, presented at Greenwich before Henry VIII and the
French ambassadors.[11]

The relatively large numbers of players, and the consequent
freedom from doubling, are evident in virtually every children's
play. In the morality *Liberality and Prodigality*, for example, "playd
before her Maiestie" probably in 1567-1568 during the Christmas
revels,[12] "all come down before the Queen" in the final scene,
when there are as many as nine to thirteen actors on stage. The
prologue declares the players to be of "childish years," and consequently boasts that the play contains no scurrility to please "the
baser sort." The play is divided into five acts. The production is
extravagant by popular standards: extras are called for with abandon, and the staging requires a "stately sumptuous throne" for
Lady Fortune (I, i), a "homely bower" for Lady Virtue (I, iii), a
"chariot drawn with Kings" (I, vi), and a scaling operation involving walls, window, and ladder (IV, iv). The play's theme is
subtly political. It probably contained a polite hint to Elizabeth
concerning the virtue of generosity in rewarding faithful subjects.
It urged her to follow a course of moderation between the extremes of Prodigality (excessive spending) and Tenacity (the
niggardliness for which Elizabeth was frequently criticized).[13]

The Stationer's Register entry for *Disobedient Child* (dated
1569) describes the play as "an enterlude for boyes to handle & to
passe tyme at christinmas." Its title page ascribes the work to a
university man, Thomas Ingelend, "late Student in Cambridge."
Although it borrows figures from the moralities like Satan, who
enters roaring "Ho, ho, ho, what a fellow am I!" (p. 307), its
tone is moderate and restrained. Like many other boys' plays its
plot is based upon the "prodigal son" theme of Ravisius Textor.[14]
In the final scene the entire cast gathers on stage with the Perorator
of the epilogue to pay tribute to the Queen, who is present: "Here
the rest of the Players come in, and kneel down all together, each

of them saying one of these verses" (p. 319). The reference to the
"Players" does not rule out the possibility of doubling,[15] but there
would have been no need for it in a boys' company of ten or
twelve. The interesting point is the tendency of writers for the
boys to provide "curtain calls" for their young actors, in order to
unify the dramatic impression with a final collective epilogue
and song.

The closing prayer for the Queen in *Jacob and Esau* (S.R. 1557–
1558) similarly calls for the appearance of all of the cast: "Then
entereth the Poet, and the rest stand still till he have done. . . .
All the rest of the actors answer, Amen." The presence of the
poet suggests the chapel-master, perhaps William Hunnis or
Nicholas Udall.[16] The title page lists "The parts and names of
the players," numbering them from one to eleven. Indication of
doubling is specifically omitted, and seems to have been foreign to
the design of the work. In any event the grouping of the characters
would permit the doubling of only two persons, Isaac's neighbors
Hanan and Zethar, who disappear after an early scene.[17] Three of
the eleven roles are for women and one is for "a little boy," Mido;
the other parts for youths or old men are entirely within the
capabilities of a children's company. The production makes an
interesting attempt at "period" costuming. The characters "are to
be considered to be Hebrews, and so should be apparelled with
attire." In staging, Issac's "tent" requires the construction of a
practical *domus*.[18] The play has been much admired as an early
"regular" comedy, Latin in structure, and "permeated with quiet
humour, that never approaches either coarseness or profanity." [19]
The refined quality of the wit in the speeches of Mido and the
"wench" Abra anticipates the pert verbal combat of Lyly's diminu-
tive pages and maids-in-waiting in *Endymion*.

Another Biblical play containing morality elements, *Godly
Queen Hester* (printed in 1561), bears evidence of production in
the royal chapel. The staging calls for the use of a "travers," or
curtained recess, from which King Assuerus emerges and through
which he departs, unlike the rest of the actors who seemingly enter
and exit by regular means. For example, "Here the kynge entryth
the trauers & aman goeth out" (ll. 140–141). Chambers notes a
similar and historical use of "her Majestes Travess" at the Easter
Communion of 1593 in the royal chapel. This "travess," or "travers,"

was evidently a private pew or compartment, screened off from view, into which Elizabeth retired when not involved in the Offertory or the taking of Communion.[20] Several passages in the play suggest a similar use of this recessed area for King Assuerus, enabling him to retire from view for meditation. At one point Hester orders an attendant to

> Call in the chapell to the intent they maye
> Syng some holy himpne to spede vs this day,   [ll. 860–861]

following which the stage direction indicates, "than the chappell do singe." Thereupon the King emerges saying

> After this prayer and our former abstynens
> To the good Lorde I call for cumforte.   [ll. 862–863]

It seems likely that the play was actually produced in the chapel by the chapel choir, using for its stage the same structures employed in religious ceremony.

Casting requirements are large, and the demand for extras is heavy and vaguely specified: "many men" (ll. 130–131), "manye maydens" (l. 188). The final scene calls for approximately ten characters in addition to the chapel choir, and probably servants for the banquet. In content the play appears to be a sophisticated political allegory of the career of Wolsey. Its message is intended for the heads of state, as in the case of *Gorboduc*. Stylistically the play abounds in mental gymnastics and rhetoric, such as the debate "whiche is most worthy honoure to attayne," or Hester's lengthy oration on the duties of a queen.[21] The populace is spoken of as a collective third person. Violence is banished from the stage: Aman is led off to be executed, and his death is reported by Arbona.

At some places the stage directions are curiously literary, intended for the reader rather than the producer. For example, at line 141 "Here entreth Mardocheus and a maiden with him." This maiden is revealed in due course to be Hester, but the withholding of this information at the start is literary suspense and, in terms of practical staging, mere confusion. A similar instance occurs in the first appearance of Aman, who is originally labeled simply as one of three unnamed gentlemen waiting on the King (ll. 14f).

Many other examples of boys' courtly theater could be cited, such as *Nice Wanton*, the Plautine *Jack Juggler*,[22] *Tom Tyler and*

His Wife, and the works of Richard Edwards and John Lyly. Because this survey is intended, however, as a selective and composite portrait of nonpopular elements in élite drama, one further illustration of a boys' play will suffice. *Appius and Virginia* (S.R. 1567–1568) is the work of one "R.B.," possibly Richard Bowers, who was Richard Edwards' predecessor as Master of the chapel children from 1545 to 1561. The cast includes a large number of women's parts: Mater, Virginia, Mansipula, and "we Ladies three" in the final scene, Fame, Doctrina, and Memory. The play is partly a morality and yet is classical in tone. It opens with ten lines of Latin elegiacs, and the range of mythological reference is considerable, with allusions to Diana, Actaeon, Nisus, Apelles, Pygmalion, Orpheus, and many others. The play glorifies chastity and is offered as an edifying spectacle to be imitated by the "deare dames" and "Virgins you, oh Ladies faire" (ll. 24, 28) in the courtly audience. Virginia disclaims any interest in marriage, for she is by her truest nature in love with Diana's gift. Throughout its course the play anticipates Lyly's preoccupation with bloodless and "platonic" love relationships. Even the lustful Appius alludes in his perverse intent to one of mythology's most curious unions:

> Oh that Virginia were in case as somtime Salmasis,
> And in Hermafroditus steede, my selfe might seeke my blisse.
>
> [ll. 427–428]

The comic element of the moralities, though present, is subdued. Haphazard's language is notably chaste for a vice character. The play deals in the materials of the English literary tradition, for the plot source in Livy had appeared in Chaucer's "Physician's Tale" and Gower's *Confessio Amantis* (vii, 5131f). The legend and the elements of moral drama, however, have been deliberately refined for the delicate taste of the court and its virgin queen.

Dramas of the schools and universities tend to similar elaboration in casting and stage design, even when consciously borrowing popular conventions. It is often observed in *Ralph Roister Doister* that the "parasite," Matthew Merrygreek, embodies more than a touch of the old Vice, and that the play combines with its five-act structure and unities of time and place a spirit of English humor that is genuine. It contains a mock battle of remarkable vigor and heartiness. Its allusions reflect schoolboyish delight not only in the names of classical and Biblical antiquity, but of the medieval heritage of romance: Launcelot, Guy of Warwick, Hercules, Hector, Goliath, Samson, Colbrand, Brute, Alexander, and Charlemagne (I, ii, 118–125). At the same time this abundance of mirth is avowedly more decorous than that to be found on the popular stage:

> Wherein all scurrility we utterly refuse,
> Avoiding such mirth wherein is abuse.
>
> .   .   .   .
>
> Mirth is to be used both of more and less,
> Being mixed with virtue in decent comeliness.   [Prologue, ll. 4–12]

The play has been variously assigned to the period of Udall's mastership at Eton (1534–1541), at Westminster (1553–1556), or to his service at Queen Mary's court.[23] Whether for court or for school, the humor depends less on burlesque action than on situation and witty dialogue, such as the cleverly ill-pointed letter with its emphasis on verbal dexterity. The parodies of the church service are in accord with the English school tradition of the boy bishop and the reign of misrule during the Christmas season.[24]

In casting, *Roister Doister* reveals a characteristic divergence from the popular stage. Of its thirteen named characters four are female and two more are boys (Dobinet Doughty and Tom Truepenny). In the battle scene (IV, viii) ten persons appear on stage simultaneously, plus "two Drums with their ensigns." For a Christmas production at school, doubling would be the writer's least concern. On the contrary, he usually had the obligation to include as many would-be participants as possible, swelling the number of players with walk-on parts such as drummers and ensign-bearers for less gifted Thespians.

Gammer Gurton's Needle (S.R. 1563), "Played on Stage Not Long Ago in Christ's College in Cambridge," also combines sophistications such as entr'act music and the Italianate setting of two houses on a street, with the slapstick farce of vice comedy. The language is at times richly profane, reaching heights of invective undreamed of by contemporary popular authors. The play is a college-man's indulgent laugh at unlearned country folk, and the parody is hyperbolic even in its name calling and abuse. For example, the following epithets and more all appear in the first fifty lines of III, iii: doting drab, old witch, old gib, ramp, rig, arrant witch, bawdy bitch, rakes, scald, jakes, glutton, drunken beast, thief, knave, old whore, scald callet, hoddypeak, dastard, sluttish toy, sir loose-breech, losel, and old tarleather. Such virtuosity of vituperation is not to be met in the truly popular drama before Shakespeare; here it has the exaggerated aspect of caricature. Of the play's ten roles, four are female and one a boy.

In neither of these two well-known plays can it be proved by internal evidence that some doubling was not employed, but the existence of a casting list for Thomas Legge's Latin *Richardus Tertius* (1580) confirms the natural impression that doubling of parts would be foreign to the nature of an amateur academic undertaking. It was written to be played at St. John's, Cambridge, by a scholar who later became vice-chancellor of the University.[25] The play consists of three parts, each subdivided into five acts. The parts are each prefaced by an arrangement of the cast for the original performance:

D. SHEPHARD, Elizabetha Regina.
Mr. FOX, Cardinalis, Archiepis: Cantu:
Mr. WHALEY, Nuntius.
L. W. HOWARD, Eduardus Rex quindecem annorum,

continuing thus through twenty-five names. In the last part, the three appearances of a Nuntius are assigned to three separate players, who take no other roles. Only a few mute extras are doubled. The play calls for a procession involving Choristers, Singing Men, Prebendaries, and Citizens, suggesting the almost unlimited number of participants available. Robert Burton's *Philosophaster,* written in 1606, revised, and finally acted in 1617 by the students of Christ's Church, Oxford, provides a similar *"Actorum Nomina"* involving twenty-seven players and no doubling.[26]

School productions inclined toward extravagance in spectacle as well as in casting. Such a performance was Richard Edwards' *Palamon and Arcite*, presented in 1566 before the Queen at Christ Church Hall, Oxford. It lasted two days. The first part ended with a much admired hunting scene in which boys, standing in the windows, shouted at the cry of hounds in the quadrangle below. On the second day a noble display was made in the lists. Other features included three altars and a splendid funeral. Spectators crowded into the hall, and the Queen was pleased. According to Anthony à Wood, "they were all Scholars that acted." Edwards spent two months at Oxford completing the play and supervising the preparation of the stage setting, which was unusually elaborate.[27]

Splendor of costuming and visual display in university drama appears in a revels of the early Jacobean period, pointing to a tradition of some antiquity. *The Christmas Prince*, held at St. John's, Oxford, in 1607–1608, consists of a series of entertainments, one of which is entitled "Times Complaint" and involves a mammoth costumed procession:

Enter first six Knighte Marsalls men in sutable liueries with links and truncheons two by two . . . After these fower Knightes in rich apparell with hats and feathers, rapiers and daggers bootes and spurres, euerie one his Lackie attending one him with torch-lighte all two by two,

and so on, ending finally with twenty of the guard. The total scene requires at least seventy-eight persons, besides musicians. Their entry is accompanied by a volley of fifty or sixty guns. All of this, and more, cost the student producers £64 5s. and obliged them "to cast about for more mony," by seeking subscriptions and finally levying a toll on the rest of the college.[28]

On occasion, school plays became a public event of some magnitude. Thomas Ashton, Master at Shrewsbury in 1560 and afterwards, produced *The Passion of Christ* in a quarry where the performance of a "mystery" had been an annual event. According to Thomas Churchyard, the seating capacity was large. He speaks of "twentie thousand men" as the number who might have beheld "Astons play." [29] Earlier, in 1538, Ralph Radcliffe set up a school in the dissolved Carmelite Priory of Hitchin, Hertfordshire, where he yearly presented a play. John Bale, who visited Hitchin and was favorably impressed, lists the following subjects in his *Catalogus*: Patient Griseldis, Susanna and the Elders, Lazarus and Dives, the Courage of Judith, the Afflictions of Job, the Condemnation of John Huss, and others.[30]

Inns of Court productions also tended to be lavish. Patronized chiefly by families of high rank, the inns were more closely connected with the court than were the universities. As a contribution to the revels, the various inns (especially Gray's and the Inner

Temple) presented a sport each year at Christmas and Shrovetide in friendly rivalry with each other.[31] *The Tragedy of Gorboduc* was written by Thomas Norton and Thomas Sackville as "furniture of part of the grand Christmas in the Inner Temple," and was presented accordingly before the Queen in Her Highness' court on January 18, 1562. Despite its freedom with unities of time and place, it is classically regular. It contains a five-act structure, uses chorus and nuntius, and banishes violence from the stage. Its message concerns the rulers of the state, and was written primarily to warn them — and Elizabeth most of all — of the dangers of civil strife attendant upon an unsettled succession to the throne.[32]

A contemporary account of the first performance describes it as

A play in the quen hall at Westmynster by the gentyll-men of the Tempull, and after a grett maske, for ther was a grett skaffold in the hall, with grett tryhumpe as has bene sene; and the morow after the skaffold was taken done.[33]

This extravagant production was for a single performance. The play was never intended for continued presentation before varying audiences in the manner of popular drama, which must rely on repetition for economic success. Thomas Norton is on record as being opposed to the existence of the public stage (1574), advocating "that unnecessarie and scarslie honeste resorts to plaies, to shewes . . . [etc.] maye be avoided." [34] Seneca was a model for this attitude of indifference toward the vulgar exigencies of repertory staging and audience. Many Elizabethan translations of Seneca and of other classical dramatists were never intended for acting at all.

The first performance of *Gorboduc* was memorable enough to require no repetition. All costumes, especially those of the dumb shows, must have been costly for single performance. The Furies are "clad in black garments sprinkled with blood and flames, their bodies girt with snakes, their heads spread with serpents instead of hair," and so on. The extravagance in personnel is no less pronounced. The dumb shows require a separate cast of at least nine players, perhaps more; four men form the permanent chorus; and the play itself, even if doubling were used, demands a minimum of eight players. All told, the apparent minimum is twenty-one. In addition the entr'act music requires a new set of instruments for each act: violins, cornets, flutes, hautboys, and drums with flutes. The entire pattern indicates a concern for lavish display rather than for economy.

Once the performance had taken place, *Gorboduc* continued to fulfill its function of teaching a political lesson — but as a work of literature rather than of repertory theater. Undoubtedly it circulated among the courtly group in manuscript before a pirated edition required publication of the authorized text. As neo-Senecan drama for the "closet," it could operate effectively through the written word. The play lacks stage action, the stage directions are sparse, the speeches are long, the debates involved in political theory. The choruses are more comprehensible on the printed page. The directions for the dumb-shows are primarily literary. Before the first act, for example, six wild men come on stage and are unable to break a bundle of fagots which are tied securely together, but easily break the individual sticks when they are separated from each other. Whereas a theatrical audience would be left in suspense at this point, the author gratifies his courtly reading audience with a key: "Hereby was signified that a state knit in unity doth continue strong against all force," and so on. The use of the past tense in these descriptions suggests literary intent rather than dramaturgic instruction to actors. The play as theater is already a part of history.

Not all productions by the Inns of Court were as lavish as *Gorboduc*. Gascoigne's *Supposes* is certainly more practicable as theater. Even this comedy, however, ends on a note that looks back from the literary printed text to the ephemeral phenomenon of a performance: *"Et plauserunt."* The text also contains marginal glosses, calling attention to the various "supposes." The actors, instead of moralizing to the audience directly as popular players were wont to do, pretend that no audience exists. Balia opens the play with "Here is nobody. Come forth, Polynesta." Both *Jocasta* and *The Misfortunes of Arthur* contain elaborate dumb-shows as in *Gorboduc*, described in the past tense, with literary explanation of the allegory introduced by such phrases as "representing unto us . . . ." *Jocasta* goes beyond *Gorboduc* in its demand for actors: *Jocasta* has twelve gentlemen and eight gentlewomen attending her, Antigone has three gentlemen and her governor, Eteocles has twenty gentlemen in armor and two pages, Creon four gentlemen, and the Priest sixteen "bacchanals."[35] *Gismond of Salerne* calls for stage machinery in its first scene when Cupid comes out of the heavens in a cradle of flowers. It is noteworthy that *The Misfortunes of Arthur* was written twenty-five years after *Gorboduc* without making any significant improvement in the type. It is again in the "Mirror for Magistrates" tradition, setting forth in allegorical guise the political arguments for the execution of Mary Queen of Scots.[36]

A final consideration before we return to the popular drama itself is the extent of the relationship between that drama and the work of the humanist school. The problem is more complex than any dealt with so far. John Heywood's *Four PP* was, after all, one of the seven plays offered by "My Lord Cardinalls players" to Sir Thomas More. Furthermore, nothing in the play itself contradicts the likelihood of such auspices. It is not a morality, but its farce is native and may be an outgrowth of that shadowy line suggested by *Interludium de Clerico et Puella*, the secular comic drama of the minstrels. Heywood was himself at various times a minstrel, player, and playwright. No doubling is possible in *Four PP* since all characters appear on stage simultaneously, a technique employed in all of Heywood's plays. Yet the cast is limited to four and is therefore well within the scope of the troupes. All the actors sing together (l. 322). Properties are elementary, and limited mainly to costuming. The Palmer introduces himself by saying "I am a palmer, as ye se" (l. 9); perhaps he carries a palmleaf, and the others might carry badges of their trades. Indications of *mise en scène* are so general that the play could be performed anywhere. The audience is near at hand, so that the players are able to jest with the bystanders. The Pedler refers to his female audience:

> Amonge the women in thys border,
> Take thre of the yongest and thre of the oldest . . .   [ll. 1070–1071]

The humor is scatological, especially in the 'Pothecary's tale of his woman patient, the "glyster," and the "tampyon." Here was material for a village assembly or for a noble banquet. In the fourteenth century Chaucer had addressed his fabliaux to the court of Richard II, and may well have read them aloud to an audience of gentlemen and ladies. The early Tudor kings appear to have retained some of this genial tolerance for broad humor, making it possible for Heywood to appeal to country and court together. Since interluders in noble livery were called upon to please a widely varying audience, Heywood found a means of bridging the gap by employing a native tradition of humor. *Four PP* has few elements of classical sophistication.

The Pardoner and the Friar gives indication of similar auspices. The scene is supposed to be a church, and presumably the audience itself serves as the congregation. Neighbor Pratt probably comes up out of the audience to join in the quarrel. The players speak to their auditors: the Pardoner says, "I say some good body lende me his hengar" (p. 123). The spectators are referred to as "maisters" (p. 119) and "worshypfull maysters" (p. 97). The language is abusive and the fighting is violent and undignified. Once again the casting is limited to four players who appear all together on stage. Heywood's debt to Chaucer and the English literary tradition is obvious.

John John the Husband, Tib his Wife, and Sir John the Priest, although modeled upon the French *Farce du Pasté*,[37] also belongs in the popular repertory. Like its French source, it has only three participants who appear simultaneously. Thus Heywood found a model for limiting his cast of characters not in the English popular theater but in fabliau literature. John John addresses the "maysters" in the audience (l. 1). The setting requires a hall: John John hands his gown to one of the audience who is "so nere the dore he myght ron away" (ll. 249–257). Properties required include a table, place-settings for the table, a stool, two cups, a pot of ale, bread, and a fireplace — all perfectly suited to any kind of banqueting hall. The humor is that of the fabliau in an anticlerical vein, presenting a vivid fight on stage.

These three popular plays are not, however, wholly typical of the humanist drama, nor even of Heywood's own dramatic idiom. A. W. Reed has noted that Heywood's plays fall into two sharply distinguished categories: the fabliaux already discussed, and the more decorous disputations known as *The Play of Love*, *The Play of the Weather*, and *Witty and Witless*. "We are, therefore, confronted with a pretty problem. There are two trilogies claimed for Heywood which are remarkably unlike, so unlike at a first glance that they appear to be the work of different minds."[38] Reed finally allows both groups to be Heywood's, but conjectures that the refined disputations must have been written more directly under Thomas More's influence.

An examination of auspices makes clear the distinction between the two groups, and suggests a reason for the remarkable differences in the works of a single author. *Weather* (printed 1533), the liveliest of the three, is too elaborate to be taken on tour like *Four PP* and its fellows. By internal indications, *Weather* appears intended for an evening entertainment at court or in the hall of a nobleman who had guests to dinner (ll. 1027–1030).[39] It requires ten players, all of whom gather before Jupiter's throne in the closing scene and "singe most ioyfully" (l. 1253). The assemblage is like those ending *Respublica, Liberality and Prodigality, Disobedient Child*, and *Jacob and Esau*. Two of the roles are women's parts, and the role of the young boy is assigned to "the lest that can play," implying that the rest are also boys. All the indications point to boys' courtly drama. No adult troupe of this size is known to have traveled publicly in England before the 1570's, or to have commanded the talents of three or more qualified boys. Furthermore, the conspicuous disregard of the possibilities for doubling rules out the likelihood of troupe performance. Without the final action of bringing all the suitors on stage at once, *Weather* could be handled by half as many actors.

The staging too is elaborate. Jupiter has a throne, and evidently is able to withdraw from public view by means of a "travers" or curtained alcove, like that used by King Assuerus in *Godly Queen Hester*, or by players on scaffolds in medieval cyclical performances (such as the *Ludus Coventriae* "Slaying of the Innocents," in which the curtain "xal unclose shewing herowde in astat").[40] In *Weather*, Jupiter announces "A whyle we woll wythdraw our godly presens" (l. 181), and the stage direction indicates "at thende of this staf the god hath a song played in his trone or Mery report come in" (l. 179). Seemingly Jupiter never exits altogether. This type of *locus* with structural *sedes* was evidently too cumbersome for the itinerant players. As will be shown, no popular text of the period indicates the need for such an arrangement.

Weather retains some of the vitality of the popular tradition. Merry Report is evidently concealed in the audience as the play begins. Jupiter asks for a volunteer to act as his "crier," and Merry

Report steps forward, chiding one of the torch-bearers: "Brother holde vp your torche a lytell hyer" (l. 98). He is even rougher with the servants of the hall in his next entry:

> Auaunte carterly keytyfs auaunt
> Why ye dronken horesons wyll yt not be.   [ll. 188–189]

Nevertheless, the coarseness in *Weather* is considerably rarer than in *Four PP*, and the whole is clearly directed to a courtly audience.

The theme is occasionally classical in tone, and subtly political. The portrait of Jupiter is probably intended both as a compliment to Henry VIII, and as a polite hint that he continue to emulate Jupiter by taking more complete control of his own government and thereby gaining greater solidarity among his subjects.[41] The pronounced element of debate follows a tradition of disguisings in the coterie drama dating from the fifteenth century. In Lydgate's entertainment at Hertford (between 1425 and 1435), for example, the Presenter supplicates the King on behalf of six peasant-husbands who plead for command of the home over their wives. After hearing both sides, the King's advocate defers sentence and orders a truce of one year's duration.[42] Other courtly precedents and analogues for *Weather* have been found: a play by William Cornish (1519) in which seven boy actors portray Sun, Moon, Wind, Rain, Summer, Winter, and Lust; and in the time of William Crane (1527) a dramatized debate between Love and Riches, in which Mercury acts as messenger and Justice as arbiter.[43]

Love (ca. 1533) and *Witty and Witless* (ca. 1520–1533) are little more than a series of disputations, and so essentially untheatrical that they seem like "closet" drama, intended for reading rather than performance.[44] They are not entirely lacking in stage techniques, however. Toward the end of *Love,* for example, appears the graphic stage direction:

Here the vyse cometh in ronnynge sodenly aboute the place among the audiens with a hye copyn tank on his hed full of squybs fyred.   [l. 1294]

"Closet" drama is not quite accurate as a description. The reference to an "audiens" provides the clue of actual forensic presentation. These elevating discourses were devised to be recited at banquets or other state occasions, perhaps by costumed gentlemen of the chapel. To maintain interest among the guests, Heywood interspersed a few passages of humor and action. For the most part, nevertheless, these dialogues dealt seriously with favorite topics of courtly debate. *Love* contains a subtle element of political satire directed at Wolsey; *Witty and Witless* owes much of its interest in human reason to Pico della Mirandola and to Erasmus' *Colloquia*.[45] Apparently it was the patrician audience that occasioned the rarified tone of the two disputations, and differentiated them from those plays which Heywood wrote for the nation at large. Heywood's plays might all have been acted at court, but clearly some were never intended for any other audience than the nobility and intelligentsia.

Of Gentleness and Nobility (ca. 1527), often ascribed to Heywood but believed by Reed to be Rastell's work,[46] offers a particularly good example of humanist drama intended solely for sophisticated tastes. The title page demonstrates the manner in which its author has combined a primary intellectual interest in debate with occasional comic diversion in the popular vein:

A Dialogue between the Merchant, the Knight and the Ploughman, disputing who is a very Gentleman, and who is a Nobleman, and how men should come to authority. Compiled in the manner of an Interlude, with divers toys and jests added thereto to make merry pastime and disport.

The disputation is the central object, and the jests are "added thereto." The topic is in the time-honored tradition of Boethius, Dante, and Jeun de Meun, and of Chaucer's "moral balade" to "Gentilesse" and the "Wife of Bath's Tale." [47] Courtly circles took cognizance of the doctrine that "Thy gentillesse cometh fro God allone" [48] without acknowledging any revolutionary social implications in the idea. The debate, here addressed to "Ye sovereigns all descreet and excellent" (epilogue), stresses the need for virtue in the ruling classes. In advocating moderation in the uses of wealth, the play also endorses Tudor sumptuary legislation.[49] The lengthy discourses, the scarcity of action, the refinement of language, are all suited for the edification of guests at a banquet. The possibility of "closet" drama is discounted by the fact that the debate is organized into two presentations. At the halfway point the speakers disperse on various pretexts and agree to assemble later for a continuation. This device, as in *Fulgens and Lucrece*, evidently enabled the banquet to resume without excessive interruption.

The added comic material too suggests a semidramatic performance, for each half of the debate contains one active quarrel. The Ploughman provides this comic relief. In the first part his entrance is delayed considerably, allowing the others a lengthy and sober discussion before his rough and scatological language creates an amusing diversion. The author actually provides a little physical violence on stage: *"Et verberat eos"* (p. 439). After this brief digression, however, even the Ploughman settles down into prolonged rhetoric. The contrast in decorum between *Of Gentleness and Nobility* and *Four PP* may be attributed to the different audiences for which they were written.

By these same standards it is evident that Medwall's *Fulgens and Lucrece* is a humanist play that borrowed from the popular tradition rather than becoming a part of it. The play was seemingly performed by professional actors, but was presented on a special occasion and in courtly surroundings. Actor "B" denies that he is a player (I, 44–56), but this appears to be a dramatic fiction. "A" later explains:

> Perde my felowys and I were here
> To day whan ye where at dyner
> And shewed you a lytyll disport
> Of one fulgens and his doughter lucres.   [II, 10–13]

"B's" apparel is splendid, so much so "That a man shall not lightly/ Know a player from another man" (I, 55–56). The function of this two-part drama as entertainment between phases of a banquet is abundantly illustrated in the dialogue. The guests have already had meat and drink when the first part commences (I, 9–10, 15–16). Boas and Reed have deduced more exact particulars: the presentation was probably at Christmas time, 1497, in honor of important visits by the Ambassadors of Flanders and of Spain.[50] Many of the play's topical references (for example, II, 389–392), and its setting in a banqueting hall, would lose their meaning in a more widely traveled or repeated performance. Like *Gorboduc, Fulgens and Lucrece* was written originally for a single important occasion.

The comic element of the play is pronounced, and exhibits many characteristics taken from popular drama. "A" and "B" continually jest with their audience. "A" orders one of the servingmen standing by to see who is at the door (II, 75). The genteel audience is also near at hand:

> This gentylman can wytnes bere
> That all this owre I haue stonde here.   [I, 1011–1012]

The staging area was probably little more than a cleared space in the dining hall. The contest of "A" and "B" for the favors of the maid Joan is lively, and brings her virginity into question (I, 900f). Still, the language is suggestive rather than broad, and obscenity is almost wholly lacking.

This native comedy is entirely relegated to a subplot. The concern of the main plot is a humanist discourse upon the familiar debating subject, *"de vera nobilitate."* Its lengthy speeches are compounded of the forensic *controversia* of classical rhetoric,[51] and its characters — unlike "A" and "B" — do not recognize the presence of the audience. *Fulgens and Lucrece* is really two plays, a debate on gentleness and nobility and a compilation of humorous skits added in the manner of a popular entertainment. The use of two parallel plots and the clever device of an "Induction" attest to the experimental nature of Medwall's writing. His epilogue recognizes the double appeal contained in the play's two elements, one addressed to "folke" and one to "gentilmen of name":

> . . . all the substaunce of this play
> was done specially therfor
> Not onely to make folke myrth and game,
> But that suche as be gentilmen of name
> May be somwhat mouyd
> By this example for to eschew
> The wey of vyce and favour vertue,
>
> . . . .
>
> This was the cause principall,
> And also for to do withall
> This company some myrth.   [II, 888–901]

The appeal is dichotomized, but the avowed emphasis is on the serious material. The humorous portion is added for diversion, as in *Of Gentleness and Nobility.* Medwall seemingly used popular entertainers rather than boys to act his drama,[52] and gave them some of the familiar scenes in which they excelled; but his auspices were unequivocally genteel. His lengthy morality play *Nature* (before 1500) makes similar and extensive borrowings from the troupe stage, and yet remains sophisticated in tone. Although conventional in type, it strives at times for a quality of thought and language that is exceptional in the later fifteenth century.[53] Humanist drama was closer to the popular theater than was the drama of the schools, Inns of Court, and boys' companies, but in the humanist plays written specifically for a limited audience a distinction in emphasis from truly popular drama can legitimately be made.

Calisto and Melibea, issued from the press of John Rastell before 1533, is also a curious blend of humanist learning and popular motifs. Although the conditions of performance are hard to determine, the play seems suited for Rastell's own experimental stage.[54] The title indicates the conscious borrowing of the old by the new: "A new commodye in englysh in maner of an enterlude ryght elygant & full of craft of rethoryk." The element of debate is pronounced in the discussion of "the bewte & good propertes of women" versus "theyr vycys & euyll condicions"; also in Parmeno's defense of joyful poverty (ll. 500f); and at the close of the play, in Danio's moral lecture to the audience on the dangers of idleness, an amazing non sequitur to the play itself but interesting for its close connection with Thomas More's ideas on idleness in Book I of *Utopia*.[55] At the same time the popular element shows chiefly in the fabliau material in the manner of *Dame Siriz* and *Interludium de Clerico et Puella*. Celestina is a woman of the world whose tales of bawdry and methods of seduction are worthy of at least distant comparison with those of the Wife of Bath and Pandarus. Danio's prophetic dream, in which Celestina appears in the figure of a "foule rough bych" (l. 961), bears a plausible resemblance to the fabliau of *Dame Siriz*.

The complex relationship of humanist drama to the popular theater may best be summarized by an analysis of John Rastell's *Play of the Four Elements* (1517–1518). No play better reflects the ambivalent attitude of humanist writers toward their public. It is chiefly a sounding-board for the exciting new ideas that More and his circle were discovering, proclaimed on the title page as "many proper points of philosophy natural, and of divers strange lands, and of divers strange effects and causes." The play is the effort of a scholar zealous to revive learning in his time. It illustrates the author's extensive acquaintance with works of natural philosophy and cosmology by such writers as Gregorius Reisch, Martin Waldseemüller, Sacrobosco, and Bartholomaeus Anglicus.[56] The play contains a purely literary preface, not for the stage but for the printed edition, promising physical explanations of the formation and decay of matter, of the earth's roundness and the roundness too of the sea upon its surface, of astronomy and meteorology.

And yet the play contains a good deal of amusing and vivid popular material, presented in such a way that the humanist and popular elements are offered as separable entities. Almost wistfully, Rastell announces on the title page that his work may be acted in two versions, one as he wrote it, and one heavily abbreviated to provide a less serious and informative drama:

which interlude, if the whole matter be played, will contain the space of an hour and a half; but, if ye list, ye may leave out much of the sad matter . . . and yet the matter will depend conveniently, and then it will not be past three-quarters of an hour of length.

The Messenger too, in speaking the prologue, finds himself caught between two camps, urging a more serious national literature and better understanding of the weighty subjects contained in this play, and at the same time apologizing for the inclusion of so much comic material to attract a wider audience:

> But because some folk be little disposed
> To sadness, but more to mirth and sport,
> This philosophical work is mixed
> With merry conceits, to give men comfort,
> And occasion to cause them to resort
> To hear this matter, whereto if they take heed,
> Some learning to them thereof may proceed.   [p. 10]

The play, like *Fulgens and Lucrece*, is really two plays, a "philosophical work" and an interlude of "merry conceits," offered for two audiences, and evidently presented under such auspices — perhaps on Rastell's stage — that the humbler sort might be induced to come of their own volition as to a public play. There is an inference of repeated performance, so that the people might take occasion to "resort."

Rastell, in a practical way, indicates specifically which parts of the "sad matter" may be left out in the abbreviated performance of his play. It is interesting to read the play in its shortened form. This version omits the Messenger's part with its anti-Scholastic manifesto ("How dare men presume to be clerks . . . And know not of these visible things inferial?" p. 9), much of the natural philosophy and scientific explanation, and — dearest of all perhaps to Rastell's heart — the plea for the commercial settling of America, with its unlimited opportunities for enriching England's treasury, triumphing over the French fishing industry, and bringing civilization and God to the ignorant savages. These passages grew out of the humanists' deepest concerns, including investments by More and Rastell in an uncompleted colonizing attempt.[57] More made a literary case for colonization in *Utopia* during these same years.

Bereft of these experimental qualities, the forty-five-minute performance that remains might almost pass for an unexceptional popular morality. Its humor is on the decorous side, as in *Fulgens and Lucrece*. Profanity and stage brawls are kept to a minimum. Nevertheless the scientific lectures are forgotten, while the hero's main business, like that of Prince Hal, is to frequent taverns, consort with rioters, sing, and dance. The casting as well as the content of the play is divided for two sorts of performance. The shorter version involves seven characters, and their parts could be handled by five actors; but for the fuller performance the Messenger is necessary, and also "if ye list, ye may bring in a Disguising" (pp. 5, 46–48), calling for an unspecified number of dancers together with greater elaboration and extravagance in costuming. This optional disguising, outgrowth of Lydgate's courtly mummings and predecessor of the Jonsonian mask, would obviously be intended for an indoor entertainment in which noble spectators of the play could dance.[58] It seems possible, then, that the cut version could have been taken on the road where lengthy discourses on science and geography would have been considered expendable.

In Rastell's drama we see a quality characteristic of the humanists: he writes with the motivation of a schoolmaster, attempting to guide and improve the populace by speaking to it in its own terms. He uses the stage as a medium, like the printing press, to promote a worthy literature in the English tongue.[59] He writes also for his intellectual peers, and it is in trying to bridge the gap that he makes his distinctive mark. Only occasionally did humanist drama become a genuine part of the popular canon, as in *Four PP*; but insofar as its writers felt a responsibility to the literature of a whole nation, their influence on the development of popular drama was certain to have effect.

IV The Popular Canon

Returning from the other schools of dramatic writing, we have now the means of assembling with some assurance a popular canon — plays homogeneous in the sense that they could have been presented under no auspices except those of a commercial itinerant stage. For many of these plays, the auspices listed in the *Annals of English Drama* are "unknown," and in most cases neither the exact location of performance nor the troupe responsible will ever be known. Indeed, these were usually plays for many places and for numerous troupes. Nevertheless the texts usually give a plain indication of their suitability for the popular stage and their unsuitability for humanist or courtly sponsorship. This evidence, following the clues found in *Mankind*, *Impatient Poverty*, *Lusty Juventus*, and *The Marriage of Wit and Wisdom*, will be summarized briefly and set in chronological order.

The period before 1500 was a formative one for the troupes, and auspices are not always clear in the transition from the mystery cycles to commercial troupe drama. *Mankind* (ca. 1471) is the most indisputably popular play of the fifteenth century, but three others may be considered as anticipating the popular stage in methods of doubling and itinerant production. *The Castle of Perseverance*, despite its large cast, may have been acted "by more or less professional actors in the way of business, before a number of villages in turn." [1] The banns do indeed imply advertisement for performance in a succession of communities:

Ye manly men of ——, thus Crist saue you all! [l. 145]

The play could not be transported without some difficulty, since the diagram in the manuscript calls for either a moat or sturdy fencing encircling the playing area: "This is the watyr a-bowte the place, if any dyche may be mad, ther it schal be pleyed, or ellys

that it be strongely barryd al a-bowt."[2] Nevertheless, the author
apparently assumed that his play would be performed in different
places under varying conditions, since he provided the alternative of
fencing in case a ditch could not be made. The performances evidently took place in the vicinity of Lincoln, around 1400 to 1405.[3]

Like *Mankind, Perseverance* was acted before a mixed audience
of the socially prominent and the multitude, for the players distinguish between the "syrys semly" who "syttyth on syde" around
the perimeter (1. 163), and the "wytys" who are in the "pleyn
place" inside the perimeter (ll. 157–160).[4] Little doubling was
possible and was probably not considered necessary. Assignment of
parts may have been similar to that in the French mystére of *Les
Trois Martyrs, Séverin, Exupère, et Félicien*, put on in 1508 by the
Chapter of St. Bernard and the municipality, in which eighty-six
characters were presented without doubling. All ranks of society
undertook the roles, and all except those who played singular parts
like Lucifer or Proserpine were expected to provide their own
costumes.[5] In *Perseverance*, the thirty-five roles may have been
divided between professional strollers and an assortment of amateurs
drafted from each locality. Even if this arrangement did in fact
exist, however, it represents only a modest beginning in the movement toward the highly mobile and practical theater of *Mankind*.

More suggestive of professional drama is the arrangement of
the late-fifteenth-century miracle, *Play of the Sacrament*, relating
the conversion of Jonathas the Jew, to be performed by nine actors:

IX may play yt at ease.   [colophon]

This earliest extant play "offered for acting" was evidently taken
on tour, as was a similar Chelmsford play in the sixteenth century.[6] However, doubling was not entirely unknown in medieval
mysteries — examples appear in the Coventry *Destruction of
Jerusalem*[7] — and the staging auspices of *Sacrament* are closer to
those of the mystery cycles than to those of *Mankind*. The east
Midland dialect, and a reference to Babwell near Bury, indicate that
the *Sacrament* may have originated in a Franciscan Priory there.
The use of scaffolded *loca* flanking a *platea* recalls the practice of
earlier religious drama. In the first Passion Play of *Ludus Coventriae*, for example, the Last Supper is enacted in one *domus* while
the Council of Jews bargaining thirty pieces of silver appears

simultaneously in another *domus,* with Judas trafficking between
the two.[8] Such movements across the *platea* from one "mansion"
to another are common in both *Sacrament* and *Perseverance.* The
building of individual structural *loca* was to prove too cumbersome
and expensive for the successors of *Mankind.*

A third precursor of the troupe play is the Macro morality,
Wisdom Who Is Christ, also called "Mind, Will, and Understanding." Like *Sacrament* its origins are at least partly monastic,
and it may have been written for St. Edmundsbury Abbey between
1460 and 1474. The play seems intended both for monastic and
more general audiences, suggesting that it was performed publicly.
One message in it concerns the serious problem of apostasy from
the monasteries; but it also contains a theme for all Christians,
written for the understanding of lay audiences.[9] Its casting appears
to be designed for an acting company of a particular size. Thirty-
odd roles are arranged with seeming deliberateness for a systematic
and symmetrical pattern of doubling by six actors and six mutes.[10]
Such a company may have gone on tour, but it was still considerably
larger than the professional troupe of *Mankind* and its successors.
None of these three plays had yet achieved the mobility and
economy in numbers of the troupe theater.

In the early period of the sixteenth century, before Henry VIII's
death in 1547, three plays emerge as unquestionably popular:
Mundus et Infans (printed in 1522), *Hickescorner* (ca. 1500–1520),
and *The Interlude of Youth* (1513–1529). They are similar enough
to warrant composite discussion. They are all anonymous and
unpretentious in style. The moral element is simple and yet pervasive, patiently teaching basic Christian ideals in easily understood
language. *Mundus et Infans,* for example, incorporates much popu-
larized sermonizing on the nature of shrift, the necessary stages
of contrition, the twelve articles of belief, and the five wits bodily
and spiritual. The actors address their audience often, referring to
them simply as "this meyne," "syrs," "felowes," "lordynges," "this
company" (*M et I,* ll. 561, 721, 743, 747), "my maysters," "the
persons here present," "men and women that here be" (*Youth,*
ll. 195, 779, 785), "soveraynes," and "sygnours" (*Hickescorner,*
ll. 2, 646). The auditors are shoved aside for entrances, taken into
confidence, lectured to, and asked for advice: "A backe felowes and
gyue me roume" (*Youth,* l. 39), "Now, semely syrs, beholde on

me / How mankynde doth begynne," "Lo, syrs, a grete ensample
you may se" (*M et I,* ll. 28–29, 721), "How saye you, lordes, shall
I smyte?" (*Hickescorner,* l. 765). The audience of *Mundus et
Infans* was seated, like the "sovereignes" of *Mankind:* "[God]
saue all this symylytude that semely here syttes" (l. 751).

Casting requirements do not exceed five players, and all three
plays offer opportunity for doubling. *Mundus et Infans* is unusually
limited, demanding only two actors for its five roles. The *mise en
scéne* is not made specific; in *Youth* the hero struts before the
audience "in thys place" (l. 201). *Mundus et Infans* was intended
for acting on the green: "Now wyll I fare on these flourys" (l. 235).
The most elaborate furnishing required is a throne for Mundus. The
broad comedy in all three plays is in the vein of *Mankind.* The
profanity is abundant and colorful, yet lacking in the pyrotechnic
versatility of *Gammer Gurton's Needle* (see previous chapter). In
one passage of *Hickescorner* (ll. 428–440), for example, such oaths
as "Kockes herte," "by Saynt Mary," "by Cockes body," "by Our
Lady," and "by Hyz" appear in nearly half the lines.

The Henrician period also contributed such humanist plays to
the popular canon as *Four PP, The Pardoner and the Friar,* and
John John. In addition, John Bale and John Skelton, well-known
literary men with affiliations at court, wrote a group of plays in
the popular manner: *Three Laws, King John,* and *Magnificence.*
The attitude of these authors toward their humble subject is not
unlike that of the humanist writers, with whom they may have
had some connection[11] — a kind of *noblesse oblige,* a willingness
to undertake the guidance of public entertainment for the sake of
crucial issues like the Reformation or the counseling of kings. Since
these plays are the product of genuine literary talent, they tend
to be more poetic, more complex, and more intricately organized
than contemporary anonymous plays. Nevertheless, many of them
appear to have been genuinely popular in that they were designed
for commercial production by adult troupes before a diversified
audience. Nor are they, like Medwall's and Rastell's dramas, concerned primarily with debating topics or new discoveries in cosmography. Their issues are national and their treatment is popular.

Bale was an ardent controversialist for the Reformation. Once a
Carmelite himself, he became the tireless enemy of monasticism.
He adopted the medium of popular drama as a means of placing

the "facts" of Catholic tyranny before as wide an audience as possible. His services were of special value to Thomas Cromwell, who succeeded Cardinal Wolsey as the man most effectively responsible for executing Henry VIII's anticlerical policies. In 1537 or thereabouts Bale formed, under Cromwell's patronage, a company of touring actors known almost certainly as "my Lord Cromwell's players" for whom he wrote plays.[12] Cromwell's accounts show payments to Bale for plays on September 8, 1538 at St. Stephen's, Canterbury, and on January 31, 1539. "My Lord Cromwell's players" appeared in Cambridge, Barnstaple, and elsewhere in the period between 1537 and 1540. Even when Bale was forced to flee the country, after the fall of Cromwell in 1540 and Henry VIII's curb on polemical drama in 1543, he still managed with unabated zeal to direct open-air performances such as that at Kilkenny, Ireland, in 1553.[13]

Bale's troupe undoubtedly performed his *King John* and *The Three Laws of Nature, Moses, and Christ*. These are eminently practical works for itinerant theater. *Three Laws* contains a specific casting list distributing fourteen roles among five actors. No such list exists for *King John,* but its stage directions indicate several doubling assignments and demonstrate that Bale was continually aware of his limitations of cast: for example, "Go owt Ynglond, and drese for Clargy" (l. 155). No more than five actors appear on stage together (ll. 2283f and 2422f). Both plays provide for part-singing involving three or four voices. In *King John,* Sedition is told to begin a song whereupon the others will "lepe in amonge" (l. 827). Staging needs are elementary, and the acting locale is referred to simply as a "place"; Sedition speaks *"extra locum"* (l. 1377). Both plays contain a good deal of broad humor and are moralities, although the historical element and the elaborate literary parody of Roman rite in *King John* are not typical of contemporary anonymous popular plays.[14]

The arrangement for doubling in Skelton's *Magnificence* (written not long after 1515) suggests use by a professional troupe. Although the play lacks a casting chart, its eighteen roles may be assigned with ease to five actors.[15] The scheme is far too intricate to have been fortuitous. In content, *Magnificence* is a political satire directed toward King Henry and Wolsey, and stylistically it contains literary debate of the courtly type. The play certainly was performed in the evening for a noble audience ("I had not ben here with you this nyght," l. 365).[16] At the same time its moral lesson is intended for general consumption, and the production is designed for popular touring. The epilogue, addressed simply to "ye that haue harde this dysporte and game" (l. 2566), stresses the insecurity of worldly glory and the daily reversals of earthly prosperity. Elsewhere the actors refer to their audience as "Syrs" and "Maysters" (ll. 1896, 1044), and jest with them in the popular fashion. Courtly Abusion, left alone on stage, struts before his admirers:

What nowe? Let se
Who loketh on me
Well rounde aboute.   [ll. 829–831]

The acting location is simply "the place" (ll. 825, 828, 1327, 1796). An itinerant troupe would have to carry few properties besides a standard wardrobe.[17] The play abounds in ribald songs, unseemly jests, and comic quarrels. The oaths, as in *Hickescorner,* are commonplace: "Cockes armes," "Cockes harte," "by Saynt Sym" (ll. 573–585).

The reigns of Edward VI and Mary were difficult times for the popular drama. The court regarded popular plays as troublesomely controversial, and Mary especially tended to prefer the boys' performances under Udall. Of the few anonymous plays probably dating from the period between 1547 and 1558, two have been introduced into the canon already because they were mentioned in *Sir Thomas More*: these were *Impatient Poverty* and *Lusty Juventus.* A third such play is the anonymous *Wealth and Health* (S. R. 1557), offered on the title page for four actors. Actually, five of the play's seven characters appear on stage together, and six actors are required to make the casting feasible. Title pages that offer plays for acting are not always reliable, especially those that fail to specify the exact doubling of parts. This one of *Wealth and Health* seems a clear case of a printer's fraud, added to attract buyers among the troupes.[18] Despite this misrepresentation, *Wealth and Health* has qualifications as popular drama. Its plain moral of prudence and foresight appeals primarily to the middle classes, and its patriotic defense of the realm's wealth against foreign interference is overly blunt for the atmosphere at court.[19] The cast is small and the requirements for production are minimal. The humor draws heavily on anti-Spanish sentiment. Much of the dramatic effect depends on visual impression or on improvised remarks from the actors: for example, "Here entreth with some iest yllwyll" (l. 281). Such stage directions indicate that the text was intended for the professional actor rather than the reader.

From the first twenty years of Elizabeth's reign a good number of indisputably popular moralities have survived, all similar enough in their auspices to be discussed as a group: the anonymous *New Custom* and *The Trial of Treasure,* George Wapull's *The Tide Tarrieth No Man,* Ulpian Fulwell's *Like Will to Like,*[20] and W. Wager's *Enough Is as Good as a Feast* and *The Longer Thou Livest the More Fool Thou Art.* All contain casting lists in which the parts are specifically divided among an exact number of players. In one, *Like Will to Like,* the list does not work perfectly for the play: Virtuous Life appears simultaneously with his casting counterparts Cuthbert Cutpurse (ll. 665–741) and God's Promises (ll. 832–895). Nevertheless "fiue may easely play this enterlude" as promised, if the part of Virtuous Life is given instead to the actor who plays Tom Collier. Such an error could have been the fault of the printer. In the other five plays, the directions for doubling are flawless; and in several cases, as in *The Longer Thou Livest,* it is nearly impossible to contrive any other arrangement of the parts that would work. Such careful attention to the casting could be justified only by a professional stage.

Staging requirements in these plays are uniformly simple, demanding only a playing area and a means of access. Stage directions are graphic and plentiful, and read as players' instructions rather than as literary guides. In *Enough Is as Good as a Feast,* for example, we find "Enter an olde man Tenant and speak Cotesolde speech," "Let the Vice weep & houle & make great lamentation to the Worldly Man," "Be going out . . . Holde him . . . Come in again . . . Cum in . . . He fighteth with them bothe with his Daggar . . . Lay holde on him," "go out al. iii, togither and make you redy straight waies" (sig. B₄ *recto* and *verso,* D₁ *recto* and E₁ *recto*). The actors are expected to improvise freely, as in *The Longer Thou Livest*: "Here entreth Moros . . . Synging the foote of many Songes, as fooles were wont," or "Here let Moros betwene euery sentence say 'Gay geare, good stufe, very well, finado', with such mockish termes" (ll. 71, 423). In *Like Will to Like,* Nichol Newfangle is directed to sing "Trim mer-chandise . . . as oft as he thinketh good" (p. 344). The stage directions pay close attention to such details of production as hand-properties, beards, and costuming. In *Like Will to Like,* "Here entereth Hance with a pot," and the Devil is accoutred in a personalized garment: "This name Lucifer must be written on his back and in his breast" (pp. 327, 310). The audience is often brought into the fun, and is addressed in terms such as "worshipful audience."

Formal act and scene divisions appear only in *New Custom,* and even here the markings leave off at Act III, scene i. Their incompleteness suggests that they are the work of the printer, William How, and not of the author. If these markings are in fact "editorial," then the generalization holds that no single popular play before 1567 was written in acts and scenes. Bale's *Three Laws* is so divided, but, as we have seen, he was a "popular" dramatist only in a qualified sense.

Another popular play of the 1570's is Thomas Lupton's *All for Money* (printed in 1578). Lupton, a writer of moral pamphlets such as *Sivqila. Too good, to be true,* and a collaborator with Barnabe Rich in his school of reform,[21] was just the sort of free-lance tractarian needed to provide a rapidly expanding popular theater with new scripts. At first glance the staging for *All for Money* seems more elaborate than anything attempted in the earlier days of the public theater. It requires some sort of "hollowe place for one to come vp in" (ll. 203f), through which a series of vices are brought before the audience. A real trap door was probably lacking, however, for Judas and Dives come from Hell through a regular entrance way rather than appearing from under the stage.[22] In other respects the play requires only a chair and an unlocalized scene. The doubling is unusually professional. Although the play lacks a casting chart, its twenty roles are arranged with apparently deliberate care for only four actors. In addition, these twenty roles are predominantly male. The farcical humor, the scatology, and the practical attention to costuming ("Here commeth in Satan the great deuill as deformedly dressed as may be," l. 446) all confirm the impression of popular theater.

The emphasis on the pragmatic and theatrical qualities is important, for no more serious imputation could be brought against these moralities than that they were anachronisms of a disappearing tradition, lacking a vital audience and written largely by well-wishing clergymen who were out of touch with the times.[23] Such cloistered dramas did in fact exist, but they have little in common with the plays just analyzed. A discussion of a few clerically erudite plays will reveal the distinction between truly popular drama and an ecclesiastical offshoot which has no place in the canon.

John Bale wrote a series of anti-Catholic mysteries that are strikingly different from his troupe performances. One of these is *The Chief Promises of God unto Man* (ca. 1538). It contains no dramatic action, and is simply a series of seven disquisitions between God and, in turn, Adam, Noah, Abraham, and others. A convenient soliloquy by Pater Coelestis between each passage of dialogue allows the mystery to be delivered by two speakers. The specification of *"chorus cum organis"* at the conclusion of each phase renders church performance convenient if not mandatory, and the work may well have been intended primarily for tours of churches. Doubtless Bale performed this work with his band of professionals, and was able when occasion demanded to stage it outdoors "at the market crosse. with organe playinges and songes very aptely"; organ music out of doors was not unknown in medieval drama.[24] These auspices do not suffice, however, to make a living popular drama of the static and expository *Chief Promises*. Bale's *John Baptist* and *Temptation* are also religious rituals rather than stage plays.

More dramaturgic than these but scarcely less cloistered is the anonymous *John the Evangelist,* of uncertain date (ca. 1520–1557). The setting suggested by the dialogue is a church, and no less than three sermons are woven into its 653 lines and are frankly directed at the audience or congregation. One of these is specifically called a "sermon" (l. 29). The play contains several untranslated Latin tags and Scriptural quotations, seemingly intended for a learned and perhaps ordained audience, or even for readers. The text contains virtually no stage directions, and there is little plot or action except for the incongruous antics of two vice figures, Evil Counsel and Idleness. These two personifications, borrowed from popular convention, appear only in a separate portion of the play, to provide an interlude between the sermons. Their humor is flaccid and contains no invective or vivid language. Apart from this brief episode the play evokes an atmosphere of intense and even mystical religiosity. It is essentially a meditation in the form of a mimetic rendition of Biblical story.

Particularly revealing of the lack of dramatic skill in this play is the clumsy shifting from scene to scene. The characters anticipate what is coming next on stage without any dramatic reason for having such foreknowledge. For example, before the commencement of the comic plot the two young protagonists, Actio and Eugenio, resolve to walk apart for "a space" in order to avoid the unregenerate Evil Counsel who is soon to be present; later, they announce, they will return to hear another sermon from the saintly John (ll. 358–365). And at the end of the comedy scene Evil Counsel and Idleness depart in order to avoid the sermon which they inexplicably know to be coming:

> I trowe than he wyll come hyther
> That layde fyrst In principio togyther.   [ll. 538–539]

These awkward transitions prepare the audience (or reader) for the ensuing scenes, but are unaccountable in terms of plot. The story of *John the Evangelist* is no more than an artificial excuse for a series of devotional messages.

One more example of this ecclesiastically sponsored moral drama is Nathaniel Woodes's *Conflict of Conscience* (printed in 1581). Although important for its similarity to Marlowe's *Doctor Faustus,* the play is scarcely professional.[25] Woodes, graduate of Cambridge and minister in Norwich,[26] offered the play for six actors under auspices not unlike those of the popular troupes: "conuenient for such as be disposed, either to shew this Comedie in priuate houses, or otherwise." The play is divided, however, into five acts (with a brief sixth act that is really an epilogue) and continental scene divisions; and instead of indicating entrances it groups the names of the actors at the heading of each scene. No single play in the popular canon adopts this method in its entirety.[27]

Conflict of Conscience has almost none of the interplay between actors and audience so common to popular plays of the period. The speeches are excessively long, and even Satan delivers a lecture of 112 lines (I, i). Stage directions are sparse. In one scene (II, ii) the marginal asides of Hypocrisy are so long and complex as to be almost unstageable. The Vice and his cohorts engage in a lengthy dialogue that allows little opportunity for visual effect; their combats are entirely verbal. They almost start to sing at one point, but beg off with the excuse that they lack a treble (II, iii) — a curious passage which attests to the universal popularity of song in professional plays of this genre, and the need for excusing its omission here. The distribution of the parts for six actors is not skillful: player one is left idle for most of the play. The total impression is one of amateurish drama, written as a cleric's serious answer to the levities of popular and supposedly "moral" theater. He has outfitted his play with the paraphernalia of casting, in order to make it serviceable to the cause of religion if anyone should care to show it "in priuate houses, or otherwise." Woodes's vague appeal to "otherwise" seems to reflect his wistful hope that the play might prove more popular than he had reason to expect. In his attempt both to restore the morality to its prime concern with matters of the spirit, and at the same time to introduce classical form, Woodes was working doubly at cross purposes with the popular convention.

In contrast to such anachronisms, the popular theater of Elizabeth's early reign demonstrated its vitality and potentiality for growth by adapting itself to the trend of the times toward secularism. The resulting hybrid moralities, the auspices of which will be examined next, were increasingly designed for London audiences and for the occasional coveted performance at court. Lewis Wager's *The Life and Repentance of Mary Magdalen* (printed 1566) is offered on its title page for four actors. Actually five are required; "foure" may be a misprint for five, since the distribution works easily with five players.[28] Nothing in the play would hinder itinerant production before local spectators, referred to in the text as "our audience" (l. 2007). Stage directions are full and sometimes vivid, and are directed to the players: "Put on a gown and a cap," or "Let Marie creepe vnder the table, abydyng there a certayne space behynd, and doe as it is specified in the Gospell" (ll. 404, 1725). The prologue emphasizes that the players expect to be paid for their performance:

> Truely, I say, whether you geue halfpence or pence,
> Your gayne shalbe double, before you depart hence.   [ll. 43–44]

The prologue also defends the twofold appeal of pious instruction and comic entertainment, urging the ignorant to benefit from the learning, and the virtuous to excuse the bawdry:

> In this matter whiche we are about to recite,
> The ignorant may learne what is true beleue.
>
> . . . .
>
> We desire no man in this poynt to be offended
> In that vertues with vice we shall here introduce,
> For in men and women they haue depended:
> And therefore figuratiuely to speake, it is the use.
>
> [ll. 52–53, 80–83]

The prologue throughout is a fervent defense of the acting profession ("Doth not our facultie learnedly extoll vertue?" l. 31) and a convincing demonstration that moralities continued throughout this period to be acted for "halfpence or pence" to appreciative national audiences, even "at the universitie" (l. 26). The presentation of this drama was by no means limited to an academic audience, for the actors "haue ridden and gone many sundry waies" (l. 25).[29] Wager became rector of St. James Garlickhithe in 1560, and even though he may have written this play earlier, the fact suggests that men of the cloth occasionally contributed to a genuinely popular drama.

Another hybrid morality is the anonymous *King Darius* (printed 1565). It is offered for six players, and although at least seven appear on stage together in one scene (ll. 676–738), many of the supporting roles are so minor that they may have required only extras. The four Kings of Ethiopia, Persia, Judah, and Media speak only a handful of lines each.[30] The production requires a banquet (ll. 611–738), but of an elementary sort that could be provided in any kind of hall. The actors refer to the auditors as "Good people," "my maisters," and "Syrs" (ll. 1, 35, 109), and jestingly bring them into the action:

> Syrs, who is there that hath a stoole?
> I will buy it for thys Gentleman; [that is, for Charity]
> If you will take money, come as fast as you can.   [ll. 109–111]

Despite his banal language and lack of sophistication, the author of *Darius* seems to have made overtures for the endorsement of courtly audiences. The rhetorical debate is of the same kind as in *Godly*

Queen Hester, though of a distinctly inferior quality. The ideas on royal equity and noble constancy are dramatized in the tradition of Heywood's controversies, even though fused with a native didacticism.[31] The play is best suited for the London drama, which had become increasingly concerned with national affairs and was accordingly welcomed by the master politician Elizabeth.

Two important hybrid moralities, Thomas Preston's *Cambises* (ca. 1561) and John Pickering's *Horestes* (printed 1567), are the first plays for which specific acting companies may be conjecturally assigned. The Christmas records at court for 1560–1561 indicate performances of various plays by the Earl of Leicester's (Dudley's) men and Paul's boys, one of which was a "huf suff and ruf." In all probability this title is a substitute for *Cambises,* drawn from the names of three of its comic characters. If so, then *Cambises* was performed by Leicester's men; for Paul's boys were not prepared to handle the rustic and rowdy humor, the violence on stage, and especially the heavy doubling which offers thirty-eight parts for six men and two boys.[32] Leicester's men, on the other hand, had precisely six master players in their 1572 roster, which included persons of importance to the future of the popular stage, notably James Burbage and Robert Wilson. Leicester's men were distinguished in their "quality" and received from the Queen in 1574 a highly favorable patent to play "Comedies, Tragedies, Enterludes, and stage playes" in the cities, towns, and boroughs of England, and especially in London. Records of their provincial touring have been found in Norwich, Oxford, Plymouth, Bristol, Ipswich, Nottingham, Gloucester, Stratford-on-Avon (in 1572–1573 and 1576–1577), and elsewhere. During the winters they frequently appeared at court, and in 1576 they established themselves at James Burbage's Theater.[33]

Cambises is precisely the kind of play with which Leicester's men could cater to an entire nation, on tour, at court, or in London. Along with its obvious popular elements, it offers political advice on the true nature of monarchy, and some surprisingly esoteric learning concerning the Greek tragedian Agathon, accurately translated from the *Eclogae* of Stobaeus (Prologue, ll. 1–6). This scholarship may identify the playwright as Thomas Preston of Cambridge, whose ability as actor and dialectician pleased Queen Elizabeth during her visit to the University in 1564.[34] Yet this university man wrote for a popular company, like Marlowe and other university "wits" in succeeding decades. *Cambises* requires a troupe of eight, and its scene is unlocalized. The setting calls for a banquet (ll. 965–1042), as in *King Darius,* and for a post in one comic scene (l. 186), but either of these could be found or arranged in most halls and inn-yards.

An "Orestes" was one of the plays performed at the Christmas revels of 1567 by Paul's boys and Lord Rich's men. Since *Horestes* was printed in 1567, the coincidence in date strongly suggests that the court performance was in fact Pickering's play. Its language is unpolished, but its message was intended for both courtiers and countrymen.[35] Like *Cambises,* it conceals beneath its unsophisticated exterior a wealth of political advice to the monarchy, concerning the problem of deposing an anointed Queen, Mary Stuart. Mary's presumed guilt in the death of Darnley and subsequent marriage to Bothwell invited comparison with Queen Clytemnestra.[36] Lord Rich's men, rather than Paul's boys, must have given the performance at court, because of the battle scenes and sieges, the drums and trumpets, the use of extras, the presentation of a hanging on stage, and especially the heavy doubling (twenty-seven roles for six players). Lord Rich's men seem to have been a company much like Leicester's men, touring in the provinces (Ipswich, York, Canterbury, and elsewhere), and evidently securing a footing in London[37] as most of the important troupes of the period must have wished to do. The staging in *Horestes* is more elaborate than that of *Cambises,* demanding several armies and a city wall (ll. 697f) which Horestes' soldiers storm and capture, but none of this was beyond the capabilities of a makeshift inn-yard arrangement.

Two popular romance plays survive from the 1570's. *Common Conditions* (published 1576) is offered for six actors, and the parts may be distributed successfully on this basis. The address to the audience recalls that of *Mankind:* "You skilfull heads, that sit in place to see" (l. 1). Staging requires little more than a playing area and a "tree" (perhaps a post) into which Common Conditions escapes from the three Tinkers (ll. 408–434). The stage directions to enter "out of the wood" or "out of Phrygia" may indicate the use of printed signs, like the *"Thebes* written in great letters upon an old door" described in Sidney's *Defense of Poesy,* or the direction in the *Spanish Tragedy*'s play within a play to "Hang up the title: 'Our scene is Rhodes'" (IV, iii, 16–17). The broad comedy, the songs, the professional Vice, the limited cast, and the extensive doubling all point to an adult company with perhaps two trained boys.

Clyomon and Clamydes (probably written in the 1570's) is more elaborate in staging, and in fact may suggest the use of a permanent London theater after 1576. Properties include a hearse and the head of a serpent. The demand for extras is unusually high: "Enter King Alexander the Great, as valiantly set forth as may be, and as many souldiers as can" (ll. 358–359). Even here, however, the phrasing indicates consciousness of limitation in numbers of actors. The stage itself must provide a prison, with a window through which Clamydes' voice can be heard speaking to Subtle Shift and a door through which Clamydes can "enter out" (ll. 872–914). Most impressive of all is the fact that Providence descends from the "heavens" and reascends (ll. 1549–1565). Such phenomena may have been the effect of revision before the first printed edition of 1599. The play was acted "by her Maiesties Players," whose activities began in 1583, and they may well have been reviving an old favorite. The total number of actors on stage at one time is nine. The broadly romantic plot, the use of drums, trumpets, and soldiers, the flagrant violations of the dramatic unities, and the lack of act and scene divisions all point to a rollicking and professionally acted popular drama.

Three plays "offered for acting" must be rejected from the popular canon, despite the prima-facie inference that plays with casting lists were intended for the professional market. One is *The Comedy of Patient and Meek Grissell* (S.R. 1565) by John Phillip, probably a Cambridge man and political pamphleteer.[38] The casting list for eight players seems patently deceptive.[39] It repeatedly violates the highly necessary admonition (in *Juventus*) that two parts assigned to one player "be not in place at once": Reason and Diligence (ll. 944–951), Countess' Maid and Diligence (ll. 1257–1280), Sobriety and Common People (ll. 1703–1718), Reason and Daughter of Grissell (ll. 1877–1976), and Countess of Pango and Sobriety (ll. 1877–1976). In addition, characters are often meeting their counterparts in troublesome adjoining entrances and exits (see, for example, ll. 216 and 1877). This hopelessly tangled casting chart, perhaps a publisher's fraud, is prefixed to a play that bears weighty evidence of having been acted by boys instead of an adult troupe. The number of female roles is too large for a popular play. Of a total of twenty-five or twenty-six, ten or eleven characters are women and three are boys —a proportion like that in *The Marriage of Wit and Science*. At least five of the eight actors are obliged to undertake feminine or juvenile parts. Characteristic too of childrens' theater are the emphasis on chastity, the overlay of classical mythology, the delicate songs (one is to the tune of "Damon and Pythias"), and the lack of low comedy. Several *domus* must have been staged simultaneously.[40] The topical allusions suggest, by their subtlety and refinement of taste, that the author was conversant with inner politics at court, like the authors of *Gorboduc, The Misfortunes of Arthur,* and *Endymion*.[41]

Thomas Garter's *Virtuous and Godly Susanna* (first printed in 1578) calls for an arrangement in staging unlike anything known to have been in use by popular troupes. Separated from its "stage" is an "orchard" with trees from which Susanna and her maids can be heard and probably seen as she prepares for her bath, and which has a functional gate that can be shut when her maids return to the main stage (l. 701). The two corrupt judges who lust after Susanna have previously gone into the orchard and hidden themselves. Almost one hundred lines of dialogue are spoken within this orchard. The acting area must have been divided by a partition running from front to back.[42] Later, in the trial scene, the playwright provides for the entrance of his *deus ex machina* with the ambiguous stage direction: "God rayseth the spirite of Danyell" (l. 1061). If this means merely that God moves Daniel's spirit to action, it is a stage direction with a curiously nontheatrical flavor. After the trial, the wicked judges are stoned to death in some unexplained manner on stage, but no opportunity is provided for their necessary removal from the stage in order that one of them may double as Satan in the ensuing scene. These difficulties suggest that the play was never actually performed.[43] The casting is far from expert. It offers only sixteen parts for eight players, and one of these (player one) is left idle through most of the play. The whole play is impractical and at times painfully amateurish, as though the author were trying to write an edifying morality for "this company gathered here" and "my maysters all," but had not perfectly comprehended the problems of his stage. The author was evidently a learned man, probably acquainted with some of the

Susanna plays in the Christian Terence. He observes the decorums of limiting the time to a single day and the scene to the city of Babylon. In his comic scenes he indulges chiefly in verbal wit, such as altering letters in words. The characters True Report and his cousin Ill Report have been at Oxford.[44] Perhaps the most telling clue is found in the Epilogue's apology for his actors' inability to sing:

> And though we cannot bewtify the same with musickes song,
> Beare with our rudenesse in that part, we troubled you not long.
>
> [ll. 1446–1447]

It is most unlikely that professional actors of the time would be unable to sing. *Conflict of Conscience*, also lacking song, makes a similar apology, and it may be that these two plays were not unlike in their amateur auspices.

Finally, the manuscript play *Misogonus* (1560–1577) has no place in the popular repertory for several reasons. Its division of the parts assigns sixteen roles (excluding prologue and epilogue) to ten actors, an excessive number for an early Elizabethan popular troupe. Four of the players undertake female parts; most of the other characters are youths, servants, or old men, roles in which boys excelled. The tone of *Misogonus* is that of a school play, combining hearty English humor and profanity (as in *Gammer Gurton's Needle*) with many classical elements. The play shows the influence of continental Renaissance drama. Like many of the plays written for schoolboys by Dutch and German humanists, *Misogonus* retells the familiar Biblical story of the prodigal son in the style of Latin comedy. The faithful Eupelas, for example, is similar to the character Eubulus in Gnaphaeus' *Acolastus,* and the wily servants Orgelus and Oenophilus behave like the parasite slaves in Plautus' comedies.[45] *Misogonus* is divided into acts and scenes, with the names of the characters occasionally grouped at the head of a scene. Stage directions are sparse and are in Latin. Why the author of a school play should wish to double even a few of its roles remains a mystery, but the author's connection with Cambridge seems likely. The text refers to Cambridge (III, iii, 72), and the "Kettering" named on the title page is not far from the university town. The cryptic "Laurentius Bariona" may identify the author as Laurence Johnson, graduate of Christ's college.[46]

In conclusion, a tabulation may be convenient. The listing that follows omits such obvious and long-established facts as that *Gammer Gurton's Needle* was a university play and *Gorboduc* the product of the Inns of Court:

Children's plays at court, containing in many cases pronounced characteristics of the morality:
Wit and Science (ca. 1530–1548)
Weather (ca. 1533)
Nice Wanton (ca. 1535–1553)
Respublica (1553)
Jacob and Esau (ca. 1547–1553)
The Marriage of Wit and Science (before 1570)
Jack Juggler (ca. 1553–1558)
Tom Tyler and His Wife (1558–1563)
Godly Queen Hester (before 1561)
Patient and Meek Grissell (ca. 1558–1565)
Disobedient Child (ca. 1558–1569)
Appius and Virginia (ca. 1559–1567)
Liberality and Prodigality (ca. 1567–1568)

University plays:
Palamon and Arcite (1566)
Misogonus (1560–1577)
Richardus Tertius (1580)

Humanist plays intended primarily as experimental drama or drama of ideas, also infused with notable elements of the native tradition:
Fulgens and Lucrece (ca. 1497)
Nature (before 1500)
Four Elements (ca. 1517–1518)
Calisto and Melibea (ca. 1516–1533)
Witty and Witless (ca. 1520–1533)
Of Gentleness and Nobility (ca. 1527)
Love (ca. 1533)

Fifteenth-century precursors of the itinerant drama:
Castle of Perseverance (ca. 1400–1405)
Play of the Sacrament (ca. 1461)

Wisdom Who Is Christ (ca. 1460–1474)

Popular plays of the late fifteenth century and Henrician period (1470–1547).

Anonymous plays:

Mankind (ca. 1471)
Mundus et Infans (ca. 1500–1522)
Hickescorner (ca. 1500–1520)
The Interlude of Youth (ca. 1513–1529)

Humanist contributions (John Heywood):

Pardoner and the Friar (1513–1521)
Four PP (1520–1522)
John John (1520–1533)

Contributions of literary men with affiliations at court (Skelton and Bale):

Magnificence (ca. 1515–1523)
King John (ca. 1530–1538)
Three Laws (ca. 1530–1538)

Popular plays of Edwardian and Marian reigns, 1547–1558:

Impatient Poverty (ca. 1547–1553)
Lusty Juventus (1547–1553)
Wealth and Health (before 1557)

Popular plays of Elizabeth's early reign, until the opening of the Theater, 1558–1576:

The Marriage of Wit and Wisdom (before 1570)
Mary Magdalen (ca. 1547–1566)
King Darius (ca. 1558–1565)
Like Will to Like (1558–1568)
Enough Is as Good as a Feast (ca. 1558–1569)
New Custom (1558–1573)
The Tide Tarrieth No Man (before 1576)
The Trial of Treasure (before 1567)
The Longer Thou Livest the More Fool Thou Art (1558–1569)
Cambises (ca. 1561)
Horestes (ca. 1567)
All for Money (1558–1578)
Common Conditions (ca. 1570–1576)
Clyomon and Clamydes (ca. 1570–1583)

Moralities and late mystery plays of cloistered and amateur auspices:

God's Chief Promises (ca. 1538)
John Baptist (ca. 1538)
Temptation (ca. 1538)
John the Evangelist (1520–1557)
Conflict of Conscience (before 1581)
Virtuous and Godly Susanna (ca. 1563–1569)

V   "Four Men and a Boy"

Moore. how manie are ye?
Player. ffoure men and a boy Sir.
            ——*Sir Thomas More,* ll. 931–932.

Now that a repertory has been established for "My Lord Cardinalls players" and other troupes of a similar professional standing, the next task is to examine in detail the composition and internal organization of these player bands. How many were they in number, how long were the plays they performed, and how much doubling were their members expected to undertake? Did their membership always include a boy and a leading actor? These are only a few of the questions to be investigated.

The play within a play of *Sir Thomas More,* already mentioned in Chapter II, provides a sort of genre painting of a "typical" troupe of mid-century or before, as viewed by a dramatist of the 1590's. The group portrait is not without a touch of satire, and should not be accepted as entirely accurate. Nevertheless, it has often served as a convenient example of the *modus operandi* of the itinerant troupes.[1] The salient features described are that the players are five in number, that the boy is expected to play all three of the women's parts, that the leading player takes the role of Vice and also tries to produce and direct the play, doing his best to cope with the crisis of a missing beard. The three other actors apparently divide the remaining roles between them. Beards are a primary means of changing character in the doubling of roles. The inexpertness of the performance is comically absurd. In this chapter and the one that follows we will test the validity of this generalized description by means of the fairly plentiful evidence found in the casting lists of popular plays and the internal evidence of the plays themselves.

As a preliminary it is interesting to note the relative lengths of plays acted by the troupes, and especially the steady increase in length during the course of the sixteenth century. Here our attempts at distinguishing acting traditions and auspices of production become useful in interpreting the data, especially during the early years of the period. For if one considers all morality plays as belonging to a homogeneous literary genre, the chronology of their growth in length is not at all clear or consistent. Gayley has noted this inconsistency, and has challenged the usual assumption that the moralities were lengthy during the early fifteenth century, became brief during the Henrician period when the professional troupes were small, and became longer as the troupes matured and prospered.[2] Numerous apparent exceptions may be cited, particularly during the Henrician period of assumed brevity. *Magnificence, King John,* and *Respublica,* to name only three, are all lengthy.

The confusion has arisen from the impulse to group all the moralities together as representing one tradition, instead of observing them in differing conditions of performance. Plays of the itinerant troupes were necessarily brief at first. The actors were relatively few in number, were playing chiefly to rural and village audiences, and had only meager resources for costuming and staging. The authors were usually plain-spoken men dramatizing a simple moral tale. Accordingly, the works of the popular canon prior to the accession of Elizabeth never exceed 1200 lines, and the average length is less than 1000 lines (plays enclosed in parentheses are antecedent to the popular troupe drama):[3]

(*The Castle of Perseverance*)	3650
(*Wisdom Who Is Christ*)	1168
(*Play of the Sacrament*)	927
Mankind	907
Mundus et Infans	979
Hickescorner	1026
Youth	786
Impatient Poverty	1100
Lusty Juventus	1167
Wealth and Health	964

Heywood's popular plays, intended for three or four actors, are correspondingly brief: *The Pardoner and the Friar,* ca. 641, *Four PP,* 1236, and *John John,* 680.

Moralities written during this same period under humanist, courtly, or ecclesiastical aegis, however, often run to considerable length. Bale and Skelton wrote popular plays, but their literary talents produced works of greater complexity and length than those of the anonymous writers, and they tended to demand more of their actors. *Magnificence* contains 1567 lines, *King John,* 2656, and *Three Laws,* 2081. Medwall is well known for his prolixity: *Fulgens and Lucrece* is divided into two parts of 1432 and 921 lines, and *Nature* into two parts of 1439 and 1421 lines. In Scotland, Sir David Lindsay's epic morality *The Satire of the Three Estates* (1540) with its 4630 lines outstrips even *Perseverance* in length. In production it hearkens back to the panorama of the cycles and employs at least thirty actors. Childrens' moralities before 1558 are occasionally lengthy. *Respublica* has 1940 lines, *Jacob and Esau,* 1836.

With the coming of Elizabeth's reign, several factors combined to augment the length of the popular play, especially the growth in size of the troupes, their increased prosperity, their gaining of footholds in London, and their experimentation with new materials of chronicle and romance:

Marriage of Wit and Wisdom	1290
Mary Magdalen	2035
King Darius	1605
Like Will to Like	1277
Enough Is as Good as a Feast	1541
New Custom	1076
The Tide Tarrieth No Man	1879
The Trial of Treasure	1148
The Longer Thou Livest	1977
Cambises	1248
Horestes	1205
All for Money	1572
Common Conditions	1904
Clyomon and Clamydes	2220

The gradual increase in the length of these plays throughout the sixteenth century corresponds to a marked degree with two phenomena to be observed next, the growth in number of players and the expansion in the amount of doubling undertaken by the individual actor. The correlation was a natural one as the popular playwrights moved experimentally toward a larger scope of dramatic activity. In the tabulation on page 72 those plays which are "offered for acting" to a specific number of players are clearly of greatest value in determining the actual size of the troupe, and are therefore indicated by an asterisk. In other cases the figure listed under "number of players" is the practicable minimum required to present the play, and thus constitutes a potential for doubling rather than proof that such doubling actually took place.

The statistics on number of actors give a rough index of troupe size at different times during the entire period, and of trends in growth of troupe size. Middle and late fifteenth-century plays are still moderately large in cast, seemingly in transition from the more lengthy and all-inclusive mysteries. In the early sixteenth century, four, five, and six actors are the usual numbers. It is not until the 1560's and 1570's that troupes of seven and eight begin to be indicated; but even at this time, groups of four to six are not unusual.[4] *Clyomon and Clamydes*, with its demand for at least ten actors, seems to have heralded the arrival of a permanent London stage. The use of extras is implied only rarely in the early Elizabethan period.

Similarly, the ratio of the total number of roles to the number of actors shows an unmistakable and parallel increase throughout the sixteenth century. *Play of the Sacrament*, the earliest play offered for acting, contents itself with only twelve roles for nine actors. Other early anonymous plays confirm this modest proportion, although it must be remembered that the number of actors tabulated below is in some cases conjectural. *Mankind* allows for doubling only one of its seven roles, and *Hickescorner* and *Youth* demand four or five actors for six roles in each instance. Other plays offered for acting in the pre-Elizabethan period also suggest that the anonymous authors were expanding their dramatic scope with caution. *Wealth and Health* allows only one instance of doubling, and in *Juventus* and *Impatient Poverty* the ratio is approximately two parts for each actor.

On the other hand, Bale and Skelton show during this same period a precocity in doubling that reflects their tendency to an-

Ratio of Total Number of Roles Presented to the Number of Players

	Total roles	Number of players
Before 1547:		
(*The Castle of Perseverance*)	35	over 22
(*Wisdom Who Is Christ*)	36	12
* (*Play of the Sacrament*)	12	9
Mankind	7	6
Mundus et Infans	5	2
Hickescorner	6	4 or 5
Youth	6	5
Heywood:		
The Pardoner and the Friar	4	4
Four PP	4	4
John John	3	3
Skelton and Bale:		
Magnificence	18	5
King John	19	6
* *Three Laws*	14	5
1547–1558:		
* *Impatient Poverty*	8	4
* *Lusty Juventus*	9	4
* *Wealth and Health* (offered erroneously for four)	7	6
1558–1576:		
* *Marriage of Wit and Wisdom*	19	6
* *Mary Magdalen* (offered erroneously for four)	15	5
* *King Darius*	21	6 (+ extras?)
* *Like Will to Like*	16	5
* *Enough Is as Good as a Feast*	18	7
* *New Custom*	11	4
* *The Tide Tarrieth No Man*	18	4
* *The Trial of Treasure*	15	5
* *The Longer Thou Livest*	15	4
* *Cambises*	38	8
* *Horestes*	27 (+ extras)	6 (+ extras)
All for Money	20	4
* *Common Conditions*	21	6
Clyomon and Clamydes	33 (+ extras)	10

ticipate trends rather than to accept current norms. *Magnificence* and *King John* exceed three roles for each actor, and *Three Laws* is not far behind with fourteen parts for five actors.

During the first twenty years of Elizabeth's reign a three-to-one ratio becomes quite common in the popular theater. In a few important cases — notably in plays which are expanding their homiletic form to include chronicle, *Cambises* and *Horestes* — the ratio of roles to players exceeds four to one. Both extant romances, *Common Conditions* and *Clyomon and Clamydes*, exceed three to one. *All for Money*, almost surely written for four actors, establishes the highest recorded level of doubling with an average of five parts for every actor.

Unquestionably the popular theater of the sixteenth century operated with doubling as one of its basic practices. In no extant popular play during this period, excluding Heywood's, do all of the characters appear on stage at once. The parts are always arranged so that at least some doubling is possible. In addition, there is with time a steady growth in the amount of doubling, reflecting a desire on the part of the playwrights and their audience to include more material and to fill the stage with an ever-increasing number of allegorical personifications and historical personages. This tendency marks a universal distinction between popular and élite theater. Occasionally, courtly drama must have employed some doubling, but only when it was unavoidable. The popular tradition found doubling to be an indispensable, inevitable, and congenial technique of dramatic construction. Accordingly, the effect produced by heavy and consistent doubling on the internal organization of plays was a phenomenon peculiar to popular drama during this period.

The statistics on doubling presented so far have dealt in terms of averages for the entire troupe, in order to give an impression of the over-all increase in doubling during the century. The roles were not divided evenly among the members of the troupe, however, and the next step must be to distinguish between the various responsibilities of the boy, the leading actor, and the remaining players. The primary documents are the plays offered for acting, especially those with casting lists. Accordingly the period covered by this descriptive report will be from the 1530's, the approximate date of Bale's *Three Laws*, to the late 1570's, with the majority of the samples falling in the latter half of this period. The attempt is to reconstruct a composite picture of a mid-century popular troupe, and to discern trends in its development culminating in the London companies of the 1580's and 1590's.

The first inquiry concerns the employment of boy actors for the women's parts. Were the female roles invariably assigned to a boy, and only to him? Was there one boy in every troupe of four, five, or six players, and only one? Was this boy actor limited to portrayal of women and children, or could he fill other roles? Does the number of boy actors tend to increase in the 1560's and 1570's as troupe size increases? J. A. Symonds' summary of the acting tradition of these strolling players, based in part on the play within the play of *Sir Thomas More*, may serve as a convenient and perhaps too widely accepted generalization which will be tested: "The leading actor played the part of Vice and undertook stage management. There was a boy for the female characters; and the remaining two or three divided the other parts between them."[5]

As it happens, investigation of the casting lists reveals no single instance to support this generalization in its literal sense. That is, no play in the group distributes its roles so that one player handles all the female parts and only female parts. Some of these plays, in fact, have no identifiable female roles at all: *Impatient Poverty, Wealth and Health, Like Will to Like,* and *Enough Is as Good as a Feast.* In such cases, the boy member — if indeed he existed for the troupe in question — would have to play an equal assortment of demanding male roles with the other supporting players of his group. In *Like Will to Like,* for example, he might be assigned to play Lucifer, Ralph Roister, Good Fame, and Severity, or perhaps Philip Fleming, Pierce Pickpurse, and Honor. The remaining sets of roles are no less thoroughly male, and in every case the supposed boy would have to perform the burlesque routines of comic villainy. The more logical assumption is that the troupes which performed these plays employed no boy.

Still other plays offer only one, or perhaps two, feminine or juvenile roles, so distributed that the person playing these roles had also to play other parts of a dominantly adult and masculine character. In Bale's *Three Laws,* for example, Idolatry "decked lyke an olde wytche" is the only female character, and doubles with Law of Moses and with Hypocrisy, apparelled "lyke a graye fryre." Idolatry appears in part of one scene only; the others appear throughout the play. Because of the scarcity of feminine roles in all of Bale's printed plays, it is probable that "my Lord Cromwell's players" consisted of five men rather than four men and a boy.[6] In *Juventus*, lacking a casting list but convincingly offered for four players, Abominable Living is the only female, and any feasible scheme for doubling requires that she double with at least two male parts, perhaps Satan and God's Merciful Promises.

In *All for Money*'s list of thirty-two *dramatis personae,* the aged Mother Croote is the only woman. Thomas Lupton plainly wrote this play for four adult actors. In fact he altered his source (a sermon by Latimer) in order to eliminate female roles. He keeps off stage a woman infanticide who bribes a judge, permitting her only to communicate by letter, and he changes the sex of a petty thief who was a woman in Latimer's account. Lupton also makes humorous use of his professional players in juvenile roles. The birth of Satan as a full-grown adult allows the actor to make comic capital out of his maturity, thereby reversing the customary quip in the boys' theater arising from the immaturity of the young actor.[7]

New Custom describes Hypocrisy on the title page as "an old Woman." Hypocrisy is assigned to player two, along with Ignorance, an "elder" Popish priest, and Edification, "a Sage." Hypocrisy is on stage for only seventy-four lines; the other parts are important supporting roles, appearing for the major portion of the play. In the later boys' companies, star performers like Salomon Pavy often imitated old men, utilizing the treble voice as a stock characteristic of stage oldsters. Such assignments, however, were the product of the peculiar casting limitations in boys' theater. The popular troupes had no reason to anticipate this practice. Instead, they were evidently more inclined to assign incidental female parts to the men, especially if the women were disfigured and unfeminine like Idolatry, Mother Croote, and Hypocrisy, or courtesans like Abominable Living.[8]

The Tide Tarrieth No Man offers perhaps the most striking example of this undertaking of female roles by a seemingly adult player. Its one female role, Wantonness "the Woman," is assigned to player four along with five other parts, all of them male and some of them vividly comic: Feigned Furtherance, Greediness, the

Sergeant, Authority, and Despair. The rapid transition from Greediness to Wantonness and then to the Sergeant is a remarkable demonstration of the flexibility demanded of this player in shifting from one sex to the other and back again. Greediness exits at line 1198, and during the absence of player four the Vice and his companion Hurtful Help "fighteth to prolong the time, while Wantonnesse maketh her ready" (l. 1215). Wantonness enters at line 1247, transformed not only in garment but in personality. She departs at line 1362, and thirty lines later the Sergeant appears to play his part. It would be unsafe to assume that this group of roles, and the others already mentioned, would of necessity require the talents of a boy.

In at least eight plays offered for acting and in *All for Money*, then, it is presumptuous to suppose that the boy had any function whatsoever. Many of these plays are pre-Elizabethan, four of them quite early: *Three Laws, Impatient Poverty, Wealth and Health*, and *Juventus*. In fact, no pre-Elizabethan play offered for acting provides positive evidence of the existence of the boy.

Early plays without casting lists, even though lacking evidence as to doubling, seem to offer few feasible roles for a boy actor. The author of *Mankind* consciously avoids female roles, for the portrayal of Mercy as a male priest ("I, Mercy, hys father gostly," l. 758) is a departure from the traditional representation of this abstraction as a woman.[9] Apart from Mercy and the title figure, the *dramatis personae* are all rude, swearing, fighting vice figures. *Mundus et Infans* and *Hickescorner* have no discernible feminine roles. Infans, despite his juvenile name, grows into "Manhood" and "Age" and has the leading role in the play. In Bale's *King John* the only woman, the widow England, doubles with Clergy. Heywood's popular plays, *Four PP* and *The Pardoner and the Friar*, provide no opportunity for differentiation of acting talents between boys and grown men. If the boy participated in these productions, he did so on an equal footing with other members of the troupe. All told, fifteen plays of the popular canon reveal no need for a boy.

Remarkably few plays — in fact, only two — appear to call for the services of one and only one boy. *Trial of Treasure* gives both of its women's parts, Trust and Treasure, to "the fourth" player, probably a boy. Even so, he is not limited to female roles. Player four must render the part of Elation, one of the boisterous companions of the Vice (pp. 271–275).

Horestes also seems to demand one boy, who performs both female and male roles. Yet additional female roles are distributed to other distinctly adult members of the troupe. The female leading role, Clytemnestra, and Menelaus' daughter Hermione, are assigned to player six. Even he, as in the case above, is burdened with some very difficult assignments: the profane and scurrilous Hempstring, who is directed to "fyght at bofites with fystes" with his Newgate companion, Haltersick (l. 389); and also Provision (ll. 926f), who acts as marshal for the kings of Greece. Allowing player six to be the boy notwithstanding, we still find that Horestes himself, the male lead, plays "a woman like a begger, rounning before they sodier" (ll. 625f). Nature, who appears to be a motherly sort of woman (ll. 400f), is played by the Vice.

In *Cambises* the adult players undertake female roles, even though the troupe includes two boys. The casting list is fairly careful to segregate feminine and juvenile roles for the last two of the eight players, and even distinguishes in ability between the leading boy and the younger boy. Player seven portrays Meretrix, Shame, Otian (Sisamnes' son), Mother, and Lady (the Queen). Shame, although a neutral allegorical figure, may have been thought of as a male role; his brief appearance at line 340 comes at a time in the play when all the adult players are busily occupied in immediately adjoining scenes, and the part appears to have fallen to the leading boy by default. Player eight is limited to Young Child (seven speaking lines) and Cupid (six lines). Notwithstanding this careful distinction, the exigencies of doubling in such a sprawling and ambitious play require that the goddess of beauty, none other than Venus herself, be rendered by the player of Lord, Commons' Cry, Commons' Complaint, Lord Smirdis, and — *mirabile dictu* — the redoubtable desperado Ruf. Thus even the later and more professionally advanced plays of the popular theater, although tending to specialize the boy's role, were constantly required by expediency to provide numerous exceptions to the rule.[10]

The Longer Thou Livest appears at first glance to come closer than any other play to fulfilling Symonds' definition of the boy's position in a popular troupe. Its sole feminine role, Lady Fortune, is the responsibility of the player whose only other part is that of

Moros, the harebrained central figure. Moros is a child at heart, if not in years, and his character might suit a boy actor's age. Yet Moros is also the leading role, requiring the sort of adept comic acting later perfected by Tarleton and Kempe. The part is the acting plum of the play, and it is hard to imagine that the leading player would yield it to his boy. Besides, the casting lists of these popular plays offer no instance of a boy actor's having undertaken the broadly comic idiom of the fool.

Three late casting lists demand two boy actors. *Cambises*, already discussed, is one of these. *Marriage of Wit and Wisdom* offers a remarkably clear case: of its six actors, two play all the female parts and do nothing else. One plays Indulgence (Wit's mother), Wisdom (the heroine), and Mother Bee. The other plays Wantonness, Fancy, and Doll. The third instance is the late romance *Mucedorus* (ca. 1590), helpful perhaps in suggesting a trend in the 1580's toward increased specialization of boys' roles. The heroine, Amadine, whose important part requires the talents of the leading boy, doubles no other roles. The younger boy, player six, has four "bit" parts: Comedy in the induction (who calls herself a "woman"), a Boy with the boar's head, who speaks no lines, Ariena (one speaking line), and an old woman. The last three characters appear only briefly in single scenes. Here, as in *Cambises*, one sees the development toward a ranking of the boy actors into a leading boy and his considerably less experienced assistant.

It is erroneous, then, to speak of "the boy" as a predictable and unchanging member of these popular troupes. His position during the sixteenth century was evidently subject to continual redefinition. Even though his function became more specialized with time, the progression was not steady. Some of the plays requiring no boy's talents at all occur quite late, such as *All for Money*, and it seems reasonable to suppose that some strolling troupes may have had one or even two boys when other troupes had none. Again, there seems little basis for thinking that boys were used from the very first solely for feminine or juvenile roles. Nearly all the early impressions of these boy actors suggest versatility and not specialization.

Nevertheless, the adult players seem always to have been reluctant to portray female characters other than those absolutely necessary for the plot. The early plays, which apparently employed no boys, tend accordingly to present as few females as possible. Even in a later play, *Cambises*, the adult player who undertakes the role of Venus does so only in an especially difficult situation, when all his fellow actors are otherwise employed; there are actually eight players on stage (ll. 872f). The limitation on the number of women's roles imposed on Shakespeare and his contemporary playwrights for the public theater is seen even more clearly in the predominantly male casts of early popular plays.

No evidence suggests that women ever acted in the troupe theater. They appeared occasionally in medieval plays on the Continent and in England. The Chester cycle assigned the play of the Assumption of the Virgin to "ye wyfus of ye town," and women were paid for appearing in a London Lord Mayor's show in 1523. Even so, such occasions are late and infrequent, with no hint of that free association of men and women found in the jongleur bands of the Middle Ages.[11] Whether owing to the moral climate of opinion or to the weakness of feminine voices, women never entered the ranks of the professional players.

Perhaps the clearest summary that can be constructed is as follows. In pre-Elizabethan times most, if not all, popular troupes appear to have performed without a boy. The adult actors avoided feminine and juvenile roles as much as they could, but when necessity demanded a woman for the plot, any member of the troupe could double such a part. Even the leading player might take a female role. When the troupes began belatedly to take on young apprentices, they evidently preferred to have two rather than one. Such boys were likely to receive female roles, but might also perform male parts. Female roles might still go to the adult players when no other arrangement was feasible. By and large, however, the tendency was toward specialization of the boys for female roles, and toward a hierarchical distinction between fully trained and less experienced apprentices. On the other hand, all-adult troupes appear to have been in existence throughout the Elizabethan era prior to 1576.

Our next concern is with the leading player. Once again Symonds' generalization, and the picture of an old morality production in *Sir Thomas More*, may serve as the basis of discussion: "The leading actor played the part of Vice and undertook stage management." To this may be added W. J. Lawrence's conclusion that the Vice enjoyed the privilege of not being doubled.[12] What evidence is there that every troupe had such a leading player? Does this leading player always take the part of the Vice? To what extent is the Vice the dominating role in the play, and does the extent of his dominance vary in different periods of the sixteenth century? How often is the leading man called upon to double other roles? How many and how demanding are these roles? These are some of the questions for which the plays offered for acting can provide documentary illustration. The inquiry presupposes that the popular plays being studied are in fact moralities containing Vice characters, a correspondence which was demonstrated in the previous chapters on canon.

In a majority of popular plays, the Vice has indisputable command of the stage. In *Three Laws* Infidelity is the recognized chieftain of "the six vyces," and is actually on stage for 1561 of the play's 2081 lines, far ahead of the nearest contender. He doubles two roles, which at first glance seem as many as any of the supporting members of his troupe. But the roles are "Prolocutor," or prologue (35 lines), and Christian Faith, who appears in the last ninety lines of the play in order to speak a sort of epilogue. Thus the leading player introduces and then apologizes for his play, as the stage manager might be expected to do. In the meantime he appears almost continually in the role of Vice, occupying the center of attention and manipulating the action.

Several other plays confirm the dominance of the Vice. In *Impatient Poverty*, Envy, although not named as such, appears to be the Vice. He is present on stage for 532 of 1100 lines, more than any other character, and doubles only with the "Sommer" (Summoner) who appears briefly toward the end of the play for 99 lines. "Idleness the vice" in *Marriage of Wit and Wisdom* doubles only with prologue and epilogue, like Infidelity in *Three Laws*. Idleness occupies the stage for 669 lines of 1290. In *Trial of Treasure*, "Inclination the Vice" is the only one of five players not required to double. All the others have at least three parts. Inclination is on stage for 723 of 1148 lines; the nearest role, Lust, is considerably far behind with 487 lines. Again, "Nichol Newfangle the Vice" in *Like Will to Like* is assigned to player five without doubling, whereas the other four players have at least three roles each — frequently four. Newfangle is an unusually dominant Vice, being on stage almost continually, for 1077 lines of a total 1277. Tom Tosspot is second with a mere 408 lines, Virtuous Living third with 265. The Vice of *New Custom*, "Peruerse Doctrine, an olde Popishe priest," has an equally dominating role. He appears in all but 110 of the play's 1076 lines. Some part of his dominance stems from his being the mankind hero as well as the Vice, converted to true Christianity at the end of the play. He is the only player of four not required to double.

In *The Tide Tarrieth No Man*, "Corage the Vice" doubles only with Debtor, a minor character appearing in one 47–line scene (ll. 1393–1439). This instance affords an illustration of the conditions under which the Vice might take such a role. The other three actors are either on stage during this scene, or are off stage preparing to appear almost immediately. In other words, the Vice may be expected to double with minor parts in a difficult situation, when the rest of the troupe is already employed. Otherwise he is left to perform his specialized and demanding role without added burden other than prologue and epilogue. Courage's role by itself is taxing enough. He is on stage for all but 420 of the play's 1879 lines, and has no near rival.

The dominance of the Vice in the plays mentioned so far can be demonstrated neatly by the position of his name on the printed casting lists. In nearly every case so far mentioned, the Vice is named first or last among the list of characters, and the grouping on the page is often such that the Vice's name receives typographical prominence. His name is first in the casting lists of *Three Laws*, *New Custom*, and *Marriage of Wit and Wisdom*. It is last in *Impatient Poverty*, *Trial of Treasure*, and *Like Will to Like*. Only in *The Tide Tarrieth No Man* is his name placed between those of other players.

In the remaining plays covered by this investigation, however, the dominance of the Vice is beginning to yield to other forces. Correspondingly, one finds in this group that the Vice's name tends to disappear from its position of prominence in the casting list. In *The Longer Thou Livest*, for example, Moros is given to player two of four players, and in *Cambises* Ambidexter is given to the sixth of eight players. In these plays, and in *Horestes* and *Enough Is as Good as a Feast,* the secularizing tendencies at work in the mid-century morality are bringing to the fore new figures and per-

sonages, often from history, legend, or romance, whose increasing
importance in the hybrid plays inevitably comes to rival and even
surpass the traditionally central function of the Vice. In *Enough*,
for example, "Couetousnes the Uice" occupies the important last
position in the casting list, but his prominence is offset by Worldly
Man, the human protagonist, in first position. Both parts are assigned without doubling, and Covetousness' 986 lines of a total 1541
are closely rivaled by Worldly Man's 870. In *The Longer Thou
Livest* the role assigned to the leading player may not accurately
be described as "Vice." Moros, like Worldly Man, is the human
protagonist, a secular figure who dominates this play instead of
the Vice. *New Custom*, already mentioned, presents a leading
figure in Perverse Doctrine who performs the function of Vice
throughout most of the play only to be transformed into the
virtuous hero at the end.

As secular figures grew in importance, the relationship between
the Vice and the leading player must have grown more tenuous
until at some point the leading player shifted his talents to a portrayal of the human hero. This tendency was already apparent in
Horestes and *Cambises*. In *Horestes* both "the Vice" and the title
role are assigned to actors each of whom play two additional parts,
but these demands are small when compared with the duties of
the other players. The actor of "the Vice" also portrays Nature
(about forty-eight lines on stage) and Duty, a minor personage in
the final scene whose real function is to speak the epilogue and the
prayer for Elizabeth, her Nobles, the Lord Mayor, and so on. The
actor of Horestes doubles as Prologue (whose part is not printed,
but is assigned in the casting list) and with "a woman like a
begger" appearing for twenty-two lines. Thus the two leading
players divide between them the labor of prologue and epilogue.
The other four players have from four to seven roles each. Horestes
and "the Vice" are on stage for nearly the same length of time:
Horestes for 521 lines of a total 1205, "the Vice" for 557. Despite
the Vice's slight edge in these statistics, however, it is evident from
a reading of the play that Horestes has taken over the central
position. The Vice is only an instrument; Horestes controls the
action and speaks the important lines.

Cambises exhibits a notably similar troupe structure. The actor
playing Ambidexter the Vice doubles only as Trial, a minor char-

acter who appears for forty lines and speaks once (ll. 405–406). Even this brief appearance might have been avoided except for a critical moment in which all the other adult players are on stage and occupied at the time. King Cambises himself is played by an actor who doubles only as Epilogue, rising like Nell Gwyn of later years to "speak the Epilogue" after having died on stage. The other adult players all take five to seven roles each. Ambidexter is on stage for 436 of the play's 1248 lines; Cambises, incontrovertibly the leading role, is on stage for 604 lines. The essential groundwork has been prepared for the later dominance of Tamburlaine, Hieronimo, and Richard III, although the gradual nature of the change may be seen in Richard's blend of the traditions of Vice and leading human protagonist.

Such an important transition raises the interesting possibility of a second leading adult player in the makeup of the popular troupes. In several of these plays, especially the hybrids, we find two players standing above the rest in importance, and distinguished from the others by doubling only in unusual cases: Worldly Man and Covetousness, Horestes and "the Vice," Cambises and Ambidexter. Significantly they are from plays performed by growing troupes: *Horestes*, six plus extras, *Enough*, seven, and *Cambises*, eight. Although it may be doubted whether a hierarchy of two leading players became fixed and standard during this period of the late 1560's and 1570's, it is reasonable to suppose that as the troupes expanded they discovered a capacity not previously feasible for distinguishing between first-rank supporting players and those who would specialize in minor parts.

This concept introduces the next topic, the manner in which the remaining roles were distributed among the supporting members of the cast. How many roles might a supporting player be expected to maintain? How does the casting list discriminate between the assignment of major roles and "bit" parts? Do the texts suggest an evolving hierarchy among the men as the troupes expand in size? Do the supporting players appear to have specialized in certain types of roles? Do the first-rank supporting players tend to be less burdened with doubling? With the answers to these questions the picture of popular troupe composition will be completed.

In many of the plays written for small troupes, and often of early date, no hierarchy or differentiation is discernible between the various supporting players. In Bale's *Three Laws*, for example, the division of parts is equalized to the point of symmetry. Apart from the assignments of Vice and the *deus ex machina,* Deus Pater or Vindicta Dei, the three remaining players have three parts apiece. Each appears as one of the three "Laws" of Nature, Moses, and Christ, and each appears severally as two of the six villains conjured by the Vice for the discomfiting of the three Laws. Thus the inner workings of the play are perfectly balanced, and the three players are on an equal footing with one another. *New Custom* exhibits a similar equalization among the three assistants of the leading player. Discounting the prologue assigned to player four, these three men assume three parts apiece. One plays two vice lieutenants and a sage, while the other two play a "Ruffler" and two virtuous men each.[13] With the leading player as Vice, the cast symmetrically opposes five workers of evil with five workers of good. *Impatient Poverty* assigns two or three roles each to its supporting players, each aggregate task being approximately equal in its demands.

Other plays written for small troupes employ a related method in the distribution of supporting roles. Each of the secondary actors receives one main supporting role, and the remaining "bit" parts are allowed to fall where they will. In *Trial of Treasure*, apart from the Vice, the roles are distributed fairly equally among the other four players, each having three or four. The main supporting roles are assigned as evenly as possible: Lust for player two, Just for three, and Treasure for four (a boy). Only player one is left with "bit" parts and little else. In *The Longer Thou Livest* every player, except the Vice, has four or five parts, and one of them in each case is a major supporting role: Wrath (1), Discipline (3), and Idleness (4). *The Tide Tarrieth No Man* provides a similar supporting structure. The assisting players each have four to six roles, one of them an important vice lieutenant: Hurtful Help (1), Painted Profit (2), and Feigned Furtherance (4). Each assistant also portrays a significant personification of virtue in the moral conclusion of the play: Faithful Few (1), Christianity (2), and Authority (4). The ten remaining minor roles are bestowed as occasion demands upon the player who happens to be most available. Small troupes evidently had no room for the apprentice actor who would specialize in minor parts only.

In the more secular plays written for larger troupes, however, a tentative internal hierarchy begins to emerge. We have already examined the evidence concerning a second player, privileged like the leading player in having fewer minor roles than his fellows, in *Enough Is as Good as a Feast, Horestes,* and *Cambises.* Further steps are taken in these and similar plays to differentiate the supporting actors. In *Enough,* for example, players two and four have relatively little to do, with two small parts each, whereas players three, five, and six appear to be the more experienced supporting men with four roles each of more general importance to the play. In *Marriage of Wit and Wisdom,* player two would appear to be "the least that can play" with four notably small parts, one of them mute (Honest Recreation).

Horestes demands two "master" players, as previously noted, and a boy. The three remaining actors are left to pick up the nineteen assorted additional roles, none of which is particularly dominant. *Cambises* has two "master" players and two boys, but with its larger troupe of eight is able to make distinctions among the four supporting players. Actors one and four handle the demanding roles of Praxaspes and Sisamnes, whereas the other two specialize in "bit" parts. Player three in particular seems to be the junior member of his troupe. His only colorful role is that of Snuf; the others are Knight, Attendance, Second Lord, Execution, Proof, and — with touching appropriateness — Small Ability. The later *Mucedorus* illustrates the direction of the trend. All major roles, Mucedorus, Amadine, Segasto, and Mouse, are single assignments, and the twelve "bit" parts are relegated to the remaining four players.

The tendency, then, is toward less doubling not only for the leading player but for his chief associates insofar as troupe size allows, and conversely toward more doubling of essentially minor roles for the hard-working second rank of players. One can see here the beginning, but only the beginning, of the later distinction between a sizable group of master players and the hired actors.

VI The Tradition of Versatility

So far, a number of distinctions have been made between the boy, the leading actor, his chief associate or associates, the supporting players, and the roles that each might undertake. It is important, however, not to confuse these distinctions with the notion of type-casting. The evidence concerning type-casting in this popular theater is fundamentally negative. The leading players avoided extensive doubling only because their major parts were sufficiently demanding in themselves. The player of the Vice was not confined to that role because the audience would tolerate him in no other dramatic capacity. Numerous indications of doubling prove the falsity of such a supposition. When necessity arises, "the Vice" in *Horestes* can double as Dame Nature and Duty, Ambidexter in *Cambises* as Trial, and Moros in *The Longer Thou Livest* as Lady Fortune. The actor of Horestes plays a woman without any apparent incongruity. Throughout this period there is never a hint of incongruity in the mixing of heterogeneous roles. Instead, the impression one receives is that of an imaginative flexibility on the part of the popular audience, and dauntless versatility on the part of the players. If this ability is noteworthy even in the leading players, it is particularly evident in the assignment of supporting roles.

Shakespeare's company, according to T. W. Baldwin, made extensive use of type-casting.[1] Baldwin's assumption is admittedly a plausible one, at least in the twentieth century, that the permanent members of a repertory company would tend to develop "lines" of acting of such pronounced individuality that the playwright would be obliged to suit his drama to their various styles. The validity of this assumption during the period of the 1580's and 1590's will be discussed in the next chapter. At present we may observe in some detail that type-casting was not a part of the heritage of the

Elizabethan company. The troupes, although organized as repertory groups, did not practice type-casting and their audiences seem not to have expected it.

The tradition of versatility goes back to the very beginnings of the professional morality stage, if, as is commonly supposed, Mercy and Tityvillus in *Mankind* were played by the same actor. Such doubling is striking because it requires the actor to portray his precise opposite in the struggle for the hero's soul. Mercy and Tityvillus are respectively the Friend and Enemy of Mankind. Although it seems odd at first to assume without proof that such an uncongenial pair would have been yoked histrionically, the supposition is in fact entirely plausible; for in plays where casting lists provide evidence, the players normally double roles that are diametrically opposed in the spiritual conflict.[2] In Bale's *Three Laws* each supporting actor plays one of the three "Laws" struggling for man's salvation, and also plays two of the lieutenant vices tending to subvert these laws. In *New Custom* one player doubles as New Custom ("a Minister"), Avarice ("a Ruffler"), and Assurance ("a Virtue"). His fellow players are similarly divided by the Psychomachia. In *Like Will to Like* Lucifer, Ralph Roister, Good Fame, and Severity are antithetically united in the varied talents of player two. This sort of doubling characterizes virtually every play and every player in the repertory. In addition, as we have seen, the players were versatile in assuming female roles along with male.

Parallel to the players' ability to divide their talents between the forces of good and evil is the ease with which they alternate between serious and comic action. That is, since the virtuous roles tend to demand serious acting and the villainous roles comic acting, the players must all have been adept at both. Serious and comic talent are equally necessary in the alternation between tragic and burlesque scenes in chronicle plays like *Horestes* and *Cambises,* "a Lamentable Tragedy, Mixed Full of Pleasant Mirth." The mixture of tragic and comic is present not only in the play but in each player. In *Cambises,* player one oscillates between Praxaspes, Counsel, and Third Lord on the one hand, and Huf and Lob on the other. Player five is capable of rendering the pitiful Sisamnes in one scene and Diligence, Cruelty, and Hob in succeeding scenes. The leading boy, although confined mainly to feminine and juvenile roles, demonstrates suppleness in shifting from the rough-

and-tumble Meretrix to the pathetic Otian who views his father being skinned alive.

Parallel again to the ability to move from serious to comic is the ease with which all of these players can portray both "straight" parts and "character" roles. In *Horestes* one supporting player is called on to perform both Menelaus and Rusticus, another player Nestor and Hodge, a third Egistus and Haltersick. The boy portraying Clytemnestra doubles with the vile Hempstring. No contrast, no changeover, seems to have been too audacious for these intrepid men and boys.

Dialect is common in character parts, and is casually distributed among the supporting players. They evidently looked on mimicry as one of the necessary skills of their "quality." The dialect mimic was not a player "type-cast" for a special role. *Common Conditions* introduces a heavy Spanish dialect in the speech of Mountagos, and mariners' terminology in the speech of the Master, Mate, Bosun, and Boy (ll. 995f). Mariners appear also in *Clyomon and Clamydes* (ll. 718f). Flemish accent is popular, appearing for example in Hans' "scomaker" and "Dat mought ic well don" in the early play *Wealth and Health*, perhaps forty years prior to *The Shoemakers' Holiday*. In *Three Ladies of London*, a popular play of 1581 (only five years later than our period), Mercatore has a marked Italian accent. Cotswold speech, the conventional stage dialect for rustics, is the most common, and must have been the sort of thing that any player could do for such comic roles as Tom Collier in *Like Will to Like*, Corin in *Clyomon and Clamydes*, Rusticus and Hodge in *Horestes*, and Hob and Lob in *Cambises*. Player six in *Enough Is as Good as a Feast* is directed to "Enter an olde man Tenant and speak Cotesolde speech" (sig. E₁ *recto*), and in *Marriage of Wit and Wisdom* Snatch and Catch entrap Idleness when they "spake like cuntrymen, to begild [beguile] him" (p. 29).

This versatility in the players presupposes an unusual flexibility in the minds of the popular audiences that accepted these rapid transformations from good to evil, serious to comic, and straight part to dramatic caricature. It was easy for courtly audiences to laugh at these "yoking of opposites" as absurd and even grotesque, and perhaps this condescending attitude was responsible (together with the greater number of players available) for the general lack of heavy doubling in sixteenth-century drama for the élite. Among those who aspired to write the "better" sort of play, classical precedent generally proposed limiting the cast to the number of players. Ancient dramatists had employed doubling, but never as extensively as in Elizabethan popular drama and never pairing such strange bedfellows as one finds linked in *Horestes* and *Cambises*. Besides, it may be doubted whether sixteenth-century neoclassicists had any clear knowledge of classical doubling practices. Perhaps they saw merely that ancient plays were decorously restrained in numbers of *dramatis personae*. Early in the century, Heywood propounded a sort of classical unity in assigning players to single parts, even in his more "popular" plays. Sophisticated drama tended generally to follow this example, since it could afford to do so with more actors at its disposal. But for popular dramatists doubling provided an ever-increasing opportunity for expansion, development, and experimentation. It was one of the more important techniques inherited by Marlowe and Shakespeare from the native tradition and not from the humanists' rediscovery of the classics.

The subject of versatility raises another question concerning popular methods of distributing roles among supporting players. Are there indications that a single part could be taken at various times during the play by two or more actors? For the audience, such halving of roles might seem no more offensive than the doubling of many roles by one actor. The practice was not unknown in cyclical drama. The Coventry play of *The Destruction of Jerusalem* assigns "Ananus" to one player and "a pece of Ananus" to another, "Mathias and Esron" to a third and "Esron his pte" to a fourth.[3] In Tudor times, however, halving or "substitution"[4] was evidently rare. The numerous casting lists afford only one instance of printing the name of a character twice, under two separate players. In all other cases, each character is assigned to one player for the duration of the action. The one exception is that of Idumeus, friend of the hero in *Horestes*, who is listed for players two and five. A scrutiny of the play suggests that this is no mere typographical error or publisher's deceit.[5] Idumeus seems at first to have been the charge of player two, who has little else to do in the early scenes of the play. At line 926, however, player two is called upon to enter as Menelaus, the rest of the actors being otherwise occupied. Hence Idumeus' entrance at line 948 seems to have been relegated by necessity to player five, who left the stage at line

926. The substitution offers the simplest way out of a casting difficulty, but its rarity suggests that the technique was used only in moments of unusual stress.

Two, or perhaps three, examples of role-splitting may be adduced in other plays. The conjectural instance of the early *Hickescorner* will be discussed later, in Chapter IX. Bale's *King John* offers in effect a portion of a casting list for its performance with occasional stage directions such as "Go owt Ynglond, and drese for Clargy" (l. 155), and "Her go owt Sedwsion [Sedition] and drese for Syvyll Order" (l. 313). These communications are imperfect, so that it is impossible to reconstruct entirely the plan for doubling. The difficulty arises in reconciling even the limited information available, when Sedition and Civil Order appear on stage simultaneously (ll. 1190–1274 and 2422–2557). Sedition had previously been directed to dress for the part of Civil Order, and vice versa (ll. 313, 555). At this point the part of Civil Order would presumably have to be shifted to another player. These directions occur only once, however, and in the early portion of the play. It is likely that the numerous revisions of the manuscript account for the discrepancy, and that in a final version Civil Order and Sedition would not have been assigned to the same player.

The third instance is from a late play, *Three Ladies of London* (1581), and concerns the boy actors who portray the three Ladies themselves.[6] The three never appear simultaneously, and the reason is soon evident despite the lack of a casting list: the playwright is working with only two qualified boy actors. His difficulty occurs in the final scenes of the play, when all three Ladies must be brought into close proximity. First, Love and Lucre are brought on stage together, and shortly thereafter Conscience and Lucre. Lucre then leaves, in order that Love may appear with Conscience; the stage direction reads, "Let Lucre make ready for Love quickly." Lucre reappears eighteen lines later as Love, with whom she had shared the stage a short time before. Thus it has been possible for all the Ladies to meet each other at last, a feat which could be engineered for two boys only by assigning one role to two players. Again, as in *Horestes*, this substitution occurs only in an unusual situation. These instances have been examined in detail in order to determine what sort of difficulty might necessitate this seemingly uncommon and irregular procedure. The conclusion is important as a basis for much of this study. If role-splitting were frequent, the casting lists themselves would be of little value as indexes of dramatic structure.

It is important, too, that halving of roles continued to be practiced only rarely after 1576. Exceptions have been found. According to the prompt manuscript of Massinger's *Believe as Ye List*, two characters, Calistus and Demetrius, were each played by different actors at a short interval. The plotter of *The Battle of Alcazar* resorted to similar expedients.[7] Nevertheless, these are atypical situations and occur at moments of peculiar casting difficulty.

The spectacle of Lady Lucre making ready for the role of Lady Love in an eighteen-line span introduces another aspect of versatility in the distribution of supporting roles. What interval of time does an actor need in changing from part to part? How frequently are actors required to make the hasty sort of change indicated in the example just cited? How does costume change enter into the determination of interval? Does the change between women's roles, or a change from one sex to the other, appear to require more time than a change between men's roles? Do some men's roles seem to have peculiar requirements of costuming that demand a longer interval? How conscious were the playwrights of these requirements? Finally, is there evidence of a need for interval between scenes in these popular plays?

Rapid change between roles is surprisingly common. Except for Bale's *Three Laws*, every popular play considered here requires at least one player to change parts in twenty-five lines or less. The examples are too numerous to be cited individually. In sum, there are at least thirty-eight instances requiring twenty-five lines or less. The authors of these plays were constantly aware of the need for rapid changing of roles. In *Enough*, for example, the actors are urged to "go out al. iii, togither and make you redy straight waies" (sig. E_1 *recto*). Commons' Cry in *Cambises* is to enter "running in, speak this verse, and go out again hastily" (l. 358), since he has only eight lines to change for Commons' Complaint.

Many plays require all the supporting players to undergo rapid transformation. In *Impatient Poverty*, for example, every actor who doubles is required to make at least one change in thirty-two lines or less. In *Trial of Treasure* every actor except the Vice has to make a change in nineteen lines or less. The demands are similar in *The*

Longer Thou Livest with changes in twenty-four lines or less. *Cambises* requires all its adult players except Ambidexter to change roles in twenty-two lines or less. Spoken even at moderate speed, twenty-five verse lines from these plays consume no more than one hundred seconds.

The supporting actor frequently makes as many as five or six rapid shifts, occasionally one right after the other. A not exceptional sequence is that of player two in *Marriage of Wit and Wisdom* who appears briefly as Honest Recreation (ll. 409–420), shifts in thirty-five lines to the part of Snatch (ll. 456–577), reappears after fifteen lines as Honest Recreation (ll. 593–673), and then changes in five lines to the role of Irksomeness. Player three in *The Longer Thou Livest* has to undergo five quick alterations in successive intervals of 24, 35, 32, 53, and 33 lines. Player five in *Horestes* goes through six changes in less than 500 lines (ll. 626–1122), with short intervals between each change.

There is evidence that the relative ease or difficulty of costume change had some bearing on the length of interval required.[8] Costumes for men were seldom overly elaborate, usually consisting simply of doublet and hose, coats, gowns of various sorts, caps or hats, beards, visors, and elementary hand props. A mere change of beards could speak volumes to popular audiences; evidently it mattered greatly whether a player appeared in "either your straw-colour beard, your orange-tawny beard, your purple-in-grain beard, or your French crown colour beard, your perfect yellow." In *The Longer Thou Livest*, for example, Moros enters in one mood "gaily disguised and with a foolish beard" (l. 1282) and later, to indicate his change of fortune, "Entre Furiousely with a gray beard" (l. 1732). In *Three Ladies of London* Dissimulation enters "having on a farmer's long coat and a cap, and his poll and beard painted motley" (p. 251). Beards could be exchanged readily by means of strings: "Here entereth in Ralph Roister and Tom Tosspot in their doublet and their hose, and no cap nor hat on their head, saving a nightcap, because the strings of the beards may not be seen" (*Like Will to Like*, p. 346).[9] For some changes of character a simple exchanging of beards probably sufficed, and could be accomplished in a few seconds.

Visors provided another means of rapid transformation, especially for more extreme changes of character. In *The Longer Thou Livest* the dire retribution awaiting the unregenerate Moros appears as God's Judgment, "with a terrible visure" (l. 1748), and as Confusion "with an ill fauowred visure, all thinges beside ill fauoured" (l. 1796). Giants and ogres could be rendered simply with the help of a visor, such as Irksomeness in *Marriage of Wit and Wisdom* who enters "like a monstor" (p. 35),[10] having a visor for his head which is carried in upon a sword after his defeat.

For bodily garments, doublet and hose were standard and need hardly have been changed in preparing for most if not all male roles. Standard costume emphasized the intimacy between actors and spectators, and was highly practicable for a limited traveling wardrobe.[11] Caps and gowns were more versatile, and might be exchanged quickly in order to provide an entirely new effect. Occasionally gowns were tailored for a specific role, like that of the Devil in *Like Will to Like*: "This name Lucifer must be written on his back and in his breast" (p. 310). In *All for Money* "Judas commeth in like a damned soule, in blacke painted with flames of fire" (l. 1440). The hero of *Mankind* must have a coat which is shortened again and again by his tormentors.

More often, players' costumes seem to run to types that could be represented by easily exchanged elements of the stock wardrobe: "Enter Lust, like a Gallant" (*Trial of Treasure*, p. 263); "Theologie commeth in a long ancient garment like a Prophet" and "Gluttonie and Pride dressed in deuils apparel" (*All for Money*, ll. 99, 485). Bale's *Three Laws* stipulates, "Lete Idolatry be decked lyke an olde wytche, Sodomy lyke a monke of all sectes, Ambycyon lyke a byshop, Couetousnesse lyke a pharyse or spyrituall lawer, false doctryne, like a popysh doctour, and hypocresy lyke a graye fryre" (p. 87).

Tudor audiences expected to find symbolism in costuming, and could readily identify a royal figure by his crown, crimson-purple robe, orb, and sceptre, a Virgin by her white garment, angels by flaxen hair and wings, Justice by a sword, Truth by a book, all in appropriate color.[12] Performers at court could always make use of available stock costumes for a "scoler," "gent.," "preste," "prentes of London," or "Colyer";[13] and although troupes on tour must have had far more limited resources than the Office of Revels, they evidently struggled to satisfy their audiences' demand for visual decorum.

That such costumes as these could be arranged in a matter of seconds is evident from the number of transformations actually taking place on stage. In *Mary Magdalen*, for example, the Vice Infidelity in disguising himself as Prudence is directed to "Put on a gown and a cap" (l. 404). The young child of *Mundus et Infans* mutates into an adolescent before the eyes of the spectators when Mundus gives him gay clothes and a new name (ll. 25f); the process continues in this manner through the seven stages of life. The title figure of *Impatient Poverty* is given a new garment on stage by Peace and is renamed Prosperity (l. 221); later, after Prosperity has relapsed into Poverty, Peace again renews his vesture of Prosperity (ll. 1051f). The phenomenon is common enough in Psychomachia drama, and illustrates the ease with which a change of cap and gown, thrown over existing apparel, could adequately signal a change in personality.

In anticipation of a rapid shift of costume, one garment could be worn over another until time for the change. In *Wisdom Who Is Christ*, "entreth Lucyfer in a dewyllys [a]ray, withowt & with-in, as a prowde galonte" (l. 324). Despite the misleading punctuation it is clear that Lucifer wears his gallant's dress underneath, not yet visible. In his devil's attire he informs the audience of his intention to beguile man in pleasant-looking disguise, and then he "dewoydyth, & cummyth in a-geyn as a goodly galont" (l. 380). Lawrence cites a similar alteration in *The Birth of Merlin*, this time on stage, when "the Devil changes to a gallant, with hat and feathers, sword and hangers, in full sight of the amazed Clown." [14]

A simple hand prop or a distinctive article of clothing could be used, like a beard or visor, to distinguish and emphasize a particular character. Feathers could suggest frivolity: "Tom Tosspot cometh in with a feather in his hat" (*Like Will to Like*, p. 317); Moros falls in love with a feather in his cap, and stumbles as he looks up to admire it (*The Longer Thou Livest*, l. 1541). Beer-pots were usually handy for the carousing wastrels of the comedy scenes: "Philip Fleming entereth with a pot in his hand" (*Like Will to Like*, p. 330). Hand props could identify professions. Art in *All for Money* enters "with certeyne tooles about him of diuers occupations" (l. 153), and Simplicity in *Three Ladies of London* enters "like a Miller, all mealy, with a wand in his hand" (p. 253).

Weapons were always available: "Enter Fraud with a sword and buckler, like a ruffian" (*Three Ladies of London*, p. 254).

The few cosmetics used were rudimentary and could be applied on stage. In *Marriage of Wit and Wisdom*, for example, Wantonness and Idleness blacken Wit's face as he lies asleep. When in *Three Ladies of London* Conscience falls from her state of moral purity, the stage directions specify "Here let Lucre open the box, and dip her finger in it, and spot Conscience' face" (p. 338).

Taking together all these means for rapid costume change, one can conjecture how an actor could shift from part to part in ten lines or less if circumstances required. Player two in *Cambises* changes from Commons' Cry to Commons' Complaint in eight lines (ll. 364–372), but the two parts are similar enough and unimportant enough that a change of beard would probably suffice. On the other hand Honest Recreation changes to Irksomeness, seemingly a very different role, in only five lines (*Marriage of Wit and Wisdom*, p. 35). In this case the probable clue to costuming is that Honest Recreation is not a noticeable figure, mute while on stage and hence requiring no special costume, whereas Irksomeness' appearance as a monster is conveyed chiefly by a "vizor" that could be donned in an instant.

The change from Piety to Ignorance in five lines (*The Longer Thou Livest*, ll. 1229–1234) also involves contrasting figures, and must have been effected by a fast exchange of gown and beard. In almost every play the actors are required to change roles on opposite sides of the Psychomachia in twenty-five lines or less. In *Trial of Treasure*, for example, we find diametric changes in less than twenty lines from Lust to Sapience (ll. 386–405), from Lust to Consolation (ll. 1040–1059), from Greedy-Gut to Just (ll. 386–405), and from Just to Greedy-Gut (ll. 520–539). There seem to have been few male costume changes which a player could not have handled in about one minute's time.

With women's costumes the difficulty was naturally greater. At times their costumes were fairly elaborate. Mary Magdalen, for example, enters "triflyng with her garmentes" (*Mary Magdalen*, l. 57), and much of the conversation in this scene hinges on the vanity of her apparel. In *Trial of Treasure* Trust is "a woman plainly [appareled]" (p. 283) and Treasure is "a woman finely appareled" (p. 288). They are played by the same actor. He is given thirty lines to change from Trust to Treasure (pp. 287–288) and nineteen lines from Treasure to Trust (pp. 297–298). The change from fancy to plain attire appears to require less of an interval than the reverse; nineteen lines is an unusually low figure, even in the popular drama, for changes in female costuming. The authors were of course not always concerned with the precise length of intervals. Nevertheless, a comparative study of minimum intervals, particularly in moments of stress, reveals a marked correspondence with the differing requirements in costume change.

Change from male to female costume seems to have been more difficult than that from female to male. The author of *The Tide Tarrieth No Man* shows an awareness of the problem which enables us to compute with some accuracy the time necessary for changing from male to female costume. Actor four, playing Greediness, exits at line 1198 in order to change for the pleasure-loving female Wantonness. During his absence, Courage the Vice and Hurtful Help strike up a time-delaying argument, "And fighteth to prolong the time, while Wantonnesse maketh her ready" (l. 1215). When Wantonness enters, she has had forty-eight lines for her change, in itself at least a two-minute interval without reckoning the time for the fight. The playwright's anxiety seems to indicate that all this time was really necessary. Appropriately enough it does not take Wantonness as long to undress as to dress herself. She is ready to play the Sergeant thirty-one lines after her withdrawal at line 1362.

Other examples confirm the impression of difficulty in changing from male to female parts. Two of the briefest intervals are as follows. Moros is allowed thirty-three lines to prepare for the role of Lady Fortune (*The Longer Thou Livest*, ll. 994–1027); and Ignorance, an "elder" Popish Priest, accommodates himself to the part of Hypocrisy, "an old Woman," after forty-four lines (*New Custom*, II, i). These minimums should be compared with the five-line intervals not uncommon in transitions from male to male parts. A transfer from female to male, although less demanding than the reverse, generally requires more time than the exceedingly rapid changes between male roles. No rigid formulas can be determined on the basis of this internal evidence, but the general practices are clear and help to complete the picture of the versatility of popular troupes.

One aspect of costuming interval remains to be considered: the evidence for short pauses between scenes, leaving the stage empty. Fairly often in these plays an actor is obliged to change roles between scenes, exiting at the end of one scene and then appearing immediately in the next as a different character. This rapid shift occurs frequently in plays otherwise perfect in the mechanics of casting, which suggests that such a method of doubling was considered legitimate. One may suppose also that even a rudimentary costume change would require a few seconds. Some time must elapse, therefore, when the Vice in *Horestes* exits at line 1121, thus ending a scene, and appears as Duty in the first line of the next scene. Similarly, in *The Longer Thou Livest* one must imagine a scene interval for player one, who exits as God's Judgment at a scene end and reappears as Exercitation in the next line. Such shifting of roles without any intervening lines occurs only at scene breaks.

Enough Is as Good as a Feast contains three such indications of scene interval, at sig. B₂ *recto*, G₁ *recto*, and G₁ *verso*.[15] At G₁ *recto*, interestingly, there is a dead man on stage during the delay: Worldly Man, who has been deserted by his fair-weather friends, and is now waiting to be carried off to Hell by Satan. Player three departs as Ignorance, and reappears in the next line as Satan. One can imagine the effectiveness of this pause, with the body of the protagonist giving mute testimony of his fall from worldly power. Other such evidences of scene interval may be found in *Marriage of Wit and Wisdom* (p. 54), and in *Cambises*, at the very end of the action, when the remains of Cambises have been carried off by his nobles and the stage is empty until he himself returns to speak the epilogue.

At least one example may be cited, however, to demonstrate that scene intervals such as these were by no means inevitable. The fifth and sixth scenes of *Cambises* are bridged by a rhymed couplet that implies virtually continuous action:

> *Mother.* My lording dear, let us go home our mourning to augment.
> *Praxaspes.* My lady dear, with heavy heart to it I do consent,
> Between us both the child to bear unto our lordly place.
>
> *Exeunt.*

Enter Ambidexter.

[*Ambidexter. (To the audience.*)] Indeed, as ye say, I have been
absent a long space.   [ll. 599–602]

Another aspect of production in these plays demonstrates the
widely versatile talents of sixteenth-century popular actors. Musical
ability, especially in singing, was as universally necessary as the
ability to shift rapidly from one role to another, or to play comic
and serious scenes in the same play. In a remarkably high percentage
of plays offered for acting, all or nearly all of the actors are
required to sing, usually as a group. In *The Longer Thou Livest*
all four players are on hand on two separate occasions to sing
(ll. 873–898, 1502–1503). The two songs in *New Custom* are each
rendered by all four actors in the troupe. *The Tide Tarrieth,*
with four players, has three songs and each is sung by a quartet.
In *Trial of Treasure* all five players join in song (p. 274). In
Lusty Juventus, Like Will to Like, and *King Darius* the number
of singers equals the number of players, and in *Three Laws* and
Mary Magdalen all but one of the actors sing.

Song was an important element in nearly all Renaissance drama,
both popular and élite. Especially in the troupe theater, song was
one of the pleasures of dramatic spectacle for which audiences
paid. The playwrights could not afford to neglect this popular
demand. Only two plays offered for acting are without song,
Virtuous and Godly Susanna and *Conflict of Conscience.* As noted
in Chapter IV, the lack of song corresponds with other peculiarly
amateurish touches in these two dramas, and the pointed apology
in both for the omission of song emphasizes its universality in the
commercial theater.

Apart from these exceptions, music was the accomplishment
of nearly every player, and its performance must have been professional. The players were naturally organized into groups of
convenient size for music, having inherited their structure from the
bands of troubadours and minstrels who previously had performed
for both public and select audiences. Accordingly the players usually
sang part songs, each player assigned a part in the harmony. In
Mary Magdalen the parts are assigned with particular care:

Infidelitie.

Nay, Mistresse Mary, we must haue a song of .iiii. partes,
At your departyng to reioice our mery hartes.

Cupiditi.
>   The treble you shall, maister Prudence, syng,
>   So freshly that for ioy your heart shall spryng.
>   Utilitie can syng the base full cleane;
>   And Noble Honor shall syng the meane.

Infid.
>   Mistresse Mary, will you helpe to syng a part?

Mary.
>   Yea, swete heart, with you with all my hart.   [ll. 756–763]

Similarly, in *Trial of Treasure* Inclination the Vice promises to "sing the treble with all my heart" (p. 274), and in *The Tide Tarrieth* Wantonnesse' three companions agree to "helpe in with a share" (ll. 1329–1336). Often the singers enter into the vocal counterpoint one after another; for example, "therefore let every man / Follow after in order, as well as he can" (*New Custom,* p. 40).

In recruiting players, these troupes must have had to take into account the proper balance of voices for singing three-, four-, or five-part counterpoint, with the players' vocal ranges so distributed that they had a bass, treble, "mean," and so on. Players had to be chosen not merely for their dramatic talents, but also for the quality and range of their voices. In addition, the players had to be of approximately equal singing ability, able to blend and to harmonize on part music. Solo performance, although known, was relatively unimportant in early popular drama. The plays that contain any song at all contain some part-singing. Early troupes did not specialize the role of singer for a particular member or members.

These players had a repertory of songs which they could fall back upon as occasion required. Frequently the playwright asks for a song without bothering to specify or to write the song himself, trusting the players to meet the demand.[16] Thus, "Here entreth Welth, and Helth synging together a balet of two partes" (*Wealth and Health,* l. 1). The "balet" is not specified. In *Three Laws,* Infidelity suggests "Synge now some myry songe, / But lete it not be longe, / Least we to moch offende" (ll. 693–695). What they sing is not recorded. The author of *The Longer Thou Livest* explicitly leaves the choice to his actors: "Sing some mery song" (l. 1503). Elsewhere in the same play, Moros the fool enters "Synging the foote of many Songes, as fooles were wont" (l. 71). The text of *New*

Custom indicates the proper place for "the first Song" and "the second Song" without particularizing; the songs would doubtless be well known and beloved by the audience. The poor Queen in *Cambises*, being led off by Murder and Cruelty, begs "Yet before I die, some psalm to God let me sing." Her request is granted, and she departs with the stage direction indicating, "Sing, and exeunt" (ll. 1118–1125). Baskervill conjectures that the song is lost,[17] but the Queen's entreaty suggests rather that she wishes to sing any well-known psalm, of the actor's own choosing. It would hardly have been composed for the occasion.

In other instances, authors specify a well-known song or psalm, not of their own devising, which will suit the action of the play. In *Three Laws* Christian Faith and the three "Laws" are directed, *"Hic ad Dei gloriam cantabunt. In exitu Israel de Aegypto, Vel aliud simile"* (l. 1953). The singers may choose any known and appropriate psalm. In *Trial of Treasure* Contentation, Just, and Trust go out with the instruction, "Here, if you will, sing 'the man is blest that feareth God,' &tc" (p. 287).

Many lyrics were, of course, written for particular plays, and some have genuine literary charm. Several are explicitly set to popular tunes, and most, if not all, were intended for settings familiar to singers and audience alike. In *Horestes* Haltersick "singeth this song to ye tune of 'haue ouer ye water to floride' or 'selingers round'" (l. 306), and Egistus and Clytemnestra sing a duet "to ye tune of 'King Salomon'" (l. 538). In *Marriage of Wit and Wisdom* Wantonness sings a song "to the tune of 'Attend the goe playe the' [Attend thee go play thee]" (p. 20). Further examples could be added. In still other cases, the lyrics that are printed may well have been popular songs borrowed or adapted for the occasion, such as *Juventus'* lovely "In youth is pleasure, in youth is pleasure" (p. 46) or *Trial of Treasure*'s hymn-like "So happy is the state of those / That walk upright and just" (p. 283).

Structurally, the music of the popular stage provides alternation of mood and change of pace. Like the comic fights and scatological jokes, music is one of the happy "routines" that periodically relieve and lighten the serious burden of the homiletic message. The important part songs often appear as a sort of coda to the central scenes of the play, both comic and serious. Group songs before exits are a standard device. In *Like Will to Like* Nichol Newfangle,

Cuthbert Cutpurse, and Pierce Pickpurse "sing this song as they go out from the place" (p. 339). In *New Custom* Avarice suggests, "But sirs, because we have tarried so long, / If you be good fellows, let us depart with a song" (II, iii). Examples appear in nearly every play. These songs frequently summarize and comment upon the preceding action. They also assume the character of entr'acte music, providing a respite and marking the end of a unit of the action.

It is curious that instrumentation is seldom indicated in these plays. A stage direction in *Like Will to Like* suggests that instrumental accompaniment may not always have been available or necessary:

Nichol Newfangle must have a gittern or some other instrument (if it may be); but if he have not, they must dance about the place all three, and sing this song that followeth, which must be done also, although they have an instrument. [p. 315]

Indications of dancing are also rare, but in dancing and playing the lack of documentation may simply result from the assumption that the players would handle such matters themselves. Comic dancing was not unknown. Hans in *Like Will to Like* "danceth as evil-favoured as may be demised [devised], and in the dancing he falleth down" (p. 329).

Only in a few late plays is singing limited to particular members of the troupe. In *Horestes* the only singers are Haltersick (player five), Egistus and Clytemnestra (players five and six), and the Vice (player one) who has a comic song (ll. 849f). Player five appears to have been chosen with particular attention to his voice, and player six is the boy. In *Cambises* the Queen (played by the leading boy) sings the only song. Wantonness in *Marriage of Wit and Wisdom* sings a solo, and Wit and Wisdom sing a duet (pp. 20, 59); of the three, Wisdom and Wantonness are portrayed by boy actors (players three and four). The tendency toward specialization in singing parallels that of isolating the female roles for boys in these later plays. Marlowe's and Shakespeare's stage developed both practices, although the tradition of versatility lived on in many ways.

We may conclude this study of the casting capabilities of these early players with a brief discussion on the use of extras. The practice of hiring extra hands to perform walk-on parts may date back to the fifteenth century if, as Brooke surmises, *The Castle of Perseverance* was enacted by a nucleus of itinerant players together with "drafted local amateurs for the minor parts in each place in which they acted." To support his theory, Brooke offers Richard Carew's description of Cornish mysteries in the sixteenth century: "The players conne not their parts without booke, but are prompted by one called the Ordinary, who followeth at their back with the booke in his hand, and telleth them softly what they must pronounce aloud." [18]

However it may have been in the large and spectacular productions of this earlier age, or in coterie plays like *Roister Doister* with its drums and ensigns and *Gorboduc* with its dumb shows, the case is altered in the professional popular drama of the sixteenth century. Strolling players from *Mankind* to *Cambises* evidently preferred to minimize their costs by hiring no extra performers. With one or two exceptions, *Horestes* and perhaps *King Darius*, the casting-list plays are arranged so that every part, even the most insignificant, is assigned to a regular member of the troupe. *Cambises'* casting chart fails to provide an actor for Marian-May-be-Good and a waiting maid; but this omission surely is oversight and not a demand for extra help, since these roles are small and can be accommodated easily by the existing troupe of six men and two boys. The practice of avoiding extras is in fact so universal that it amounts to an unwritten code among popular playwrights. The itinerant players simply could not afford to hire help, or wished to avoid the time-consuming hazard of training new assistants in each new place of performance. They evidently preferred to be independent and mobile, ready to put on an interlude at a moment's notice. As a result, the troupes were severely limited in the scope of their stage spectacle, and had to fall back on other means of creating the illusion of a large cast.

The advent of a semipermanent popular theater in London, with advantages of increased revenue and fixed location for at least part of the year, was bound to stimulate growth in numbers, both of regular actors and of extras. Once hired men could be engaged for more than a single performance, the problem of training them in their limited services became less acute. The hiring of musicians also became more feasible. Of the plays with casting lists, *Horestes* alone indicates how a prosperous troupe in the 1560's might have begun to employ a few extras. Its casting list fails to provide for "men," drums, and trumpet, who appear in the battle scenes throughout much of the play (ll. 400–449, 454–504, and 680–837):

Go and make your liuely battel and let it be longe, eare you can win ye Citie, and when you haue won it, let Horestes bringe out his mother by the armes, and let ye droum sease playing and the trumpet also.

[at ll. 725–726]

Such demands occur at times when most of the regular players have other assignments and hence are not free to double as the rank-and-file. The number of men in arms is nowhere specified, but there must have been enough to supply a token army for Horestes and for Egistus simultaneously (ll. 754f).

Here for the first time an author distinguishes between "bit" parts assigned to a trained player, and those relegated to the extras. The role of a "Sodyer" is assigned to players two and five for those occasions when a soldier has to speak and act: for example, "Enter a woman like a begger, rounning before they sodier; but let the sodier speke first" (ll. 625f). The extras are employed only for marching and battle, and reply only in unison to the stirring words of their chieftains (see ll. 474–475 for example). By and large, however, the use of extras lies outside the scope of this study because it lies outside the practices of the popular troupes. Only in the late *Clyomon and Clamydes,* bearing evidence of production on a London stage, does one find the expansive demand for all stagehands available:

Enter King Alexander the Great, as valiantly set
forth as may be, and as many souldiers as can.   [ll. 358–359]

VII Doubling Patterns in the 1580's and 1590's

Since we are considering the early popular dramatists as the professional precursors of Marlowe, and will soon trace the development of a dramatic structure in the plays themselves as a means of demonstrating the origins of Marlowe's structural method, it is important at this point to outline the continuity in troupe structure between the itinerant players and the later London companies. To what extent was Marlowe subject to the same necessity for doubling as were his predecessors, and to what extent was he favored by the same tradition of versatility? Was the structure of Marlowe's drama dependent upon the organization of his company in the peculiar manner of the earlier plays?

Fortunately, certain documents have survived from the later period of Marlowe's dramatic activity which indicate how these companies were composed: the number of regular actors, hired men, and boys, the method of distributing roles, the extent of doubling, and other aspects we have been studying in the earlier theater.

The relevant documents in the late 1580's and 1590's are seven so-called "plots," which are in effect skeletal outlines of plays, prepared for the convenience of the acting company.[1] Apparently these plots were posted backstage, so that during the play the company members or their "manager" could determine the order of entry of the actors, the proper time for special hand-props or furniture on stage, the proper time for special sound effects or music, and so on. In brief a plot was simply a scene by scene account of what was needed, in the way of either persons or things, to keep the play moving. For example, the plot of *The Battle of Alcazar* begins like this:

```
                  Enter a Portingall   mr Rich: Allen   to him
        sound                          1 Domb shew
        s[e]nnett   Enter Muly Mahamett  mr Ed: Allen,  his sonne
                    Antho:Jeffes:  moores attendant : mr Sam, mr Hunt
                    & w. Cartwright : ij Pages to attend the moore
                    mr Allens boy,   mr Townes boy :  to them  2
                    young brethren : Dab:& Harry: : to them
                    Abdel[m]enen  w. Kendall :          exeunt
```

From such a plot one can determine what actors played what roles, and hence how the company doubled parts.

The seven extant plots, edited by Greg,[2] cover a period from the late 1580's to about 1602. The majority of the plays thus plotted were acted by the Lord Admiral's company at the Rose Theater and later at the Fortune. The earliest two, *Dead Man's Fortune* and *2 Seven Deadly Sins*, may have been acted at the Theater and/or the Curtain around 1590 or shortly before. Three of the seven plots are preserved in such mutilated manuscripts that they may as well be dismissed at the start: *Dead Man's Fortune*, *2 Fortune's Tennis*, and *Troilus and Cressida*. It is unfortunate, too, that only one of the seven plots, *The Battle of Alcazar*, relates to an extant play, and even here the relationship is confused by the fact that the plot seems to have been based on an abridged form of the play.[3] Nevertheless, from the four best-preserved plots one can make certain generalizations. These four are *2 Seven Deadly Sins*, ca. 1590, *Frederick and Basilia*, ca. June 1597, *The Battle of Alcazar*, ca. 1598–1599, and *1 Tamar Cam*, ca. October 1602.

As the accompanying table indicates, the companies by 1590 are considerably larger in size than were the mid-century troupes.[4]

Play	Actor sharers	Hired men	Boys	Total
2 Seven Deadly Sins	8	8	6	22
Frederick and Basilia	5	7	4	16
Battle of Alcazar	11	7	8	26
1 Tamar Cam	10	6	6	22
Average	8.5	7	6	21.5

Performers for these plays may number as many as twenty-six instead of the eight used in *Cambises*. It is primarily the number of hired men that has burgeoned, however, rather than of regular players. The company members, commonly addressed as "Mr." in the plots, are now usually "actor sharers" who jointly own their company and divide the profits. They number eight or nine as compared with *Cambises'* six; nor does their number seem to have risen' much above ten during Shakespeare's lifetime. Neither has the number of boys increased greatly from *Cambises'* day. The average roster of boy actors is around six, and *Alcazar* has as many as eight; but usually only two of them undertake what appear to be important roles. The rest are younger apprentices, "Allen's boy" or "Towne's boy," who play the parts of pages and ladies in waiting, and are seen but seldom heard. It is primarily the hired men, virtually unknown before *Horestes,* who have expanded the ranks. Their number, usually around seven, could be augmented by the attendants and gatherers of the playhouses who occasionally appeared on stage to increase the swelling scene. In the plot of *Frederick and Basilia,* for example, attendants and gatherers play soldiers, lords, guards, and confederates.[5] Thus, whereas an average troupe in the 1570's might consist of five or six men and one or two boys, we find in the late 1580's and 1590's an average company of eight or nine actor sharers, two leading boys and perhaps four less experienced boys, about seven hired men, and enough "supers" and stagehands to bring the total to approximately thirty.

Despite the inevitable growth in size, however, the company's organization resembles that of the troupe in the 1570's, and is in fact the natural outgrowth of tendencies at work during that period. Doubling is still a primary technique of dramatic organization. The twenty-two actors of *2 Seven Deadly Sins* handle approximately sixty roles (in all three parts of the play), the sixteen of *Frederick and Basilia* approximately twenty-seven roles, the twenty-six of *Alcazar* approximately fifty-five roles, the twenty-two of *1 Tamar Cam* approximately seventy roles (including the procession). Because of expanded resources in personnel the need no longer exists for a ratio of four parts to one actor, but the average in the plots is still generally two or three parts for each.

The distribution of the doubling within the company is also a heritage from the earlier popular stage. The leading actor appears in many if not most of the scenes and dominates the action. In none of the four plots is the leading actor required to double. Mr. Edward Allen plays Sebastian in *Frederick and Basilia,*

Mahomet in *Alcazar,* and the title figure in *1 Tamar Cam.* In this last role he appears in eleven of the play's nineteen scenes.

The leading actor has his chief supporting actors, who also are spared from doubling many roles — a tendency which began in the larger troupe plays of the 1570's, like *Enough Is as Good as a Feast, Horestes,* and *Cambises.* As the companies grew larger, they assigned more master players to single roles. *Alcazar,* for example, requires no doubling for its four central characters, Mahomet, Sebastian, Abdelmelec, and Captain Stukeley. *1 Tamar Cam* does not double the parts of Artaxes, Otanes, and the title figure. Otanes is on stage in fourteen of the play's nineteen scenes.

It does not follow, however, that the actor sharers left all the doubling of minor parts to the hired men. Once the three or four central roles had been distributed, the rest of the "Masters" proceeded to carry as many of the lesser roles as possible, as had the supporting players in the 1570's. Even important secondary characters are often doubled with minor parts.[6] The Persian Shah in *1 Tamar Cam,* who appears throughout the play, doubles as an Oracle in one scene and as a Tartar in the final procession. The Mango Cham also doubles as a Tartar, and the seemingly important Colmogra (who appears in eight scenes) doubles as Artabisus. In *Alcazar* Edward Jubie plays Calsepius Bassa in Act II and Avero thereafter, and Robert Shaa changes from the Irish Bishop to the Governor of Tangier, and perhaps Celybin. Harry [Condell] plays Ferrex and a Lord in *2 Seven Deadly Sins,* and Sly plays Porrex and a Lord.

In several instances the lesser of the players, even those addressed as "Mr.," are assigned no important roles and must content themselves with six or seven "bit" parts, like players two and three in *Cambises.* In *Alcazar,* for example, "Mr. Sam" Rowley (who in *1 Tamar Cam* plays important supporting roles and was listed by Henslowe as sharer in 1598) must portray a Moor attendant, Pisano, messenger, devil, and Death. Dick Jubie, who in *Alcazar* is the leading boy, in *1 Tamar Cam* must play Chorus, Trebassus, Diaphines' spirit, trumpet, messenger, and Cataian.

The more capable of the hired men regularly appeared in six or more walk-on roles. In *1 Tamar Cam,* Thom. Marbeck, for example, has eight assignments: noble, attendant, Pontus' spirit, hostage to the Shah, rebel noble, guard, captain, and Bactrian. He figures in several of these roles more than once, and as a result appears on stage in nearly every scene. "Black Dick" in *Frederick and Basilia* serves as guard, messenger, servant, confederate, and soldier. His fellow player, Thomas Hunt, appears as servant, guard, lord, messenger, and soldier.

It is evident that on the popular stage of the 1590's there was still little thought of incongruity or grotesqueness in the pairing of such roles. The tradition of versatility was as much alive as ever, and it seems likely that the only reason Mr. Edward Allen did not double also was that his parts were generally more demanding than those of his assistants. It would not have been improper or "out of character" for him to do so.

T. W. Baldwin, in *The Organization and Personnel of the Shakespearean Company*, reaches the opposite conclusion. Even as early as the 1580's and 1590's, he argues, type-casting was basic to the production of plays by a London company. Type-casting affected not merely the leading actor and clown, but all the masters and not a few of the hired men. Once each player had developed a certain "line" of acting, he — and the playwright — re-enacted that "line" in play after play. The "line" was based generally upon the player's physical appearance and his character as an individual. "These men did not act; they were themselves." [7] Accordingly, Shakespeare, like other playwrights, created dramatic character simply by recording brilliantly the personalities of his acting associates. "The play was regularly fitted to the company, not the company to the play." [8] When an actor left the company, his replacement was expected to continue the same "line."

This is not the time to review Baldwin's study, nor even to defend Shakespeare, Marlowe, and other writers against the narrowing concept of determinism implicit in Baldwin's view of their creativity. It is relevant, however, to defend the actors against the charge that they could or would not act "out of character," and to that end some brief account must be made of Baldwin's method. He bases his argument for type-casting upon five plays with lists of assigned actors in the period 1626–1632, such as *Believe as Ye List* and *The Wild Goose Chase*. With these lists he attempts to define the "line" of each actor during that period. Even here Baldwin runs into apparent contradiction. The "line" that supposedly emerges for John Lowin is as follows:

His is the bluntly humorous, bluff character. To him falls the impolite villain, the gruff counsellor, the plain-spoken friend. He is the cruel tyrant Caesar, revelling in blood even from his youth; the honest Jacomo, who is an exceedingly lame Iago and could have given Lowin but little joy; the equally honest Flaminius, relentless devil incarnate, hounding the hero for love of evil, of brusk, imperious manner, haughty and over-bearing; the wise old counsellor Eubulus, who mistakes blunt impudence for plainness of speech, humorous withal; the equally humorous and blustering Belleur, the brave but bashful lover . . .[9]

Baldwin continues with the assertion that "Lowin had certainly been taking this line as early as 1612–13." Even if this were a "line" of type-casting and not a fair definition of Lowin's remarkable range of ability, it cannot safely be carried back ten or fifteen years into a period when few acting assignments are known, without evidence that such stability was common. Yet Baldwin retraces the hypothetical careers of persons concerning whom he knows far less than of Lowin. Furthermore, his logic of working backwards depends heavily on the unproved assumption that departing actors were succeeded by identical types. By such means he arrives, for example, at the career of Thomas Pope, whose Shakespearean "line" includes Armado, Parolles, Quince, Speed, Falstaff, Sir Toby Belch, Petruchio, Philip the Bastard, Mercutio, Aaron, Benedick, Fluellen, Mowbray, Casca, Jacques, and Shylock. "Pope was thus the high comedian and gruff villain of the company."[10] In such instances it appears that what Baldwin calls a "line" of type-casting and what this present study refers to as "versatility" are hardly distinguishable.

Circular reasoning enables Baldwin, once he has conjecturally assigned parts to an actor, to deduce particulars about that actor's personal appearance. Thus Joseph Taylor was a handsome young man, strongly built, of brown complexion and curly hair.[11] Yet at other times Baldwin allows for great diversity between the actor's appearance and that of his roles. Of Burbage he concedes, "His characters are pretty well divided between comparative youth and age, as occasion might demand."[12]

In his eagerness to determine acting assignments for all the characters in Shakespeare's plays, Baldwin formulated his assumption of type-casting in order to trace his evidence back from early Caroline drama to Shakespeare. That assumption of type-casting remains unproved even in the 1620's and 1630's. The question deserves careful reappraisal,[13] for it is entirely possible that as the London companies grew more select in auspices and more classical in orientation, the literalist notion of type-casting may have asserted itself. In any case Baldwin's method cannot safely account for the theater of the late sixteenth century. The heritage of the troupes as manifested in the seven extant plots affords a more direct method of investigation.

The versatility of rapid change from one part to another, implying ease of certain costume requirements, is as common in these plots as in the earlier plays. Without the texts of the plays themselves it is impossible to measure exact intervals, but the proximity of two parts for a single actor is frequent in the plots. Thus, in *2 Seven Deadly Sins*, J. Sincler and R. Cowley both play a captain and musician within a single scene (xiii). In *Frederick and Basilia*, "Black Dick" appears both as messenger and soldier in scene xviii. In *1 Tamar Cam*, Dick Jubie must change from messenger to Trebassus within the course of III, iii, and Thos. Marbeck and W. Parr both appear as attendant and guard in IV, i. Thos. Parsons doubles as Persian and guard in I, iv, as messenger and guard in III, iii, and as nurse and guard in IV, i. In many other instances, two parts for a single actor are listed in adjacent scenes.

Feminine and juvenile parts are by the 1590's usually limited to the boy actors, but the instance just cited of Thos. Parsons playing a nurse as well as Persian, messenger, and guard in *1 Tamar Cam* proves an interesting exception. We have here either a man playing a woman's role or a boy playing a succession of adult roles. Perhaps with unintentional fitness, the plotter has assigned Parsons a place in the final procession as "Hermaphrodite." At any rate, the shift from male to female roles was not unknown.

It is more difficult to speak of versatility in shifts from "straight" parts to character parts and serious to comic, since we lack the texts for all the plots except *Alcazar* and so must conjecture what many of the characters were like. Some of the changes required of the hired men ask little imagination, such as attendant, guard, messenger, soldier, and the like. Others, however, appear to have more substance. In *1 Tamar Cam,* there are shifts from Colmogra to Artabisus, Assinico to Bactrian, Ascalon spirit to Crim, and Pitho Satyr to Moor. In *Alcazar*, where we are able to follow the narrative, we find the Irish Bishop (who is plotting to overthrow Protestant England with Stukeley, Jonas, and Hercules) doubling with Don de Menysis, Governor of Tangier. Actors frequently change sides in the battle, as their predecessors had crossed and recrossed the lines of the battle for Mankind's soul. Edward Jubie impersonates Calsepius Bassa, Abdelmelec, lieutenant, and also Avero, who is a follower of the King of Portugal. Charles similarly changes back and forth from Abdelmelec's army (as Zareo) to Portugal's (as Barceles). Sam shifts from Pisano (a captain of the Moor) to devil, Portuguese soldier, and Death.[14]

The virtuosity of these public players may be traced by yet another means: the contrasting types of acting ability required of them in different plays. From a variety of sources, such as the actor lists of Ben Jonson's plays and records of payment at court, it is known that Richard Burbage, for example, starred not only in his famous roles as Richard III, Hamlet, Hieronimo, Lear, "the greued Moore, and more beside," but also appeared in Jonson's comedies: *Every Man in His Humour, Every Man out of His Humour, Volpone,* and *The Alchemist.*[15] Harry Condell played the part of the Cardinal in *The Duchess of Malfi,* but also had an important assignment in *Every Man in His Humour* and *Every Man out of His Humour.* Hemmings undertook various roles not only in Jonson's comedies but in his tragedies, *Sejanus* and *Cataline.* These actors were ready to play a tragic role one day and a comic role the next. Burbage, though famed as a tragedian, must also have excelled in some important role in *Volpone* and *The Alchemist.*[16] The audience who viewed this dexterity must have been as flexible in imagination as the players were versatile in performance. Indications of type-casting are limited to a few special personages such as the clown.[17] Otherwise, Renaissance dramatists were remarkably free from the need to conform in the creation of character to company capabilities or types.

To sum up the evidence: except for the leading player and one or two of his chief assistants, the actor sharers or "Masters" were content to double one minor role, or perhaps two, in addition to their major part. The Masters did not all assume leading roles, for there were usually more actor sharers than major parts. Those who played supporting roles doubled heavily, often as many as six or seven small parts to an actor. Supporting roles were also assigned to hired men who were capable of playing six, seven, or even eight parts. Players often changed roles in adjoining scenes, or within a single scene — a practice which seems to indicate great flexibility on the part of the players and the audience, and considerable rapidity of some costume changes. Extras were employed in abundance, and for large battle scenes or processions every man and boy in the employment of the company might be pressed into service, including gatherers, tire-men, and stagehands. Finally, as was generally true in the earlier plays, the plots demonstrate a conscious attempt to avoid halving of roles between two actors.[18]

It was not until the seventeenth century, with the growing tendency toward coterie theater, that the London companies developed a distaste for excessive doubling. Lawrence cites the performance of Thomas Heywood's *The Silver Age* for which two companies temporarily merged in order to present thirty-two characters. In the late sixteenth century one company would have undertaken the task without hesitation.[19] This disavowal of the honest means by which earlier players had aspired to greatness signaled the end of an era, for it was the part of the élite drama to sneer at the convention of doubling. Marston, in his induction to *Antonio and Mellida*, is pointedly reluctant to allow a single pairing of roles, forced upon him and the boy actors by vulgar "necessitie." [20] Such scorn for the Tudor popular drama, and the Jacobean emphasis on "decorum" in casting, indicate a new spirit of literalism in the theater anticipating the proscenium arch and use of women for female roles.

The point of this study so far has been to describe a resemblance in organization between the popular dramatic troupes before the advent of the London theaters, and the companies of Marlowe's and Shakespeare's day. In the ensuing chapters, after we have analyzed the dramatic structure of the earlier plays in terms of troupe composition, we will then be in a position to evaluate the structural debt of high Renaissance dramatic literature to its humble popular predecessor. That is, the aim is to establish a parallel between the structure of the troupes and the resulting structure of the drama. The factor is only one among a great many elements, of course, that combined to produce the miracle of the late sixteenth-century theater. This study in no way pretends to offer a complete explanation of that miracle, or to suggest that Elizabethan dramatists were merely the product of their theatrical environment. This is only one approach, to analyze certain popular aspects of structure in the Renaissance theater that have been hitherto neglected.

VIII The Origins of Popular Dramatic Structure

Now, semely syrs, beholde on me
How mankynde doth begynne.
—— *Mundus et Infans,* ll. 28–29.

Throughout the Tudor period, writers for itinerant troupes faced a peculiar and exacting challenge that was destined to produce a characteristic structure in the plays they wrote. Commercial theater is at all times dependent upon the preferences of its audience and the conditions of its staging, but seldom has a theater movement had to deal with a more inexorable and conflicting set of circumstances than those of the late fifteenth and early sixteenth centuries. On the one hand the troupes were severely limited in personnel, staging facilities, and finances. On the other hand they inherited from the late medieval stage a predilection for inclusiveness of characterization, elaborate mechanical and visual contrivances, and sumptuous production. In short, the self-contradictory objective of the troupes was to achieve a maximum of scope with a minimum of means.[1] Their efforts to reconcile these opposites laid the foundations for popular dramatic structure on the English professional stage.

In the age when the popular moralities began to flourish, the great medieval cycles were waning, partly because of profound alterations in the economic system that had fostered them and partly because of calculated governmental opposition to their Catholic intent.[2] Moralities had the advantage of greater independence from Church doctrine, and were accordingly more flexible in doctrinal content — Catholic one day and violently anti-Papist the next, concerned with spiritual matters in one reign and with politics or social problems in another. The cycles perished with the Middle Ages while moralities bridged two worlds, advancing and then retreating with each shift in the unpredictable winds of controversy. As a result, this Protean drama gradually fell heir to the sizable and receptive audiences of the trade cycles. The players moved forward readily to fill the demand, and realized that they were expected to provide a similar kind of entertainment.

To do so was no easy matter, however, for at its height medieval drama was an achievement of impressive splendor.[3] Before the end of the fourteenth century, medieval pageants had featured machine-operated descents and ascents from overhead. Hell-mouths belched smoke, and could be opened and closed to display souls in torment. Storms, earthquakes, flaming swords, burning altars, and God speaking from a cloud were popular effects. In civic street pageants, large casts of allegorical personages acted out didactic lessons on statecraft in the guise of Biblical or homiletic story. Non-cycle miracles and moralities such as *Perseverance* had introduced all this colorfully symbolic spectacle into the very beginnings of the professional drama. In subject matter, troupe performances had to satisfy popular taste for bustling plays, crowded with incident and covering the entire range of mortal and immortal existence. The players needed to emulate the most stageworthy qualities of plays like *Perseverance*, the *Noah* plays, and *The Second Shepherds' Play*: *Perseverance* with its pageantry and festive spectacle, its thirty-five characters, its various platforms, its panoramic inclusiveness, and its glorious battle between the seven Deadly Sins and the seven Cardinal Virtues; the *Noah* plays or *The Second Shepherds' Play*, with their hearty burlesque and brawls, and their vivid portrayals of English lower-class life. The tradition of the minstrel added the ingredients of song, dance, and secular farce. A vital commercial drama, in catering to public audiences, could not omit except when absolutely necessary any of these elements which had become so much a part of the national taste in theater.

Deprived as they were of the means to achieve multiple staging and elaborate scenic effects, the strolling players inevitably chose the expedient of casting as a way to imitate the scope of medieval drama. They had only themselves and their costumes, set upon a makeshift stage, with which to produce a modified pageant play. In the face of their severely limited numbers, the players had essentially three practical alternatives: the employment of supernumeraries, the reduction of the cast of characters to a manageable size, or

doubling. All these methods were tried, as the new theater groped
its way forward by experiment toward the goal of a thriving commercial drama. *Perseverance* may well have used supernumeraries.
Wisdom Who Is Christ seemingly did so, with its evident division
of cast among six speaking characters and its twenty-nine silent
parts designed for six mute players, probably boys.[4] But this solution was evidently abandoned in the early years of the sixteenth
century, as has been shown above in the tabulations on use of extras. It was discovered to be the least economical of the three
methods, and was therefore the first to be discarded.

Reduction of *dramatis personae* was much more widely employed
as a solution, particularly in the earlier sixteenth century. We have
seen in studying the ratio of parts to actors that early plays like
Mankind, Hickescorner, Youth, and *Wealth and Health* employed
a smaller number of roles as the simpler and more obvious means
of meeting troupe limitations. *Play of the Sacrament,* with its
twelve parts for nine players, suggests an intermediate point in
the process of change between *Perseverance* and *Youth.* The technique was mechanically satisfactory, but achieved its success at the
expense of the pageantry so deeply ingrained in the native conception of homiletic drama. In this sense it was destined to remain
a temporary expedient until popular playwrights could evolve more
skill in doubling.[5] Doubling was thus the third and most satisfactory solution, and reigned supreme during the years from mid-
century to the advent of the London theaters.

Since our object is to study plays in which doubling is fundamental to structure, we shall be concerned primarily with the mid-
century period when the techniques of doubling became fully
understood by popular authors. In many earlier plays such as *Mankind* and *Youth,* the occasional doubling of a single role may be
thought of as incidental rather than integral to the method of con-
structing a play. A few early plays, however, provide important
exceptions, and these deserve careful investigation as forerunners of
a new system. Perhaps the first of these is the interlude of *Mundus
et Infans.* The casting of this play is anomalous, for it demands
only two players.[6] It seems unlikely that troupes were ever quite
this small, and one can only assume that the author had some
special reason for casting it in this manner. It is virtually incon-
ceivable that he did so inadvertently, for the doubling is executed

with precision and considerable ingenuity. At any rate, the play offers the earliest opportunity for observing the full effect of doubling upon dramatic structure.

Mundus et Infans relates the life story of its hero, who passes from childhood (with the name of Infans) through the various stages of man's life until he reaches old age. The pilgrimage is essentially a spiritual one, and the hero is the universalized man who had prevailed in the moralities of the previous century — for example, Humanum Genus in *Perseverance* and Mankind in the play named for him. The plot of *Mundus et Infans* is also a carry-over from the fifteenth-century morality: the Psychomachia, or struggle for the soul of man by the personified forces of good and evil. This simple plot, deriving its name and origin from the fourth-century *Psychomachia* of Prudentius, had been and was to remain astonishingly popular in the native English drama.[7] Other basic plots had occasionally found their way into fifteenth-century moralities — the Debate of Body and Soul, the Parliament in Heaven, and (in *Everyman*) the Summons of Death — but the Psychomachia always maintained its popular lead. The plot of *Mundus et Infans* follows the pattern already conventional, of innocence corrupted by evil into a state of degeneracy, an encounter with God's grace resulting in conversion to goodness, then a relapse, and finally recovery to salvation.

Mundus et Infans can be viewed, therefore, as a rewriting of the story of *Perseverance* in a briefer scope and for a reduced cast of characters, performed by an even more severely limited number of actors. In place of 3650 lines and thirty-five speaking parts, *Mundus et Infans* contains only 979 lines and five speaking parts.[8] The author's technique for creating the effect of the Psychomachia with only two players is a simple one, and basic to the rest of our study. Since the hero, Infans, is on stage for nearly all of the play, thus demanding the full attention of one player, the other player must alternate between the two sides of the Psychomachia, portraying first an Enemy to Man and then a Friend to Man. Player two in his role as Mundus corrupts Infans, then exits at line 236 leaving the hero (by this time grown to Manhood) to revel in his worldly iniquity, and reappears at line 288 as Conscience in order to bring about Manhood's first conversion. And so the alternation proceeds. The unavoidable effect upon structure created by such an arrangement is clear: the opposite members in the struggle cannot be brought face to face with one another. Man must be exposed first to good and then to evil.

In *Perseverance*, of course, the phases of retrogression and conversion are just as discernible, but the opposing forces act simultaneously, with the Good and Bad Angels exchanging hard words, and the seven Deadly Sins and the seven Cardinal Virtues trying to outface each other on the field of battle. Since in *Mundus et Infans* the stage is alternately dominated by good and evil, the whole tenor of the play shifts accordingly. Periods of elevated discourse change place with periods of merriment, intrigue, and worldly argument in behalf of physical pleasure. The casting limitation has induced a structure of scenic rather than panoramic effect, alternating between serious scenes and comic scenes, godly and depraved, instructive and entertaining.

The simplest arrangement of this alternation would be to have only three characters in the play: the hero, his good angel, and his evil angel. *Mundus et Infans*, however, presents two personifications in each camp: Mundus and Folly representing damnation, and Conscience and Perseverance representing salvation. Since all four are played by one actor, Mundus cannot meet with Folly, and Conscience cannot meet with Perseverance. Here the author applies a technique as simple as that of alternation. He suppresses one character in order to bring on another. Of the four personifications who struggle for the hero's soul, three appear on stage only once. Mundus appears first and tempts his pupil into a worship of worldly vanity, and exits at line 236 to disappear permanently from the play. Conscience's act of conversion is followed by the sole appearance of Folly for 177 lines, after which Conscience returns only to be deliberately suppressed in order that Perseverance may succeed him to the end of the play.

Structurally, this sort of suppression eliminates the possibility of bringing together all the characters at the conclusion of the drama, or tying together all the strands into a compact literary form. Instead, characters and episodes must be abandoned. As the play progresses it tends to organize itself around different groups of personalities. The early portion of *Mundus et Infans* deals with the corruption of infancy by the blandishments of worldly riches and power; the later portion concerns the temptations to carnal folly, the sins of the flesh. The structure of the plot is essentially linear and episodic, organized by theme and variation rather than by a direct and organic relationship of each part to a single whole. *Mundus et Infans* is really two plays despite its brevity, with two parallel states of degeneracy and two conversions.

The two parts are not, however, merely successive and repetitive. They are related by a progressive sequence that justifies the suppression of one character for the benefit of introducing another. Suppressed characters are succeeded by their own homiletic offspring. Worldly pomp and vanity naturally give rise to frivolity and abandoned living, and thus Mundus gives way to Folly. Similarly, Conscience is the first step in the reclamation of a fallen soul; once Conscience has done his work and salvation is in progress, Perseverance must ensue. In this way the author has made a virtue of limitation.

The progressive introduction of new characters was certainly not unknown in fifteenth-century moralities. *Perseverance*, for example, brings God and his four daughters Mercy, Righteousness, Truth, and Peace into the final episode, in order to determine the fate of the dead hero's soul. In fact a progressive and episodic structure was basic to the whole intent of medieval drama, with its day-long cycles extending from the creation of the world to the crack of doom. What the troupes did was to derive from this principle a scheme of dramatic construction that intentionally suppressed a character to make room for his homiletic successor.

A third structural concomitant of the doubling pattern in *Mundus et Infans* is symmetry. Once again it is important not to ascribe the origin of the concept solely to institutional development, for symmetry was unquestionably a vital structural principle of late medieval art. One need only recall the ornate architectural balance of the late Gothic masters of painting, such as the Van Eycks and Roger Van der Weyden, to recognize its permeating influence in the fifteenth century. The spirit of the age has been defined as one of balanced contrast between cruelty and mercy, between obsessive fear of death and a mystical perception of indwelling joy.[9] In the drama the very essence of the Psychomachia is a symmetry of contrasting forces, with Man and his soul at the focus. Accordingly, in *Perseverance* one finds the seven Deadly Sins offset by the seven Cardinal Virtues, Good Angel by Bad Angel, and the like. Speeches are often carefully balanced, as in the first orations of World, Devil, and Flesh, each from his own scaffold.[10]

Asymmetrical elements prevail, however, in the staging of *Perseverance*. Four of the five platforms belong to the World, Flesh, Devil, and Covetousness, leaving only one platform and the castle itself to present God and his loyal subjects. The forces of evil dominate the action. In *Mundus et Infans*, on the other hand, the symmetrical balance of the opposed forces is reinforced and even made necessary by the fact that the opposing numbers have to play each others' parts. The result is to equalize the positive and negative forces of the Psychomachia. The exigencies of doubling have converted an artistic conception of symmetry into a theatrical formula.

A fourth structural effect of doubling in *Mundus et Infans* is the constant and systematic use of soliloquy. The stage monologue was not invented for the occasion; but its employment in pageant plays like *Perseverance* is practically nonexistent, whereas in *Mundus et Infans* its function is vital. It repeatedly occupies the interval required for the brief costume changes of player two. At lines 236–288, 494–522, and 699–713 the hero is left alone on stage while his fellow player prepares for a new role. His three meditations are of convenient length, from fourteen to fifty-two lines. They are all essentially end-of-scene soliloquies, acting as theatrical punctuation between the phases of degeneracy, conversion, relapse, and recovery.

In each case these soliloquies provide the means for commentary on the action that has just concluded. In the first instance, when Mundus has departed, the hero (by this time called Manhood) boasts of his daring, especially in war, and vows allegiance to the seven Deadly Sins. In the second, having been stirred to reform by Conscience, Manhood rededicates himself to the task of virtuous living, but as yet he sees no reason to despise the world, even though he sees that the World and Conscience are at strife. His vacillating state of mind prepares the audience for his relapse in the ensuing scene. In the third soliloquy his feelings are again ambivalent as he longs for pleasure and yet fears for his soul:

> The Worlde and Folye counseylleth me to all gladnes;
> Ye, and Conscyence counseylleth me to all sadnes, —
> Ye, to moche sadnes myght brynge me in-to madnes.   [ll. 709–711]

These soliloquies are useful both as mechanical bridge for the doubling formula and as structural bridge for the progression of the alternating plot.

Not all soliloquies need act as doubling aids, of course. Mundus' first appearance on stage is intended solely for the revelation of his proud character. Such soliloquies at the openings of plays are common, serving as prologue. They often are detachable from the play itself, like the "banns" of the earlier medieval plays from which they are descended. Also, Conscience's end-of-scene soliloquy (ll. 721f) provides a necessary commentary on the recovery phase of the play without the excuse of a doubling change. Conversely, the need for costume interval does not always require soliloquy, as at line 744 when Conscience exits leaving the stage bare, and returns shortly as Perseverance, allowing the silence of scene interval to fill the time. Nevertheless, the function of soliloquy in these plays of limited cast reinforces its value to the plot. The result is an ever-increasing use of this dramatic technique which was so much a part of the later Elizabethan stage.[11]

Still another instance of medieval expansiveness reduced into the limited scope of *Mundus et Infans* is that the personifications tend to represent many qualities of sinfulness or virtue. Several attributes are often compressed into a single character. The numerous medieval divisions and subdivisions in the allegory of both good and evil can no longer be portrayed individually on the stage. As a result, Mundus, and especially Folly, have to "stand in" for the World, Flesh, and Devil and their lieutenants the seven Deadly Sins.

This compression of character is both implicit and explicit in the text. Mundus himself is of course World, and betrays the pride befitting his exalted station; perhaps he also speaks wrathfully and enviously toward those who despise his gifts (ll. 1–24). More explicitly, the term "Folye" is equated with all the seven Deadly Sins:

> *Manhood.* Folye? what thynge callest thou folye?
> *Conscience.* Syr, it is Pryde, Wrathe, and Enuy,
> Slouthe, Couetous and Glotonye, —
>   Lechery the seuente is:
> These seuen synnes I call folye.   [ll. 457–461]

And when Folly enters a short time later, he pointedly identifies himself with Covetousness and the sins of the flesh:

> For I am a seruaunt of the lawe;
> Couetous is myne owne felowe, —
>   We twayne plete for the kynge;
>
> . . . .
>
> By my feyth, syr, into London I ran
> To the tauernes to drynke the wyne;
>
> . . . .
>
> In feythe, syr, ouer London-brydge I ran,
> And the streyght waye to the stewes I came,
>   And toke lodgynge for a nyght;
> And there I founde my brother, Lechery.   [ll. 576–596]

Mundus and Folly, especially the latter, have absorbed the vice functions personified by some fifteen characters in *Perseverance*.

This compression is of additional interest when we realize that Folly is the "Vice" of his play. *Mundus et Infans* was written seemingly before any such term was in general use, but Folly is without doubt one of the ancestors of Nichol Newfangle and Ambidexter. He indulges in comic profanity and scurrility, makes ribald comments about his female auditors, jests about friars, fights a ludicrous duel with Manhood, and in a series of asides keeps the audience posted on the intent of his machinations, sinister beneath their comic exterior:

> A ha! syrs, let the catte wynke!
> For all ye wote not what I thynke,
> I shall drawe hym suche a draught of drynke
>   That Conscyence he shall awaye cast.
>
> . . . .
>
>   Lo, syrs, this Folye techeth aye,
> For where Conscyence cometh with his cunnynge,
> Yet Folye full fetely shall make hym blynde:
> Folye before and Shame behynde, —
>   Lo, syrs, thus fareth the worlde alwaye!   [ll. 649–652, 695–699]

This early "Vice" derives his bag of tricks from the several divisions and subdivisions of sin in medieval allegorical drama, all compressed into a single generic or root evil. The Vice is, in his dramatic origin, this epitome of evil. Two structural factors, then, contribute to the creation of this remarkable figure: the need to fit a previously expansive representation of vice into the limited capabilities of a small troupe, and the emergence of a leading player whose acting talents suited the engrossing tactics of the Vice manipulator.[12] In *Mundus et Infans* the Vice is not yet all-powerful, but his dramatic origins are admirably clear.

The deliberate compression in both the vice figures and their opposites may also be seen by comparing *Mundus et Infans* with its likeliest source, a fifteenth-century poem called the "Mirror of the Periods of Man's Life or Bids of the Virtues and Vices for the Soul of Man."[13] The poem is a debate, not unlike the earlier medieval verses on the "Debate of Body and Soul," and it carries the newborn child through the various ages of Man. Its cast of tempters and defenders is sizable, including Bodily Gifts, God's Commandments, the Pleasures, the Seven Works of Mercy, the Creed, and in the hero's twentieth year seven attendant Virtues and seven Vices. All these abstractions in the poem are reduced by the dramatist to five characters for his two players. Mundus and Folly take the place of the seven Vices, whereas Conscience and Perseverance must absorb the functions of Bodily Gifts, God's Commandments, and the rest. The poem equates the word "folly" with all the sins, thereby giving the dramatist an appropriate name for his Vice.

Another method of compression in *Mundus et Infans* creates the illusion of expansiveness by referring to characters who never appear but are identified by name. This is in fact the means by which Folly suggests the generic nature of his personality; he casually drops the names of Covetousness, his "owne felowe," and "my brother, Lechery." Whereas a play like *Perseverance* might have produced these personages on stage, Folly must be content to evoke their presence by naming them, and then incorporating their behavior into his own.

A related technique used to expand the cast is that of employing alternate names and pseudonyms. The renaming of the hero adds to the apparent list of characters in two ways. As he progresses from childhood to old age he is given a series of different names to correspond with the stages of his life: Infans (or Dalliance), Wanton, "Loue, Lust, Lykynge in-fere," Manhood, and Age. These titles actually change with him in the speech-prefixes of the text. In addition, he is given pseudonyms which indicate a state of mind rather than a phase of existence. These names are not recorded in the speech-prefixes. Folly labels Manhood as "Shame" to indicate his relapse; and, at the last, Perseverance bestows upon the contrite Age the accolade of "Repentance." These pseudonyms follow the pattern of progressively suppressed character, like the real personifications of the play. The over-all effect is to create a cast, apparent or real, of some thirteen personalities, sequentially distributed as the story shifts from infancy and youth to repentance and old age.

Alternation, progressive suppression, symmetry, and compression — these are the primary effects of troupe composition upon the structure of *Mundus et Infans*. The play may not have been the first morality to combine these characteristics, but in the absence of other texts it stands as a landmark; and its simple design for two players, even if atypical, provides an admirably clear illustration of the principles to be pursued in the later drama. Understandably in this early experiment, the mechanics are often awkward, letting the bare bones of the skeleton show through. In particular, the necessary exits are baldly or inadequately motivated. Suppressed characters disappear without any ostensible reason. Mundus, for example, departs with the words:

> Now wyll I fare on these flourys;
> Lordynges, haue good-daye!   [ll. 235–236]

Conscience, having raised Manhood from his fallen condition, evidently cannot remain to support his protégé in the times of trouble that are sure to follow, but the reason for this enforced absence is not given:

> Nowe fare-well, Manhode; I must wende.   [l. 487]

Such technical difficulties were inevitable at first, but equally inevitable was their removal in the course of time through improvement of the basic pattern.

One play prior to *Mundus et Infans*, during the formative years of the late fifteenth century, deserves consideration in accounting for the origins of popular dramatic structure. *Wisdom Who Is Christ* illustrates clearly the compression of the seven Deadly Sins into a lesser number of personifications for the sake of limited casting. The play is transitional between *Perseverance* and *Mundus et Infans*, both in date (ca. 1460–1474) and in size of troupe, and so may help explain how the technique of compression evolved. *Wisdom Who Is Christ* strongly suggests by its internal organization that it was intended for five to six speaking actors with six boy "mutes." The plot is again that of the Psychomachia. Mind, Will, and Understanding, the attributes of Anima the soul, are instructed by heavenly Wisdom in the true path of salvation, and are warned of their three great enemies, World, Flesh, and Devil. Nevertheless they fall easy prey to Lucifer's insidious argument of riches, pleasure, and power (that is, world, flesh, and devil) and fall into the characteristic patterns of sinfulness that are the very opposites of their godlike natures. Finally they are called to account by Wisdom, and they and Anima are chastised and cleansed. The four recognizable phases of the plot are the soul in innocence (ll. 1–324), temptation and fall (ll. 325–551), life in sin (ll. 552–876), and repentance (ll. 877–1168).[14]

The compression of the seven Deadly Sins is again produced by absorbing the individual sins into their generic medieval roots. The scheme was common in medieval thought, and *Perseverance* offers a dramaturgic precedent in its division of the seven Deadly Sins into three groups: Satan is represented as overlord of Pride, Envy, and Wrath; Flesh is overlord of Sloth, Gluttony, and Lechery; and World occupies the pivotal point of the seven sins, the *radix malorum*, with his lieutenant Coveteise. But whereas *Perseverance* presents all the sins and their captains in full splendor, together with their opposite virtues, *Wisdom* is thrown back on the expedient of a reduced version of the classic seven to three, Pride, Covetousness, and Lechery. Lucifer plans his attack on the human race in these terms:

> I xall now stere hys mynde
> To that syne made me a fende,
> Pryde, wyche ys a-geyn kynde,
>   And of synnys hede;
> So to couetyse he xall wende,
> For that enduryth to the last ende;
> And on-to lechery, and I may hym rende,
>   Than am I seker the soule ys dede.   [ll. 528–535]

Accordingly, when the three protagonists are perverted into sin by Lucifer's treachery, they assume the evils most precisely opposite to themselves. Mind becomes Pride or Maintenance (support of wrong), Understanding becomes Covetousness or Perjury, and Will becomes Lechery. These three generically represent all the failings of mankind. Each has a band of six followers (seemingly played in turn by six mute boys) who augment the attributes of their three masters. Maintenance calls forth Indignation, Sturdiness, Malice, Hastiness, Vengeance, and Discord. Lest the audience should misapprehend their significance, Will comments:

> Thes meny, thre synnys comprehende,
> Pryde, Invy, & wrathe in hys hestis.   [ll. 718–719]

Perjury calls in six Jurors, Wrong, Sleight, Doubleness, Falsehood, Ravin, and Deceit, who are ready to pronounce any verdict for a bribe. Lechery summons Recklessness and Idleness (Sloth), Surfeit and Greediness (Gluttony), and Adultery and Fornication (Lechery). The seven Deadly Sins are rearranged to suit the capabilities of these three adult actors together with six mute dancing boys.

This grouping and contrasting of theological abstractions is carried to some lengths in *Wisdom* and is portrayed with great precision. The accompanying scheme reveals the symmetry of corresponding concepts in the play's thought and characterization.[15]

(1) *Soul in Innocence*			(2) *Temptation and Fall*	
Mind	Father	Faith	→ Devil	Suggestion
Understanding	Son	Hope	→ World	Delight
Will	Holy Ghost	Charity	→ Flesh	Consent

(3) *Life in Sin*			(4) *Repentance and Salvation*	
Pride	Maintenance	Force	→ Confession	Perfection
Covetousness	Perjury	Deceit	→ Contrition	Truth
Lust	Lechery	Prodigality	→ Satisfac- tion	Chastity

Such elaborate correspondences were basic to the thought of medieval authors and dramatists, who associated each of the twelve Apostles with an article of the Creed and each of the seven Deadly Sins with a petition of the Lord's Prayer.[16] Their dramaturgic significance in *Wisdom* lay in providing a key to a casting formula. The playwright found ready at hand a system of theatrical shorthand based upon the equation of one philosophic abstraction with its many components and opposites.

The symmetry of these devices is clearly related to the structure of the troupe. One player is required for the part of Anima, the center of the spiritual conflict. The player who portrays Wisdom (or Christ) probably doubles as Wisdom's chief enemy, Lucifer. The three generic virtues, Mind, Will, and Understanding, are transformed into their own spiritual opposites. Six boys are sufficient to perform in turn the six retainers of Maintenance, Lechery, and Perjury, the "vi small boys in the lyknes of Dewyllys" who "rennyt owt from wndyr the horrybyll mantyll" of Anima (l. 917), and the five wits (virgins) attending Anima in other scenes. The clearest indication of doubling in all these successive appearances of five or six mute performers is that "vi small boys" must suffice to represent the seven Deadly Sins exorcised from Anima by Wisdom, implying that only six mutes were available. Once again, as the

		Forces of Good	Forces of Evil
	Player 1	Anima	
	Player 2	Wisdom (Christ)	Lucifer
5 speaking	Player 3	Mind	Maintenance
actors	Player 4	Will	Lechery
	Player 5	Understanding	Perjury
6 boy super-numeraries		5 wits (virgins)	6 retainers of Maintenance, Lechery, and Perjury; 6 devils

players move from one side of the Psychomachia to the other, the play shifts scenically from serious and didactic instruction to an essentially comic and satiric portrayal of evil. *Wisdom Who Is Christ* therefore appears to have been transitional in reducing the full panoply of the Psychomachia in *Perseverance* to a feasible scope for a limited troupe, by the methods of compression of personified abstraction and symmetrical pairing of opposites in the spiritual struggle.

The Pioneering
IX Contributions
of Bale and Skelton

Apart from the distinctive *Mundus et Infans,* anonymous popular drama of the Henrician period made only faltering contributions to the development of a dramatic structure based on extensive doubling, since most playwrights chose the simpler expedient of limiting their *dramatis personae.* Paradoxically, the greatest advances during the period in this predominantly popular movement were made by two well-known authors, John Bale and John Skelton. They both maintained some connection at court and in ecclesiastical circles, and both were conscious literary artists, two facts demanding some justification if we are to consider their works as part of a drama that was essentially nonliterary (see Chapter IV above).

The conscious and sophisticated use of a native tradition can often produce results that are artificial when seen from the point of view of that tradition. The artist can revive obsolescent forms, as did Sir David Lindsay in his *Satire of the Three Estates* (1540) with its panoramic and non-doubling structure hearkening back to *Perseverance* and its type.[1] In such an antiquated display the practical theater could find only a restatement of the casting problems that it had yet to solve. Literary drama with a "popular" flavor can also be conspicuously ahead of its time, like Medwall's *Fulgens and Lucrece,* which employs a double plot more skillfully developed than any for another half century.[2]

Unlike Lindsay and Medwall, who merely borrowed indigenous elements of structure for courtly benefit, John Bale actually contributed plays to the popular repertory. He wrote for professional actors and numerous local audiences. For that reason his adept solutions of technical problems were employed where they could be known and imitated by popular dramatists.[3] *Three Laws* is the earliest extant text to publish a full casting chart. The chart is partly atypical; it is printed at the end of the play rather than in its later customary position on the title page or second leaf. Its ratio of parts to actors — fourteen parts for five actors — is considerably more advanced than that of its popular contemporaries like *Youth* or *Hickescorner*. Yet its technical improvements constituted an innovation rather than a radical change, for the casting chart came into extensive use in the years immediately following Bale's model.

Three Laws contains a Psychomachia figure named Christian Faith, but he is only nominally the center of the play, and makes his first appearance belatedly in the last 120 lines of the 2081–line work. The play really concerns the battle between Christian Faith's three spiritual defenders, the Laws of Nature, Moses, and Christ, who are led by Deus Pater, and six spiritual enemies, captained by Infidelity the Vice. In Act I, God instructs the Law of Nature to protect man in his state of innocence, the Law of Moses to correct man in his fallen condition, and the Law of Christ to redeem man into heavenly grace. Subsequently the three Laws are subverted each in turn by Infidelity, who calls forth two assistants to accomplish each task. Act II records the overthrow of Nature's Law by Idolatry and Sodomy, Act III the overthrow of Moses' Law by Ambition and Covetousness, and Act IV the overthrow of Christ's Law by False Doctrine and Hypocrisy. In Act V, God as Vindicta Dei destroys Infidelity with three scourges, water (Noah's flood), sword (the defeat of the Israelites), and fire (the Last Judgment). God then restores to health his three Laws and bids welcome to Christian Faith, the subject of these cosmic struggles.

The symmetry of the design is evident even in briefest outline. With the seldom-seen hero in the center, God stands opposite to Infidelity, and each of the three Laws faces two opponents. The relation of the symmetry to the troupe is equally evident. There are five players. The first doubles as Infidelity and Christian Faith, and the fifth presents God.[4] Each of the three remaining actors portrays one of the Laws and two of the vice lieutenants — not his own opposites whom he must confront, of course, but one enemy standing in opposition to each of the other two Laws. Thus Acts II, III, and IV contain every possible combination of the three players. Acts I and V frame the inner acts of the play, just as players one and five are a sort of obbligato and thorough bass to the strong inner voices of players two, three, and four.

The structure of the play is, if anything, too controlled, and the

	Act II (*Downfall of* *Nature*)	Act III (*Downfall of* *Moses*)	Act IV (*Downfall of* *Christ*)
Player 2	Law of Nature	Covetousness	False Doctrine
Player 3	Idolatry	Law of Moses	Hypocrisy
Player 4	Sodomy	Ambition	Law of Christ

pattern of intrigue in the three middle acts tends to be repetitive. The high degree of organization is Bale's literary imprint, and was not carried over entirely into anonymous popular drama. As we have seen, the five-act structure was not adopted by anonymous writers. Nevertheless, Bale's plan offered an intelligent and sophisticated form, constructed nominally upon the classical premise of five acts[5] but in reality constructed upon native practices of symmetrical alternation and suppression. The native drama, derived from the loosely joined day-long cycles of the fourteenth century, needed discipline above all else, and Bale's contribution was to reveal the inner consistencies and correspondences inherent in that drama.

The configuration of the number three, based on the tenets and symbols of medieval Christianity but also closely related in *Three Laws* to the structure of the troupe, permeates the fabric of the play. The three Laws correspond to the progressive steps in the awakening of the soul to true righteousness: first, man's instinctive Right Reason, then outward conformity to a code of moral conduct, and finally inner awareness of transcendent mystery. These steps, together with their inevitable opposites in the dual nature of man, form the natural basis for medieval allegory of the individual soul. The same phases also represent the history of the world as seen by the Middle Ages: innocence, transgression, and finally redemption; or pleasure, exile and punishment, and reconciliation:

> Of Innocency first, of hys transgressyon than,
> Than the longe season, wherin he was afflycted,
> Fynally the tyme, wherin he was redeemed.   [ll. 72–74]

Correspondingly the provinces of the three Laws in man's pilgrimage are represented by the heart, the tablet, and the testament (ll. 109–138). In sixteenth-century terms the six spiritual enemies personify three stages of ecclesiastical decay leading to the Reformation: at first the idolatry and moral laxity of the Roman Clergy (who are accused of sodomy, ll. 572–573); next the legalistic drive for temporal power of ambitious bishops and covetous ecclesiastical lawyers; and finally the violent methods of the Inquisition, represented by False Doctrine and Hypocrisy, who threaten to burn the "schismatic" Law of Christ at the stake unless he renounces his faith. Subsequently, in the emblematic reworking of the figure three, God destroys Infidelity (and by implication his lieutenants) with a triple scourge, water, sword, and fire. All these correspondences, achieving medieval scope through the equation of a primary quality with its many corollaries and antitheses, are strikingly reminiscent of *Wisdom Who Is Christ* and *Mundus et Infans*.

The skillful use of alternation and progressive suppression of character in realizing this tripartite scheme offered a lucid model for practical theater. Players two, three, and four each assume a new role in each inner act, leaving behind a series of suppressed personifications which represent the individual, historical, and controversial allegories. Acts II, III, and IV are variations on the structural theme, with each player assigned a different part in each repetition and elaboration. With such a constant interchange of parts, soliloquy functions repeatedly as a structural bridge. Following Act I, Law of Nature remains on stage alone after the departure of God and the other two Laws, before the arrival of Infidelity and, a short time later, of Sodomy and Idolatry. At the end of Acts II and III, the unhappy Law who has just been defeated comes before the audience to comment on his wretched plight, while the troupe readjusts for the next variation of intrigue.

Entrances and exits are better motivated than those of *Mundus et Infans*. For example, as Act I ends, it is natural for God, Law of Moses, and Law of Christ to leave the stage, since God has deputized Law of Nature to teach mankind his first lesson:

> Christi lex.
> Here styll to tarry, I thynke it be your mynde.
> Naturæ lex.
> My offyce ye knowe, is to instruct Mankynde.
> Moseh lex.
> Than God be with yow, we leaue ye here behynde.
> *Exeunt. [manet Naturæ lex]*

Other entrances and exits have a similar logic. The transitions seem effortless because they are expected, and the costuming intervals are always sufficient for the players. Bale's technical facility is impressive for his time.

Unfortunately, inconsistencies in manuscript, combined with an imperfect and confused indication of doubling procedures, render Bale's *King John* an unsatisfactory subject for a study of structure in its relation to casting. The play evidently achieves its economy of casting through two sorts of doubling: one in which two entirely different characters are played by the same actor (such as Clergy and Widow England), and the other in which an allegorical character becomes a new person by assuming an alternative name. The latter has made *King John* justly famous as a Renaissance play. The transformation of the generic figures Sedition, Private Wealth, Dissimulation, and Usurped Power into the historical figures Stephen Langton, Pandulphus, Symon of Swynsett, and the Pope offers a striking illustration of the secularizing trend at work in sixteenth-century art and life. It should be remembered, however, that the combining of universal allegory and topical allusion was by no means peculiar to *King John*, and was in fact a standard means by which authors could achieve the compression of character appropriate to a small-troupe play.

A better play for our purposes is John Skelton's *Magnificence*, which, although lacking a casting chart, possesses a consistency of organization that invites comparison with Bale's *Three Laws*. It relates the story of the Psychomachia in secular guise, since the hero Magnificence is at once a generic type of potentate and a thinly veiled representation of Henry VIII. He is the central figure in a fiscal and political struggle between Wealthful Felicity and Measure on the one hand and, on the other, a rogue's gallery of courtly parasites such as one finds in the "Ship of Fools" literature or in Skelton's own "Bowge of Court." The orthodox moral structure of *Magnificence* is apparent beneath the novelty of its secular content. Following the usual saga of the mankind figure, Magnificence falls away from the virtuous counsel of Measure to indulge in the various extravagances advocated by his conniving courtiers. Inevitable retribution takes the form of Adversity and Poverty, leading the King eventually through Despair to Good Hope, Redress, Sad Circumspection, and Perseverance.

According to R. L. Ramsay, Skelton evidently constructed *Magnificence* for five actors. There are never more than four speakers on stage at once, but a casting for four players "can be done only by splitting a single part between two actors in at least four cases, — the parts of Felicity, Fancy, Measure, and Cloaked Collusion." [6] With five actors instead of four, the casting works easily and naturally. On the other hand, the notion of a larger cast renders inexplicable the care with which Skelton reshuffles his staging in order to avoid the meeting of various characters. "Thus Folly, Counterfeit Countenance, and Courtly Abusion apparently remain strangers to each other, evidently because one actor took all three parts." [7] Ramsay's argument is sound enough that we are scarcely hampered by the lack of a casting chart. The scheme of *Three Laws* would appear as self-evident if it too had failed to provide the documentary information.

Magnificence offers eighteen parts for its five actors; and since the leading actor playing *Magnificence* cannot double — he is present on stage with every other character — seventeen parts remain for four actors. This represents an increase in doubling over Bale's *Three Laws*, and is in fact the most ambitious undertaking in troupe drama of Henry VIII's reign. Yet its technique was sufficiently practical that any popular dramatist could profit from its example.

Skelton's structural method of distributing seventeen parts for the supporting actors is to arrange his play into four distinct phases, each with a new cast. These phases are prosperity, conspiracy and delusion, overthrow and retribution, and restoration of the hero to happiness.[8] In the progression from one phase to another, characters are superseded in groups. Skelton shows his awareness of the plan by dividing the "names of the players" (following the last words of the text) into four units with marked spacing between.

[1] Felycyte	[3] Fansy	Dyspare
Lyberte	Counterfet counte.	Myschefe
Measure	Crafty conueyaunce	
	Clokyd colusyon	
	Courtly abusyon	[4] Good hope
[2] Magnyfycence	Foly	Redresse
	Aduersyte	Cyrcumspeccyon
	Pouerte	Perseueraunce

This progression, shown in the diagram, corresponds so nearly to the phases of the play that very few characters exist before, or continue past, their appropriate phases. The exceptions to this rule are indicated in parentheses, and all such appearances are brief.

Phase 1: Prosperity	Phase 2: Conspiracy and delusion	Phase 3: Overthrow and retribution	Phase 4: Restoration
(ll. 1–401)	(ll. 402–1871)	(ll. 1872–2534)	(ll. 2535–2567)
Felicity	(Felicity)		
Liberty	(Liberty)	(Liberty)	
Measure	(Measure)		
Magnificence	Magnificence	Magnificence	Magnificence
	Fancy		
	Counterfeit Countenance		
	Crafty Conveyance	(Crafty Conveyance)	
	Cloaked Collusion	(Cloaked Collusion)	
	Courtly Abusion	(Courtly Abusion)	
	Folly		
		Adversity Poverty Despair Mischief	
			Good Hope Redress Circumspection Perseverance

Of these four separate phases, the second contains the largest cast with its ten characters, three of whom appear for a short time only. Ten roles are less taxing for five players than eighteen. Skelton has reduced the casting difficulty by dividing it into manageable segments.

Within the phases, moreover, on a smaller scale, a similar orderly suppression enables the limited number of actors to present a maximum number of characters. Phase three, containing nine characters, makes particular use of this technique. The figures of overthrow and retribution are so arranged that their successive appearance is an expression of the homiletic aim of the play, as well as a convenience in casting: Adversity is followed by Poverty, then Despair, and finally Mischief. Similarly, in the final phase Good Hope can disappear after having paved the way for Redress, Circumspection, and Perseverance.

The longest and most complex phase, the second stage of conspiracy and delusion, employs another method of overcoming casting limitation: a constant reshuffling and alternation of the characters. Of the ten personages, seven are more or less continually present (Magnificence and the six agents of vice), so that Skelton is occasionally driven to some lengths to make his scheme feasible. No doubt Ramsay is correct in his opinion that these exigencies create "a number of awkward oddities in the dramatic arrangement of the scenes." [9] Some clumsiness was inevitable in an experimental design of such complexity. The characters are spaced in such a way that no more than four ever appear simultaneously; the fifth man was available for use as prompter and sound-effects man.[10] This "full-stage" configuration of four players is attained again and again, each time composed of different personages, permitting nearly all the possible combinations of four (ll. 573–689, 1375–1400, 1409–1458, and 1629–1725).

Between these full stages are generally one or more soliloquies, serving both to reveal character and to occupy time needed for changes of role. Skelton makes a virtue of this necessity, for the monologues of the several villains contain the play's most brilliant writing. They are usually in Skeltonic doggerel, as Counterfeit Countenance announces in the first of these speeches:

> But nowe wyll I, that they be gone,
> In bastarde ryme, after the dogrell gyse,
> Tell you where of my name dothe ryse.   [ll. 407–409]

The characters are carefully rearranged so that each of the villains except Folly holds the stage alone in comic soliloquy: Counterfeit Countenance, 403–493, Cloaked Collusion, 689–744, Courtly Abusion, 825–911, Fancy, 968–1043, and Crafty Conveyance, 1327–1374. Magnificence too appears alone (1457–1514). Thus the second phase of *Magnificence* corresponds in structure to the inner three acts of *Three Laws*, since in both the possibilities of combination are explored systematically until the maximum in permutation has been reached.

This repeated variation in *Magnificence* appropriately creates an atmosphere of intrigue during the phase of conspiracy and delusion. Conspirators appear and disappear, giving the impression that something mysterious is going on behind the scenes. Perhaps these incessant manipulations unduly lengthen the action. Nevertheless, the device not only solves a casting limitation but is structurally relevant to a dramatic presentation of duplicity. The hints of deviltry off stage are as effective as the visible machinations on stage.

Skelton handles this invisible presence well, and motivates exits and entrances by this unseen world of intrigue. He keeps the palace of Magnificence off stage, where the actual successes of the conspiracy are taking place. The *locus* of the dialogue is some indeterminate meeting place of the villains, where we overhear them plotting further moves and gloating over recent achievements. The conspirators insinuate themselves one by one into the service of the prince, return and disappear, consult one another, and generally augment the mischief until Magnificence's delusion is complete. Thereupon the play is ready to enter a new phase, of progressive sequence leading to correction of abuses and the restoration of normality.

Magnificence is a morality that has undergone a degree of secular transformation. Its hero represents a limited range of human experience when compared with Mankind or Humanum Genus, and its vice figures are courtly, satiric types rather than generic derivations of the seven Deadly Sins. The interest is historical rather than timeless; the political advice to a prince is specific and practical rather than generic and spiritual. Secularization is one of the unmistakable developments in the chronology of the English moral play, and *Magnificence*, like *King John*, represents a significant step forward.

Nevertheless, the late medieval structure remains intact, through the continuity of the professional troupe. *Magnificence* is alternately serious and comic as the actors shift from virtuous counselors to conniving parasites. When Felicity, Liberty, and Measure are replaced (conjecturally) by Cloaked Collusion, Counterfeit Countenance, and Crafty Conveyance, the tone of the play changes entirely. Another such transformation brings the action to a suitably dignified and didactic conclusion. As in other moral plays the key to this symmetry is that evil is the reverse of good, and as such —

like the bearded women in *Macbeth*, sailing in a sieve — is seen as grotesque, ludicrous, comic through exaggeration and distortion, and yet ultimately fearful. The individual actors, like the plays themselves, embody this antithesis, oscillating between straight and character parts, normality and excess, the believable and the absurd.

In dwelling on the dramatic work of these literary figures, Bale and Skelton, there is the danger of creating an impression of undue precocity in the development of dramatic structure before Edward VI's reign. In the humbler plays forming the bulk of the popular repertory, it is not until the 1540's that a true successor to *Mundus et Infans* appears with sufficient doubling to justify full analysis of the influence of casting upon structure. Before going on to that period, however, we should briefly examine three early plays in order to see just how far Bale and Skelton were ahead of their anonymous contemporaries.

The early *Mankind* (ca. 1471), written for five players, makes an interesting although unskillful attempt at an abbreviation of the seven Deadly Sins. Mercy warns Mankind that his four jolly companions are in reality his great enemies:

> Ye haue iij aduersarys, — he ys master of [t]hem all, —
>> That ys to sey, the dewell, the world, the flesch; &
>>> [I] the tell
> That Newgyse, Now-a-days & Nought, the world we may
>> [t]hem call;
> And propy[r]lly Titiuilly syngnyf[ie]th the fend of helle;
>
> The flesch, — that ys the vnclene concupiscens of your body;
>> These be your iij gostly enmys in whom ye haue put your
>>> confidens;
> Thei browt yow to Myscheffe to conclude your temperull glory.
>
> [ll. 876–882]

This attempt at some sort of structure in the allegory is evidently an afterthought, instead of a preconceived plan for the entire play. The author has failed to provide any allegorical characters who represent the sins of the flesh; Mercy has to gloss over this omission as best he may. Mercy also hints vaguely at a generic quality in Mischief that is not borne out in the action. The author probably introduced his comic characters when he needed them, rather than striving for an accurate allegory.[11] Nevertheless, his desire to

schematize the seven Deadly Sins suggests a rudimentary but growing concern with the need for compressing character in a troupe
play.

The other most characteristically popular plays before 1547 are
Hickescorner and *Youth*. Like *Mankind* they double only one or
two characters. Even with such a minor technical problem, however,
both playwrights show concern over the feasibility of the plan. That
is, the doubling of one or two characters, as modest an achievement
as it seems, was not fortuitous in either play and was not engineered
without noticeable effort by the authors. These playwrights are
beginning to deal with the puzzle of the doubling formula in its
most elementary form.

Hickescorner tells the story of the tribulations and final rewards
of its central figure, Pity, who is befriended by Contemplation and
Perseverance but in their absence falls prey to the evil intent of the
three villains, Freewill, Imagination, and Hickescorner. In the central comic scene (ll. 156–544) these villains unite to jeer at Pity,
to deride his piety, and then to set him in a pair of stocks. They
leave him disconsolately alone on stage. In soliloquy (almost certainly necessary for a costume change) he inveighs against the
corruptions of the times, until finally he is discovered and set free
by Contemplation and Perseverance. At this juncture Perseverance
curiously anticipates the happy conclusion of the play with the
following prophecy:

> I thynke they wyll come hyder agayne,
> Frewyll and Imagynacyon bothe twayne;
> Them wyll I exorte to vertuous lyvynge
> And unto vertu them to brynge
> By the helpe of you, Contemplacyon.   [ll. 615–619]

The reader is surely justified in asking here, why not bring back
Hickescorner, the title character, as well? And should not Pity, the
central figure, take part in the conversion of Freewill and Imagination? These omissions, however, were not merely the result of
forgetfulness on the part of Perseverance. The writer is preparing
for a final scene in which only four characters appear, Contemplation, Perseverance, Freewill, and Imagination. The implication is
that only four actors are available; no more than four ever appear
on stage simultaneously. Hickescorner is simply not heard from

again, suppressed presumably for casting reasons. Pity is dispatched to arrest the malefactors and somehow fails to return with them, evidently because the actor has to assume the role of Imagination. Thus the play ends, rather lamely no doubt, lacking its title role and its hero. The attempt is clumsy, but the effort itself is significant. If, as seems likely, the play was in fact cast for four players, the role of Imagination would have been split between two actors (those doubling as Contemplation and Pity), introducing another awkwardness that was later abandoned (see Chapter VI, above).

The motivations for exit are also clumsy when compared with those of Bale and Skelton. Early in the play, Pity must be separated from his virtuous counselors in order that he may be exposed to the jibes of the three villains. The author fails, however, to give him any reason for leaving the safe companionship of his friends:

Pyte.　　　　　Fare-well, good bretherne here,
　　　　　　　A grete erande I have elles-where,
　　　　　　　　　That must nedes be done.

　　　　　　　. . . . .

　　　　　　　Syrs, nedes I must departe now;
　　　　　　　Ihesu me spede this daye!
Perseverance.　Now, brother Contemplacyon, let us go our waye.
　　　　　　　　　　　　　　　　　　　　[ll. 145–155]

All in all, the writer of *Hickescorner* seems to have been defeated rather than assisted by his limitations.

The structure of *Youth* is similar to that of *Hickescorner*. It has six characters, five of whom appear simultaneously. The only doubling possible is that of Lady Luxury, who appears in the play until line 540, with Humility, who appears only after line 556. Even this maneuver leaves the mark of a defect upon the play. Briefly, the situation is that Youth, the Psychomachia hero, has rejected the good advice of Charity, and has gone off to the tavern (l. 540) with his tempters, Pride, Riot, and the strumpet Luxury (again, a reduced approximation of the seven Deadly Sins). The despised Charity, in chains, is rescued after a necessary soliloquy by Humility (l. 556), and these two defenders of virtue are soon confronted by two of the villains and the fallen hero, recently returned from rioting. But Lady Luxury is pointedly missing in this confrontation. Youth states explicitly to his tavern companions, "I wyll be ruled by you two" (l. 612), rather than three as before. The absence of Lady Luxury, like that of Hickescorner in the previous play, is never explained. Neither can be attributed to any logical and progressive suppression of character; each is merely an imperfect expedient. Orderly suppression of character is to become a dominant feature in later plays, but its success will be defined in terms of its appropriateness to the homiletic progression of the plot. In these early plays suppression is not yet utilized as a structural virtue.

The comparison of these rudimentary and far from flawless attempts with the impressive achievements of Bale and Skelton suggests how much the early troupe drama had to learn from its own mistakes, and from the guiding hands of the *literati* who lent their talents to its form. Since the problems and successes of *Mundus et Infans* were in some ways oversimplified and not typical, it is perhaps fair to state that the era of any consequential doubling in the anonymous popular drama did not really begin, so far as is known, until the 1540's. It is with the plays of Edward VI's and Mary's reigns, therefore, that we are next concerned.

X
The Intermediate Morality: Repetition, Expansion, and Elaboration

Probably the earliest play having a casting list, apart from Bale's *Three Laws*, is the anonymous *Impatient Poverty* (ca. 1547–1553): "Foure men may well and easelye playe thys Interlude." The title page lists ten parts for these four men, but since "Impaciente pouerte, Prosperyte, and pouerte" are all names for the single hero in the various stages of his career (compare Infans, Wanton, Manhood, and so forth, in *Mundus et Infans*), the actual number of distinct roles is eight. Although this two-to-one ratio represents considerable advance over *Hickescorner* and *Youth*, the playwright of *Impatient Poverty* is still noticeably short of the high level set by Bale and Skelton during the Henrician period.

Impatient Poverty offers a lesson in practical Christianity. The beleaguered hero learns by his own mistakes that the golden rule of "Love thy Neighbor" offers not only spiritual consolation but also material prosperity, whereas impatient wrath, envy, and riotous living bring financial ruin as well as moral bankruptcy. The play is therefore a somewhat worldly interpretation of the Psychomachia, a partially secularized and limited view of man's spiritual odyssey, less inclusive and less metaphysical in scope than the earlier moral plays like *Perseverance*, *Wisdom*, *Mundus et Infans*, and *Youth*. This narrowing and particularizing of subject matter has long been acknowledged by literary historians as a second or intermediate stage, occupying the middle years of the sixteenth century, in the development of the moral play from its early spiritual orientation to its late hybrid union with the secular elements of chronicle and romance.[1] In the intermediate morality the chief personages are usually neither timeless abstractions nor historical men and women, but social and ethical types.

The intermediate trend happened, perhaps by historical accident, to come at a time when troupe plays were just beginning to experiment with casting lists. The combination was in any event a favorable one for the development of structural methods. With its constant reworking of the Psychomachia plot in the context of current social problems, the intermediate morality gave popular dramatists an opportunity for perfecting a limited technique through repetition of a basic pattern. Inevitably a structural formula took shape under these conditions, and became codified into practices which were to continue on into the period following the disappearance of the intermediate morality.

In *Impatient Poverty*, the first of this group of plays, one finds the imperfections of an early attempt. It is really a patched revision of an even earlier play, and this revision may partly account for its chaotic design.[2] As in *Youth* and *Hickescorner*, the anonymous playwright or reviser is inept in handling his limitations. The structure of the play suffers accordingly, failing to derive any meaningful pattern from the necessary suppression of character.

The saga of the hero, Impatient Poverty, is actually straightforward and conventional enough. He learns from Peace to live in concord with his fellow men, and earns as his reward a new garment and new name of Prosperity. Thereafter he falls into a state of Poverty through the machinations of the Vice, Envy. Finally he hearkens once again to the counsel of Peace and receives anew his vestment of Prosperity.

Confusing this simple outline, however, are a number of structurally unrelated episodes. The second scene introduces an argument between Conscience and Abundance, the point of which is to denounce Abundance's practice of excessive usury. After this single appearance, Conscience is driven into exile and disappears from the play. Neither he nor Abundance ever meets Impatient Poverty or adds anything to the main story. Another digressive episode depicts the antics of a French professional gambler named Colehazard. In a third digression, the usurer Abundance encounters a Summoner who has a warrant for his arrest on a complaint of adultery; Abundance has to purchase legal immunity with a bribe.

These episodes all satirize usury and gambling, and have legitimate thematic relevance in a play that advocates a moderate and peacefully gained prosperity. But the episodes are fragmented in cast and uncertain in their structural relationship to the plot of Impatient Poverty's temptation. The suppression of characters is undisciplined. No progressive homiletic idea can explain Conscience's disappearance before the play is half over. Envy, the Vice, simply vanishes in the final scenes in order that player four may undertake the unrelated role of the Summoner. Scarcely any incident in the play is completed: Abundance is not brought to justice, Colehazard appears once and is never heard from again, and Conscience is never restored to grace. The moral ending completes the story of Impatient Poverty, but not that of the several personifications who have no direct relationship to the hero.

This anarchy of form would seem to follow from the fact that the author or reviser has made clumsy use of his acting personnel. Instead of pairing characters who would be expected to appear in contrasting scenes, he has assigned to one actor the personages who should work together. Peace and Conscience can never meet for this reason, and as a result their problems are never related, and Conscience cannot be resurrected for the final scene. Abundance and Misrule (a companion of Envy) ought to conspire with one another, but paradoxically because they are played by a single actor they can never be united. Accordingly, Abundance's exploits must remain tangential to the play.

Indeed, Abundance's story might almost stand as a second plot if it had continuity and focus to distinguish it from, and at the same time relate it to, the main plot. Lacking such a focus, it is random and confusing in structure. The adventures of Abundance, the Summoner, and Colehazard may well constitute the late additions to the text, for it is these digressive episodes that have warped the design of the older plot. If Conscience too is added,[3] we may account for all of the atypical doubling by postulating a theme of topical farce superimposed upon an early morality.

Impatient Poverty is valuable in demonstrating the difficulties to be overcome in the intermediate morality, but one must not assume that its loose design is characteristic of the type. R. Wever's *Lusty Juventus*, written about the same time, reveals a greater understanding of the principles of organization inherent in late medieval drama. It is another intermediate morality, characteristically narrowing its general plot of spiritual conflict into a topical allegory of the Reformation. The Vice, Hypocrisy, turns out to be a loyal emissary of the Pope, and Juventus is both a universal mankind figure and a Protestant in Tudor England. The ratio of doubling, like that of *Impatient Poverty*, is still modest. Four players assume nine roles, one of which, the Prologue, might be played by anyone. Unlike the author of *Impatient Poverty*, however, Wever has handled his relatively simple problem with skill and foresight. He has turned the need for suppression and alternation into a virtue by shaping the plot to his limited troupe.

Wever begins with a structural plan clearly in mind. In the prologue he outlines his scheme for a progressive homiletic story:

> As in this interlude by youth you shall see plain,
> From his lust by Good Counsel brought to godly conversation,
> And shortly after to frail nature's inclination.
>   The enemy of mankind, Satan, through Hypocrisy
> Feigned or chosen holiness of man's blind intent,
> Forsaking God's word, that leadeth right way,
> Is brought to Fellowship and ungracious company,
> To Abhominable Living till he be wholly bent.   [p. 46]

Thereafter, the prologue promises, Juventus shall be retrieved from sin by God's Merciful Promises. Thus Wever gives the names of his *dramatis personae,* stressing the logic of their sequential appearance: Good Counsel, Satan, Hypocrisy, Fellowship, Abominable Living, and God's Merciful Promises.

These personifications are grouped into three phases of Juventus' spiritual odyssey: conversion, degeneration, and recovery. The phases correspond to the scene divisions of the play. Wever permits the stage to be empty on only three occasions, to divide the prologue from the first phase and the other phases from each other (pp. 46, 62, and 89). The last of these scene divisions must involve a time interval, since four characters exit at this point and one of the four actors must prepare hastily for a new role.

The divisions are clearly reflected in the casting. With the one exception of the hero, each phase has a cast separate from that of the scene preceding or following. The scheme resembles Skelton's *Magnificence*, though simplified considerably. It reduces the casting difficulty by dividing the whole into separate and manageable segments. Characters are suppressed in groups, as the actors alternate from one side of the Psychomachia to the other. The exact casting is not specified ("Foure may play it easely, taking such partes as they thinke best") but any feasible plan requires that Juventus play only himself (except possibly the Prologue), while

	Prologue	Phase 1: Conversion	Phase 2: Degeneration	Phase 3: Recovery
Forces of Good	Prologue	Good Counsel Knowledge		Good Counsel God's Merciful Promises
The hero		Juventus	Juventus	Juventus
Forces of Evil			Satan Hypocrisy Fellowship Abominable Living	

the others shift from virtue to vice, from moral sententiousness to comic invective. Phases one and three employ only three actors, perhaps leaving the fourth man free to act as prompter and stage-hand (see discussion of *Magnificence* in Chapter IX). Phase two with its five roles demands at least one suppression, and thus it comes about that Satan entrusts the unfolding of his diabolical schemings to his son Hypocrisy and his followers, leaving the stage to them.

Alternation is therefore Wever's basic method, structurally juxta-posing serious and comic scenes. He also employs a limited amount of progressive suppression which is justified in terms of the homiletic development. Satan is no longer needed once he has prepared the way for his chief instrument on earth, Hypocrisy. Knowledge in phase one is succeeded in phase three by God's Merciful Promises to signify that mere knowledge without divine guidance is not enough to redeem fallen man. The casting suppressions are moti-vated and natural, not haphazard and inexplicable as they were in *Impatient Poverty*.

The devices used by Wever to shift from a practically full stage of virtuous figures to a full stage of vicious figures deserve attention. He employs a monologue at the beginning of the second phase to facilitate the transition (pp. 62–63), a method encountered before. In addition, he removes his characters from the stage one by one as the first phase ends and introduces them one by one in the ensuing scene. Good Counsel departs first, then Knowledge, and finally Juventus. In the following scene, Hypocrisy appears after

Satan's soliloquy, next Juventus, then Fellowship, and lastly Abominable Living. In the final phase, again, the forces of good enter one by one: Good Counsel first, then Juventus, and finally God's Merciful Promises. The device has its homiletic and dramatic value as well as casting convenience, for the characters are able in this manner to reveal their personalities singly. Form and content are merged here as they were in the employment of end-of-scene or beginning-of-scene soliloquy. This method of building by steps from one full stage to another is used increasingly in the early Elizabethan period.

Wever's tidy formula is appropriate not only to theatrical limitation but also to the structure of any progressive homiletic story. As man advances through his spiritual odyssey he finds himself surrounded by new personalities, new temptations, new rewards and fears. The story of *Pilgrim's Progress* is episodic, but it is so because one experience leads to another, and because good and evil alternately prevail as Christian moves uncertainly forward toward salvation. It is of course illogical to criticize Bunyan for surrendering to a linear plot, since he aspired to nothing more complex than the unadorned chronicle of a quest. It is equally illogical to charge Wever and others like him with lack of structural consciousness. Method harmonizes with intention in *Juventus*, indicating the achievement of a modest yet clearly defined artistic goal.

The anonymous *New Custom* (1558–1573) resembles *Juventus* in several ways. Both plays are offered for four actors. The amount of doubling is only slightly higher in *New Custom*, with eleven parts for the four actors in place of the previous nine. The satire of *New Custom*, like that of *Juventus*, is directed against the counter-Reformation. The central figure is "an old Popish Priest" named Perverse Doctrine. In *New Custom* there is an innovation, however. Perverse Doctrine is the leading exponent of evil throughout most of the play, but ultimately becomes a convert to Protestant virtue and is renamed Sincere Doctrine. First as tempter and then as mankind hero he is doubly the center of attention, and the structure of the play follows his career from original degenerate state to final penitence and reward. The earlier phase found in previous plays, of an original state of grace from which the hero falls into evil, is missing here. *New Custom* has a long phase of plotting and delusion, followed by a phase of conversion.

Perverse Doctrine has a number of spiritual friends and enemies who vie for his allegiance: on the Protestant side, two ministers called New Custom and Light of the Gospel, and on the Catholic side, Ignorance, Hypocrisy, Avarice, and Cruelty. The long first phase (Acts I and II of the three-act total) alternately records the comic depravity of the Catholic villains and the sobriety of their opponents. In the second phase (Act III) the vicious figures are permanently suppressed to make room for a series of personifications who form the ladder of the hero's ascent to ultimate spiritual victory: Edification, Assurance, and God's Felicity. The play is thus divided, like *Juventus* and *Magnificence*, into essentially separate casts for the divided segments of the action. The renaming of the hero emphasizes the separation.

	Phase 1 (*Acts I and II*)	*Phase 2* (*Act III*)
Forces of Good		Edification
		Assurance
		God's Felicity
	New Custom	New Custom
	Light of the Gospel	Light of the Gospel
The hero	Perverse Doctrine	Sincere Doctrine
Forces of Evil	Ignorance	
	Hypocrisy	
	Avarice	
	Cruelty	

The near symmetry of the design is reflected in the casting chart, which assigns to each supporting actor two followers of vice and one of virtue, or the reverse, two followers of virtue and one of vice. This balance permits a systematic exploration of the various

Ignorance	an elder Popish Priest	
Hypocrisy	an old Woman	Player 2
Edification	a Sage	
New Custom	a Minister	
Avarice	a Ruffler	Player 3
Assurance	a Virtue	
Light of the Gospel	a Minister	
Cruelty	a Ruffler	Player 4
God's Felicity	a Sage	

possible combinations of the actors, producing as in *Magnificence* the rapid alternation and variation of groupings so congenial to a plot of intrigue. The play adds little to the method, but indicates how the lessons of Bale and Skelton were consolidated in the anonymous drama.

In the phase of conversion, the playwright presents six characters with four actors by means of progressive suppression, evidently by this time a conventional technique. New Custom and Light of the Gospel begin the scene; once Perverse Doctrine has accepted their teachings, however, New Custom sees that his usefulness has ended and he departs "for a season." When Edification takes his place, Light of the Gospel soon makes his excuses:

> Fare you well, now you are not alone,
> For this small while I must needs be gone.   [p. 50]

Like New Custom he exits never to return, although both have promised to do so. After a suitable interval the actor of New Custom reemerges as Assurance, and shortly the player of Light of the Gospel appears as God's Felicity. The play ends with these four on stage, while New Custom and Light of the Gospel convey a sense of their presence by their promises to return. The clever staggering of these exits and re-entrances appears in the accompanying chart. By such technical precision, *New Custom* shows a small

		Act II, iii		*Act III, i*				
		1– 151*	152– 176	1– 17	18– 180	181– 198	199– 212	213– 238
Player 1	Perverse Doctrine	X	X		X	X	X	X
Player 2	Ignorance	X	X					
	Edification					X	X	X
Player 3	Avarice	X						
	New Custom			X	X			
	Assurance						X	X
Player 4	Cruelty	X						
	Light of the Gospel			X	X	X		
	God's Felicity							X

* Line numberings are mine.

but noticeable advance over *Juventus* in amounts of doubling and complexity of design, and achieves a fuller presentation of the bustling spectacle which the popular drama was striving to achieve.

George Wapull's *The Tide Tarrieth No Man* gives the pattern still more versatility. The doubling ratio is noticeably increased: eighteen parts for four actors, with two players assuming six parts each. With better than four parts to each actor the ratio is higher than that of Bale or Skelton, in fact higher than that of any other period in English drama before or since. Yet this complexity is achieved by an elaboration of the basic formula followed in *Mundus et Infans*.

Wapull's play offers a series of demonstrations of the idea that time waits for no man. It applies the proverb in two cases, that of the evil man who seeks epicurean delights, and that of the virtuous man who seeks God before it is too late. The mission of the Vice, Courage (whose name indicates rash and intemperate pride) is to "encourage" his pleasure-loving protégés to seize the moment of pleasure while it lasts. He persuades the Courtier to involve himself in a ruinous loan in order to have fine clothes and jewels. He reminds the maid Wantonness that her beauty cannot last forever, and counsels her into a rash elopement with her lover Wastefulness. Greediness is encouraged in his usury, and No Good Neighborhood is assisted in extorting a lease from his unoffending tenant. Even the virtuous hero Christianity is obliged at first to be a time-server to policy and riches, until Faithful Few and other godly friends turn his thoughts wholly to religion before it is too late.

The two constructions placed on the proverb, to use time while time serves, operate to divide the play into two phases: a long series of plotting scenes relating the misadventures and scheming alliances of the Courtier, Greediness, and other miscreants, and a shorter phase of retribution for the evil and recovery for the good. Like *New Custom*, then, *Tide Tarrieth* omits the earlier phase of innocence and fall. Even more than *New Custom*, this play divides its cast between the two phases. By means of this division, the playwright reduces his total cast of eighteen: twelve in the first phase and eight in the second. The second phase is structurally the more simple of the two. In its progression from retribution to

	Phase 1 (ll. 1–1439)	Phase 2 (ll. 1440–1879)
Forces *of* *Good* *and of* *Retribution*		Faithful Few Correction Authority Despair Christianity
The victims	The Tenant The Debtor	
Forces *of* *Evil*	Courage the Vice Greediness Hurtful Help Painted Profit Feigned Furtherance No Good Neighborhood The Courtier Wastefulness Wantonness The Sergeant	Courage the Vice Greediness Wastefulness

reward, the standard figures of Despair, Authority, and Correction make only brief and quickly suppressed appearances.

The episodes of the first phase are organized as variations on a theme, as in Skelton's *Magnificence*. Courage the Vice stands at the focal point of the action and is on stage almost without cessation. From this central position he conducts a series of cleverly interwoven intrigues with secular social types who represent the sinful excesses of man: the Courtier (pride), No Good Neighborhood and Greediness (envy and covetousness), and Wastefulness and Wantonness (the sins of the flesh). Greediness' house is off stage, like the palace in *Magnificence*, providing plausible motivation for many exits and re-entrances. Courage is assisted in his machinations by three henchmen, Hurtful Help, Painted Profit, and Feigned Furtherance, who act as his errand boys and consequently are coming and going all the time. The victims of these plots, the Tenant and the Debtor, appear briefly at sporadic intervals to bewail their unhappy fates. The rash love affair of Wastefulness and Wantonness is introduced late (ll. 836–856 and 1139–1392), after the other intrigues are well under way.

This constant interplay creates an impression of brilliant skulduggery. The Vice receives one embassy and then another, dispatches his lieutenants all in different directions, and is inevitably left alone in the intervals to comment on the action, to gloat, or to amuse the audience with his witticisms while his fellow actors prepare for new entrances. The plan calls for more shifting of parts than was found in the simple outline of *Juventus*, which relied instead on permanent suppressions. By this interchange, Wapull manages to keep alive at least four related episodes concurrently, and vividly suggests the continued presence of the twelve personages involved.

Unity is provided by the theme. The play contains a formidable variety of comic material, and the various segments of plot must remain episodic because of the impossibility of meetings between so many of the *dramatis personae*. Nevertheless, the materials offer a number of examples of the play's proverb. These examples are tied together by the all-important Vice, the leading player, relieved of any important doubling. Because he focuses so much episodic material, relating the various elements to each other through the force of his character, it is imperative that he represent all aspects of evil. He is the constant entity in the midst of constant variation, and yet of course is changeable as the Vice must be. His acts and interests are episodic and involved with different persons, and yet he proceeds always with a fixed motive. Contrasts unite in his personality, just as a number of varied episodes unite in the play's proverbial theme.

In *Impatient Poverty, Juventus, New Custom*, and *Tide Tarrieth*, the intermediate morality has carried the conventional Psychomachia from its clumsy beginnings to a highly professional and competent exposition of a standard formula. It is not until the end of Mary's reign that the anonymous drama reaches levels of technical proficiency equal to those achieved much earlier by Bale and Skelton. Once these levels are attained, however, the future of the popular drama lies in finding new materials and new patterns of structure, rather than in further polishing the old. With the intermediate morality, the conventional Psychomachia has developed to full maturity.

XI
Dual Protagonists
and a Formula
for Homiletic Tragedy

The Tide Tarrieth No Man, discussed at the conclusion of the previous chapter, is actually something more than a fulfillment of the conventional Psychomachia. It signals a new direction for the structure of the morality. Whereas previously the mankind hero was invariably subjected to the alternating influences of good and evil, and so underwent a series of transitions from degeneracy to recovery, *Tide Tarrieth* has no such faltering personality at its center. The nominal Psychomachia figure is Christianity who, although he must pay lip service to the ways of the world, is never actually enamored of vice. His spiritual conflict is brief and unconvincing, a sop to the convention. Moreover, his foil, Greediness the usurer, is no more likely to turn from evil to good than Christianity is likely to turn from good to evil. Greediness perseveres in villainy until Despair finally persuades him to commit suicide; Christianity suffers hardships at first but perseveres to a victorious end. The other personalities are also either steadfast in virtue or irrecoverably sinful, except for the minor figures Wantonness and Wastefulness. Their conversion is a peripheral incident, since neither occupies the central position formerly accorded the Psychomachia hero.

This bifurcation of the central mankind figure results from the increasing structural tendency in the intermediate morality to alternate camps of godly and profane figures. Serious and comic are more separated in *Tide Tarrieth* than has been the case before. The pattern shifts now from a struggle for the soul of a universal man to a series of contrasts between those who are unquestionably saved and those who are irreparably damned. In the history of ideas, this phenomenon appears related to the growth of Calvinism in Reformation England. The emphasis in this study, however, is on the creation of a dramatic formula depicting human failure — a formula that developed from the structure of the Psychomachia.

This pattern of two opposed protagonists becomes pronounced in several intermediate popular plays of the 1560's and 1570's. One such is the anonymous *Trial of Treasure* (1562–1567), possibly by W. Wager.[1] Its theme is the danger of coveting riches and fleshly pleasure, since time will eventually convert these gifts into "dust and rust." The trial of "Treasure," in other words, will prove the goddess to be false in man's hour of need. The gallant who learns this bitter lesson is named Lust. He leads a brief life of extravagance, assisted by Inclination the Vice, Sturdiness, Pleasure, Greedy-Gut, Elation, and of course Treasure ("a woman finely appareled"), until Time and God's Visitation end his frivolous existence. Lust's counterpart is fittingly named Just, a God-fearing soul who never deviates from the true path, following the good counsel of Sapience, Contentation, and Trust ("a woman plainly [appareled]"), and eventually receiving his well-earned reward from Consolation.

With the morality protagonist thus divided into two, *Trial of Treasure* contains two thematically contrasted strands of plot, parallel throughout the play, with two groups of characters alternately occupying the stage and only rarely confronting one another.

	Scene 1 57–165*	Scene 2 166–404	Scene 3 405–519	Scene 4 520–614	Scene 5 615–741	Scene 6 742–1039	Scene 7 1040–1148
							Time
							Consolation
Forces of Good					Contentation		
					Trust		
			Sapience				
	Just		Just		Just		Just
Forces of Evil	Lust	Lust	(Inclination)	Lust		Lust	(Inclination)
		Inclination		Inclination		Inclination	
		Sturdiness					
		Greedy-Gut		Greedy-Gut			
		Elation					
						Pleasure	
						Treasure	
Forces of Retribution						Visitation	
						Time	

*Line numberings are mine.

Lust and Just hurl defiances at each other in the opening scene in
order to establish the contrast of their personalities, but thereafter
never cross paths. The teams of opposing forces move with them in
alternate scenes. The only exception to the precise segregation of
casts is the Vice, who is by nature omnipresent and would be
expected to bedevil the forces of good. Even he appears chiefly with
Lust and his fellows. All the rest occupy alternate scenes, and are
played by the same four supporting actors who shift back and forth
from virtue to vice.

Within each separated strand, the playwright further reduces
his casting problem by a progressive sequence of characters. In
the early comic scenes, Lust is tempted into a dalliance with Carnal
Cogitation (a personification who never appears) by Inclination's
henchmen, Sturdiness, Greedy-Gut, and Elation. These three are
permanently suppressed before Treasure and then Pleasure make
their appearances (ll. 772, 823). The sequences follow as a result
of the story, for Treasure is the fruit of Lust's now unbridled
"inclination," and Pleasure is always the concomitant of Treasure:

> *Pleasure.* Whereas she is resident, I must needs be;
> Treasure doth Pleasure commonly precede.   [p. 290]

Pleasure is also the first to depart from Lust in the sequence that
leads to the end of the play. After God's Visitation pronounces
his warning, Pleasure can stay no longer:

> Nay, there is no remedy; I must away;
> For where God doth punition and pain,
> I Pleasure in no case cannot remain.   [p. 295]

His departure anticipates the inevitable destruction of Treasure and
Lust. Soon all that remain are the exemplars of virtue: Just, Trust,
Consolation, and Time "with a similitude of dust and rust," the
sobering remains of Lust and Treasure. These homiletic progres-
sions and alternations are thoroughly traditional in method, except
that they are now employed in a formula of divided paths for
two protagonists.

The new structure of dual protagonists in *Trial of Treasure*
alters the moral statement of the play. In the earlier drama the
message was one of hope for Mankind, Juventus, or Impatient
Poverty. Each exhibited the characteristic weaknesses of the human

race, fell into evil ways, and forgot the teachings of his virtuous counselors, but was inevitably reclaimed to prosperity and virtue. In *Trial of Treasure* the contrast of an unredeemed protagonist and an unassailably virtuous protagonist implies the separation of the human race into irreconcilable camps.

The result is the introduction of the theme of failure and punishment for personalities who represent human types. In earlier moralities only evil itself had been punished, in the figure of the Vice and his henchmen. In *Trial of Treasure*, distinctly human shortcomings receive dire retribution. The fate of Lust contains within it the potentiality for a formula of homiletic tragedy, which will mature in subsequent plays that admonish men to virtue by emphasizing the danger of spiritual defeat.

Ulpian Fulwell's *Like Will to Like Quoth the Devil to the Collier* contains a similarly divided structure. Indeed its title is intended to suggest the division of mankind into the evildoers who inevitably prefer depraved company like their own, and the virtuous who as inevitably follow the path of good. Like *Tide Tarrieth*, this play illustrates a proverb didactically:

> The name of this matter, as I said whilere,
> Is, Like will to Like, quoth the Devil to the Collier.
> Sith pithy proverbs in our English tongue doth abound,
> Our author thought good such a one for to choose,
> As may show good example, and mirth may eke be found,
> But no lascivious toys he purposeth for to use.   [p. 307]

The prologue stresses the separation of two paths at some length. The virtuous will befriend one another and come ultimately to reward, whereas the vicious will flock together until inevitable punishment comes upon them:

> For the virtuous do not the virtuous' company mislike.
> But the vicious do the virtuous' company eschew:
> And like will unto like, this is most true.
>
> . . . .
>
> Herein, as it were in a glass, see you may
> The advancement of virtue, of vice the decay:
> To what ruin ruffians and roisters are brought;
> You may here see of them the final end:
> Begging is the best, though that end be nought;
> But hanging is worse, if they do not amend.

The virtuous life is brought to honour and dignity:
And at the last to everlasting eternity.   [pp. 307–308]

The perspicacious author goes one step further to identify the separateness of these strands with the traditional alternation between serious and comic:

And because divers men of divers minds be,
Some do matters of mirth and pastime require:
Other some are delighted with matters of gravity,
To please all men is our author's chief desire.
Wherefore mirth with measure to sadness is annexed:
Desiring that none here at our matter will be perplexed.   [p. 308]

The two contrasting forces in this play are to represent the comically degenerate and the solemnly devout. The author combines satiric comedy with edifying homiletic teaching to produce a "measure" or mean that unites pleasure with instruction. The complementary nature of comic and serious is common to all Psychomachia drama, but here it implies also the separation of mankind into the depraved and the righteous.

The clarity of the author's plan results in a decidedly neat and recognizable structure in the play itself. The virtuous hero is appropriately named Virtuous Life, and the godly company that he prefers to keep consists of Good Fame, God's Promises, and Honor. The vicious are more numerous. Nichol Newfangle the Vice has a host of companions who generally appear in pairs: Tom Collier and Lucifer, Tom Tosspot and Ralph Roister, Cuthbert Cutpurse and Pierce Pickpurse, and two Flemish rogues, Philip Fleming and Hans. The instruments of retribution are Severity and Hankin Hangman. The play is apportioned to these groups in four distinct phases: (1) the rioting and carousing of the evil companions, (2) reassurance and consolation for Virtuous Life, (3) retribution for the villains, and (4) reward for the good. The distinctions in cast, as will be seen from the chart, are so rigidly maintained that only in one brief scene do the contrasting sides confront one another.

The comic scenes are longer and more vivid than the serious ones, and contain more varied characters. The inevitable result is a mounting emphasis upon the failings of mankind, rather than the triumphs. None of the many rogues makes any serious attempt

	Phase 1: Rioting and carousing 37–664*	Brief confrontation 665–741	Phase 2: Reassurance 742–895	Phase 3: Retribution 896–1211	Phase 4: Reward 1212–1277
Forces *of* *Good*			Honor God's Promises Good Fame		Honor Good Fame
		Virtuous Life	Virtuous Life		Virtuous Life

Forces
of
Evil
	Nichol
	  Newfangle
	Lucifer
	Tom Collier
	Tom Tosspot
	Ralph Roister
	Hans
	Philip
	  Fleming
	Cuthbert
	  Cutpurse
	Pierce
	  Pickpurse
		Nichol
		  Newfangle
		
		Cuthbert
		  Cutpurse
		Pierce
		  Pickpurse
				Nichol
				  Newfangle
				Lucifer
				
				Tom Tosspot
				Ralph Roister
				
				Cuthbert
				  Cutpurse
				Pierce
				  Pickpurse	

Forces *of Retri-* *bution*				Severity Hankin Hangman	

* Line numberings are mine.

at reform. The theme of *Like Will to Like*, reiterated time after time, is punishment and destruction for a misspent life. Since the play has no mankind hero to reclaim to virtue, it dramatizes human failure. The tone is predominantly satiric and denunciatory rather than morally positive.

As a corollary of this emphasis on vicious behavior, the author dispenses with the hitherto customary progression of "reward" personifications at the play's end. He simply recalls Good Fame and Honor to announce a happy conclusion for Virtuous Life. (*Trial of Treasure* similarly lacks "reward" figures.) Since Virtuous Life has never been in danger of falling into evil, he needs no succession of regenerating agents to replenish his spiritual health. The reward phase is correspondingly short (ll. 1212–1277) in relation to the punishment phase, and exists only as an edifying standard against which to measure the fall of the numerous lost souls.

Technically, the playwright exerts special care in elaborating the structure of his comic scenes. Clearly the vicious characters cannot all meet at once, because the troupe is limited to five players. Yet

the theme of "like will to like" requires as much convivial companionship as possible. Fulwell's solution is a sequence of paired
characters. Tom Collier and Lucifer are first, since their names
appear in the proverb of like will to like, "quoth the Devil to the
Collier." After illustrating literally the theme of the play, they make
their exits before the arrival of Tom Tosspot and Ralph Roister,
the second pair of companions in licentious living. Philip Fleming
and Hans perform in a brief satire of drinking, swearing, and
general horseplay, aimed primarily at immigrant labor from the
Low Countries. Cuthbert Cutpurse and Pierce Pickpurse then amuse
the audience with accounts of their recent robberies. Nichol Newfangle the Vice encourages all these scoundrels, and soliloquizes
between episodes, facilitating costume change (pp. 317, 332–333,
344–345, and 355–356). He manipulates the pairs — usually one
pair at a time — until his double dealings have brought Cuthbert
Cutpurse and Pierce Pickpurse to the gallows and have reduced
Tom Tosspot and Ralph Roister to beggary. In the last episode of
retribution, Nichol is himself carried off on the back of Lucifer
to eternal punishment. By sequence in pairs, the author creates
nine "birds of a feather" in the carousing scene with only five
actors. Their groupings present an inventory of social evil: vile
language, rioting, heavy drinking, thievery, and beggary. Nichol,
played by the leading actor, partakes of all their villainous practices
and so must be related generically to every sort of vice.[2] He represents the godless "new Gyse" of abandoned living in mid-century
England, as seen from a Calvinist point of view.

Another play with a cast entirely divided between good and evil
is W. Wager's *Enough Is as Good as a Feast*. Its theme is worldly
ambition and covetousness, and its structure is again a rhetorical
amplification of a proverbial title in a positive and a negative
sense. Worldly Man is the protagonist who cannot be content with
"enough," and who therefore follows the fatal counsel of the
Vice Covetousness until his soul is irretrievably damned: "Stowt
he is and in any wise wil not bow" (prologue). Worldly Man's
opposite is suitably called Heavenly Man, a person for whom the
modest rewards of a humble life are sufficient. Just as surely as
Worldly Man goes to eternal torment, Heavenly Man receives
assurances of contented abode with the faithful. As in *Like Will to*

Like, these two protagonists meet only in the opening scene in order to establish the polarities of the theme. Thereafter they and their respective supporters follow separate paths. Actually, Worldly Man undergoes a brief conversion to virtue in this first scene, but soon relapses into settled impenitence.

The prologue of *Enough*, as in that of *Like Will to Like*, recognizes the division between the mirthfully profane and the instructively godly. The prologue speaks of the auditors as having congregated to amuse themselves as well as to "haue intelligence" of the moral lesson. Accordingly the actors are to "touch" abuses and praise virtue, appealing both to the "affections" and to the reason of the audience. This traditional twofold appeal to humor and seriousness corresponds in *Enough* to the division of mankind into sinners and saints.

The phases of *Enough,* after the prologue, are as follows: (1) A scene of confrontation between Worldly Man, Heavenly Man, and Contentation (contentment). The unregenerate Worldly Man is callous at first, but wavers and then sincerely renounces his mercenary ambitions. (2) The Vice Covetousness and his lieutenants Temerity, Inconsideration, and Precipitation discredit Worldly Man's pious mentor, Enough, and win their protégé back again to vice. (3) Heavenly Man briefly comments on the pitiable spectacle of Worldly Man's recusancy. (4) A number of Worldly Man's victims, Tenant, Servant, and Hireling, plead for mercy and are haughtily refused. Worldly Man, at the height of fortune, exults in his power. (5) Retribution falls as Worldly Man is visited by Prophet, God's Plagues, Ignorance (with the Physician), and finally Satan. Worldly Man is carried off to Hell. (6) Heavenly Man receives promises of reward from Contentation, Enough, and Rest. These phases correspond with the division into scenes. A bare stage separates all but phases four and five, which merge naturally enough since both are concerned with the presentation of evil. The bare stage is not employed at any other point.

Even more than in earlier moralities, the attention centers on the comic and vicious characters, both in length of scenes and in number of personalities. The virtuous appear seldom and briefly. Phase three, for example, is only twenty-one lines long. The use of progressive sequence for the forces of good is limited. In the final scenes, Rest is the only new personification of reward, the others having been reintroduced from earlier scenes. The reason for such lack of emphasis on reward, as in *Trial of Treasure* and *Like Will to Like*, is that Heavenly Man has never wandered from the true path and hence requires no elaborate process of recovery and indoctrination.

The scenes of vice, on the other hand, are rich and varied, with a new set of characters for each phase. Temerity, Precipitation, and Inconsideration take part only in the plotting and temptation scene, and are then permanently discarded in favor of the three victims of Worldly Man's power; and so the narrative and the casting move together in groups of characters, ending in the punitive figures who pronounce Worldly Man's doom. The general movement is one of spiritual decline. The emphasis on Worldly Man's harsh but deserved fate is scarcely alleviated by the brief final scene of consolation for the godly. Worldly Man is the central figure to the extent that Heavenly Man cannot possibly claim to be. Worldly

	Phase 1: Confrontation 93–280	Phase 2: Relapse 281–939	Phase 3: Moral comment 940–960	Phase 4: Victimization 961–1187	Phase 5: Retribution 1188–1465	Phase 6: Reward 1466–1541
Forces of Good	Contentation Heavenly Man	(Enough)	Heavenly Man			Rest Enough Contentation Heavenly Man
Forces of Evil	Worldly Man	Worldly Man Covetousness Temerity Precipitation Inconsideration		Worldly Man	Worldly Man Covetousness	
Victims				Tenant Servant Hireling		
Forces of Retribution					Prophet Plagues Physician Ignorance Satan	

Man so dominates the play that the leading actor may have taken his part (see Chapter V) rather than that of the Vice. *Enough* teaches by negative example, displaying the bitter fruits of a life spent in ambition and covetousness.

In portraying defeat, the popular morality has begun to evolve a formula for homiletic tragedy. "Tragedy" is a term always in need of definition. Here tragedy is used to indicate plays ending in defeat.[3] In the light of the complexities of classical and Renaissance tragedy, this definition is absurdly simple; but in the context of sixteenth-century faith, defeat before God, though simple, is sobering enough. The downfall of a protagonist in homiletic drama implies his eternal spiritual death. The story of Worldly Man, Lust, Tom Collier, and others is one of failure according to the religious beliefs of audience and playwright. Instead of the alternating and progressive rise of the hero from fallen innocence to spiritual victory, we find in these dramas the progressive decline of the corrupted man to ultimate damnation. A native English structure for homiletic tragedy has been created out of indigenous materials, by the reversal of emphasis from the positive to the negative side of the Psychomachia. The formula has in fact grown out of the satiric and "comic" material of the earlier plays, which always tended to dominate the stage until it evolved a final pattern of destruction and catastrophe out of its own viciousness.

In the popular dramatic tradition of the 1560's and 1570's, then, the concept of mixed drama — the mixture of the comic and tragic in a single play — takes on new meaning. The well-known type of "Lamentable Tragedy, Mixed Full of Pleasant Mirth" (the extended title of *Cambises*) traces its origins to the view that vicious behavior is at once funny and terrifying as a spectacle, admirable and yet grotesque, amusing but also edifying as a perverse distortion of moral behavior. In the popular plays after mid-century the scenes of comic licentiousness produce their own catastrophe. The figures at the end of the story, who previously signaled the triumph of the successful protagonist, now emphasize the punishment of the tragic protagonist. In *Enough*, Prophet, Plagues, Physician, Ignorance, and Satan far outbalance Rest in the series of figures introduced in the last two phases.

The theory of homiletic tragedy in *Enough* and similar plays owes little to the *de casibus* tradition:

Tragedie is to seyn a certeyn storie,
As olde bookes maken us memorie,
Of hym that stood in greet prosperitee,
And is yfallen out of heigh degree
Into myserie, and endeth wrecchedly.[4]

These plays do not portray great and famous men who overreach
themselves until they suffer inevitable decline of fortune. Nor
are these plays in the mainstream of the *vanitas vanitatum* school,
with its rejection of the world and all its frivolities, since their
practical advice is often worldly in a positive moral sense. Their
theme, stated as simply as possible, is that evil is the reward of evil.
This homiletic tragedy differs from other tragic expression in that
a comic treatment is at once its source and its staple ingredient.
Even the downfalls are often comic. For example, Lucifer jokes
with the audience as he drags the dead Worldly Man off to his
eternal punishment, bidding all Worldly Men in the audience to
follow the fallen hero's example. "Yea, and after death I will
prouide a place, / For you in my kingdome for euer to reign,"
says Lucifer, and he promises the audience they will fare no worse
than he himself: "That is to lye burning for euer in pain" (sig. G_1
verso). This is a wry joke about a serious matter, everlasting damnation. Nichol Newfangle's last exit in *Like Will to Like*, on the
back of the Devil, has a similar comic bravado that is as desperate
in tone as a sardonic gallows-speech.

Despite the comic villainy and satire, nevertheless, these unredeemed sinners evoke a sympathetic response for tragic suffering and
death. The protagonist is Man, however narrowed into the topical
mold of the intermediate morality. If such a man can fail utterly,
then so may anyone. The responsibility for failure lies in this
man's impenitence. He contains within him a mixture of good
and evil, but the evil so predominates that he is born to damnation.
Still, the potential for good persists in him, so that his inability to
respond to virtuous instruction is not without its element of pity.
The Psychomachia itself had been incapable of this tragic configuration, with its Christian emphasis on perfection and other-
worldly redress;[5] but a shift in the balance from forgiveness to
retribution, ushered in by Calvinist theology, made possible a
drama of an amusing and yet devastating spiritual degeneration.

Evil protagonists like Worldly Man do not even remotely illustrate

the Aristotelian definition of tragic flaw, for they are all so compounded of flaws that they are devoid of grace. They in fact conform
to no declared artistic pattern of tragedy, other than a popular concept of man's evil as declared in many proverbs. Some are Biblical:
pride goeth before a fall, or the reward of sin is death (as Faustus
comments drily to himself in a passage that is at once comic and
despairing). Many such proverbs provide titles of the plays, such
as "the tide tarrieth no man," and "like will to like."

Another proverb-title that captures perfectly the spirit of the inherent evil in man, treated in comic manner and yet leading to
tragic conclusion, is *The Longer Thou Livest the More Fool Thou
Art*. The proverb implies a denial of hope for the protagonist,
and the prologue emphasizes his forlorn condition:

> By him [Moros] we shall declare the vnthriftie abuse
> Of such as had leuer to Folly and Idlenes fall,
> There processe, how their whole life they do spende,
> And what shame they com to at the last ende.
>
> . . . .
>
> Holsom lessons now and than we shall enterlace,
> Good for the ignorant, not hurtfull to the wise;
> Honest mirth shall com in, and appeare in place,
> Not to thaduauncement, but to the shame of vice;
> To extoll Vertue, without faile, is our deuise.   [ll. 52–68]

In this mixture of "holsom lessons" and mirth, the spectacle
of Moros is at once deplorable and amusing. Wager is subjecting
viciousness to ridicule. The auditors are supposed to recognize and
scorn their own depraved instincts, viewed at a satiric distance in
the grotesque comedy of vice.

The Longer Thou Livest goes one step beyond *Enough* or *Like
Will to Like* in the development of a structure for homiletic
tragedy. Wager strictly limits his virtuous personages to the functions of warning, moral comment, and retribution. That is, he
presents no virtuous hero whose upward climb toward salvation
offsets the decline of Moros. We find no counterparts of Heavenly
Man, Just, or Virtuous Life in this play. Of the fifteen characters
in *The Longer Thou Livest*, only six — Exercitation, Discipline,
Piety, People, God's Judgment, and Confusion — uphold the standard of righteousness, and their achievements are all negative. The
first three fail in their attempts to make Moros listen even momen-

tarily to counsels of reason and faith. "People" appears briefly to lament the prosperity of foolish and wicked men like Moros. God's Judgment and Confusion are the agents of punishment. The restoration of order in the final scene is at best a negative compensation, a summary of failure. The fool has come to a bad end, explain the virtuous survivors, but we may learn to live better by his fearful example.

Moros' false friends who accompany him during the long comic scenes consist primarily of two groups of three characters each: Idleness, Wrath, and Incontinency (ll. 571–993), and Ignorance, Cruelty, and Impiety (ll. 1234–1652). The configuration of three is used symbolically and symmetrically, as it was in *Three Laws* and *Wisdom Who Is Christ*. Moros has three virtuous counselors, Exercitation, Discipline, and Piety. The two sets of three depraved counselors are obviously intended as counterparts to the three virtuous counselors, just as Infidelity's six vice lieutenants were specifically assigned to oppose the three Laws in Bale's play. Ignorance and Idleness are the foils of Exercitation (virtuous industry), Cruelty and Wrath the foils of Discipline (the agent of divine correction), and Impiety and Incontinency (disobedience) the foils of Piety. Moreover, the three virtuous abstractions represent the same division between natural, social, and divine law as in Bale's play. Exercitation operates by the law of nature, Discipline is a legalistic controller like the law of Moses, and Piety's province is the soul where the law of Christ dwells. Use of protective pseudonyms for the villains augments the symmetrical pattern of three.

		Pseudonym		*Pseudonym*
Exercitation	Idleness	Pastime	Ignorance	Antiquity
Discipline	Wrath	Manhood	Cruelty	Prudence
Piety	Incontinency	Pleasure	Impiety	Philosophy

Not surprisingly, the casting is also arranged by threes. *The Longer Thou Livest* employs four actors, and Moros requires the full attention of the leading player except for minor doubling as Lady Fortune. The three supporting players, like actors two, three, and four in Bale's *Three Laws*, present three counselors to virtue and six counselors to vice. Each player takes the part of one worthy and two villains: Exercitation, Wrath, and Cruelty; Discipline, Incontinency, and Impiety; and Piety, Idleness, and Ignorance.

The technical virtuosity of *The Longer Thou Livest* is brought fully to bear on Moros' unregenerate decline. Progressive suppression appears only among the vicious characters, as Moros moves downward toward damnation from Idleness, Wrath, and Incontinency to Ignorance, Cruelty, and Impiety, and then to God's Judgment and Confusion. The play has no chief Vice; the central figure is a human protagonist. His centrality focuses the play upon his failure to learn.

In this play, and perhaps in *Enough*, the choice role for the leading player is no longer an allegorical abstraction, but a human individual who suffers defeat in the context of the Christian morality. That he is comic in his depravity does not alter the seriousness of his damnation. His plight is in fact strikingly similar to that of Doctor Faustus, except that Faustus is more explicitly a figure from legendary history. Once the generic name of Moros the fool is replaced by the specific name of Faustus the impenitent sinner, the structural pattern exists for a protagonist who is tragic and yet comically degenerate, and who is both an individual and a universal example of spiritual failure.

T. Lupton's *All for Money* (ca. 1577) may well be chronologically the last of the unhappily ending intermediate moralities. Technically it is a tour de force, for with thirty-two parts to distribute among four actors it resorts to nearly every staging contrivance developed in the popular repertory. The resulting medley, even if somewhat muscular in its craftsmanship, is a convenient index to the intermediate period. *All for Money* lacks a casting chart, but the internal evidence for a cast of four players is as logically incontrovertible as the evidence for five players in Skelton's *Magnificence*. The total of thirty-two characters is arranged with great care so that no more than four ever appear at once, and the opportunities for changing of parts are skillfully provided.

All for Money, like previous "homiletic tragedies," elaborates a familiar proverb. It demonstrates repeatedly that man's desire for gold is the source of evil. The spectacle is both humorous and sobering: Lupton declares on the title page that his play is "a Moral and Pitifvl Comedie," and the prologue prepares the audience for a "pleasant Tragedie." The use of these terms is no more indiscriminate than in *Cambises*, for this play is a mixed drama of derisive comedy leading to moral defeat. The author's plan is to illustrate his proverb with various social types, "plainly representing the manners of men and fashion of the world noweadayes." The play therefore shares the "intermediate" characteristic of a topical satire, concerned with specific problems of human behavior and yet treating these problems in terms of allegory and universal types.

All for Money contains six scenes, each a separate episode involving a distinctive cast of characters. Of the thirty-two characters, only three — Money, who is one of the protagonists, Sin the Vice, and Damnation — appear more than once. *All for Money* is perhaps more rigidly compartmentalized into episodic segments than any play examined so far, and makes greater use of systematic suppression.

The six scenes alternate between good and evil: (1) the virtuous norm as exemplified by Theology, Science (knowledge), and Art (craftsmanship), who agree not to labor dishonestly for private gain; (2) the genealogy of the vice characters and their plot to pervert mankind through avarice; (3) a debate on the proper uses of money,[6] comparing the merits of Learning with Money, Learning without Money, Money without Learning, and Neither Money nor Learning; (4) the corruption of various social types by Sin and All for Money; (5) retribution for the evil worshippers of money, Judas and Dives; and (6) restoration of order by Godly Admonition, Virtue, Humility, and Charity. As the accompanying chart reveals, the scenes of virtuous conduct are brief, together constituting only 443 lines of 1572 in the play.

The unity of *All for Money*, as in so many popular "episodic" plays, is the singleness of theme (man's greed) manifested in a variety of episodes.[7] This theme becomes more important than the fate of individuals. Characters are drawn to illustrate a single motif of human behavior, and are given no more depth than is necessary to make a point. The full course of their lives has no relevance here. It is the course of the moral formula that is all-important: the genealogy of sin, the analysis of its origins, motivations, and processes, the depiction of its worldly success and ultimate downfall — all seen in the perspective of moral uprightness, the beginning and end of virtuous living. The parts succeed each other as *exempla* to a homily, written for an audience that perceived a rich totality in matters of faith. The success of the play lies in varied illustration, in "multiple unity" and gathering of impact, not in the crisis of the individual moment.

Lupton's technique in producing this sequential unity is proficient, though the effect is somewhat contrived at times. Lupton devotes his greatest efforts to the second and fourth scenes, the genealogy or evil and the corruption of society. In the first of these, four actors portray eleven vice characters who appear regularly one after another. Since three virtuous personages have just left the

Scene 1 99–202	Scene 2 203–605	Scene 3 606–907	Scene 4 908–1439	Scene 5 1440–1525	Scene 6 1526–1572
					Admonition Virtue Humility Charity
Theology Science Art					
		Learning with Money Learning with- out Money Neither Learning nor Money			
			Moneyless		
		Money without Learning			
	Money Adulation Mischievous Help Pleasure Prest for Pleasure		Money		
	Sin		Sin		
	Swift to Sin				
	Damnation			Damnation	
	Satan Gluttony Pride				
			All for Money Gregory Graceless William with the two wives Nichol Never out of the Law Sir Lawrence Livingless Mother Croote		
				Judas Dives	

stage, Lupton introduces the vice figures one at a time, elaborating the character of each. Money appears first, and then Adulation. When Money is suddenly taken ill, Adulation calls for the assistance of Mischievous Help. These two comrades help Money to deliver himself of a son, Pleasure, with the "fine conveyance" of the "hollowe place." The stage now contains its full allotment of four players. While Pleasure identifies himself, Money and Mischievous Help quietly slip away, so that when Pleasure feels the pangs of oncoming birth he can call for the assistance of Prest for Pleasure. With the birth of Sin the stage is full once again. Pleasure and Adulation, having been superseded by this continuing genealogy, depart. Sin thereupon feels his hour approaching, and with the aid of Prest for Pleasure (who has remained) and Swift to Sin (who now enters), he brings forth Damnation. The stage is filled for the third time. Sin is now left alone to mark time with an amusing account of his influential position in the world of affairs, until he is joined by Satan, Gluttony, and Pride. The scene ends with a necessary and yet appropriate soliloquy by Sin, while the actors prepare for the next episode.

The lengthy fourth scene, depicting the corruption of society, uses a simpler technique of suppression to deploy the players among nine parts. Two players, in the roles of Sin and All for Money, do not double at all in the scene. Sin's business is to present a series of petitioners to the corrupt judge. The petitioners appear singly, and are evidently performed in turn by the two players who are not constantly on stage. Six petitioners come forward in this manner, though the list could go on indefinitely. The structure of the scene is like that of Heywood's *Weather*, in which Jupiter receives the requests of eight suitors in turn. There is, however, an important difference. Heywood gathers all his petitioners for the final judgment scene, so that any doubling is impossible, whereas Lupton dismisses his personages permanently in order to present new ones.

Like the preceding plays, *All for Money* stresses the dark side of human nature. The virtuous, outnumbered more than two to one by the villains, are relegated to brief scenes of commentary and debate. They have no hero to reclaim, no goal to provide continuity in their sequential appearance. The personages of the final scene, although appearing there for the first time, are not the progressive figures of regeneration found in the earlier Psychomachia. They are choral figures without function in the plot. Lupton's techniques of progressive appearance and vivid characterization have been lavished only on the followers of vice, and the theme of comic villainy leading to its own destruction belongs to them alone.

We have been following two strands throughout the intermediate morality, the maturing of technical facility in matters of suppression, alternation, soliloquy, motivation of exits, and the like, and the evolution of an increasingly secular homiletic tragedy. Both were important for the future of Elizabethan drama. Mechanical versatility in framing popular drama provided the practical experience in stagecraft needed by an expanding professional theater. Homiletic tragedy prepared the way for more intense portrayal of sympathetic character than was feasible in the conventional Psychomachia. Before either could contribute directly to secular drama of the late Renaissance, however, the popular theater had to adjust its world of moral and social abstractions to include specific historical personalities and legendary heroes.

XII The Transition to Chronicle

During the 1560's and 1570's, when the intermediate morality was reaching the high point of its development, the popular stage began to reach out into new areas of subject matter. Heretofore limited to allegorized personifications and universalized social types, even when dealing with contemporary English problems such as the Reformation, immigrant Flemish labor, or extravagant new fashions in clothing, the popular drama now began to introduce named characters from chronicle, romance, and Biblical story. Historical personages had indeed appeared earlier in literary plays like Bale's *King John*, but these experiments reached the popular movement only after a characteristic lapse in time. Not until the first two decades of Elizabeth's reign, with the popular troupes centering their activities more and more in London, did secular chronicle or romance become a staple of troupe repertory.

Despite the importance of this secular growth as a transition to the later Renaissance stage, one must not urge too arbitrary a distinction between the hybrid morality and its intermediate predecessor. The popular tradition evolved experimentally and gradually, so much so that the overlappings are often more apparent than the differences. By the 1560's the intermediate plays had grown more and more worldly in their aspect, producing finally a satiric tragedy of the English contemporary scene. On the other hand, the early chronicle and romance plays began as an amalgamation of historical or romantic figures with the familiar personalities of the allegorical drama. "Pure" chronicle or romance was not attempted on the troupe stage; virtually all popular plays from this period contain significant elements of the morality.[1] During this entire period of transition, individualized figures are introduced with moral types in plays that are secular in their setting and moral in their aim. The gradual introduction of these individuals was only one further step toward adapting the native homiletic drama to its function of commentary on contemporary life. In such a continuous tradition, the established patterns of the Psychomachia and the homiletic tragedy had a paramount influence in shaping a stage formula for history and romance.

Perhaps the easiest path of transition from moral play to specific history was through the medium of Biblical story. Scriptural hybrids were popular in the early part of Elizabeth's reign.[2] Scriptural material was of course common in the medieval pageants and cycle plays that continued to be performed in English villages and towns long after the commercial theater had turned to the Psychomachia. The introduction of Biblical narrative into the commercial drama in the 1560's was not, however, a return to an older form of dramatic entertainment.[3] It was the substitution of individual biography for abstract representation. These Biblical plays tended to envisage their heroes and heroines as flesh-and-blood people rather than as religious personifications. The Psychomachia continued its regular course, except that Biblical figures replaced more generic protagonists.

An example is Lewis Wager's *The Life and Repentance of Mary Magdalen*, which merges Biblical narrative with the familiar pattern of the morality. Mary Magdalen, Simon the Pharisee, and Christ appear along with Infidelity the Vice, Pride of Life, Cupidity, Carnal Concupiscence, and other abstractions. The Biblical and moral elements combine easily, since Mary's biography of sin and penitence fulfills all the specifications of the traditional Psychomachia plot of happy ending. Wager has chosen a familiar Biblical narrative of spiritual conflict leading eventually to salvation, and has tailored it to the morality pattern merely by adding the progression of personified figures who usually accompany such a moral struggle.

The five phases of the plot may be enumerated as follows. After the prologue, (1) Mary falls prey to Infidelity and his lieutenants Pride of Life, Cupidity, and Carnal Concupiscence. (2) Simon the Pharisee plots with Malicious Judgment to entrap Christ, by inviting Him to a banquet in order to question Him on doctrinal matters. (3) Mary enjoys the brief splendor of her sinful life with Infidelity until the Law of God moves her to a Knowledge of

Sin. Mary thereupon suffers in despair until Christ drives out Infidelity and Mary's seven Deadly Sins. Faith and Repentance assist in the task of redemption. (4) The chief Biblical episode follows. Simon, Malicious Judgment, and Infidelity fail to ensnare Christ on theological questions, while Mary confirms her faith by washing Christ's feet with her tears. (5) Justification and Love reward Mary for her faith.

Although Mary's narrative is the usual one of spiritual struggle, Wager does not content himself with repeating the structural formula of the older Psychomachia. His important contribution is to divide the play not simply into alternating scenes of serious and comic, but into alternating scenes of the historical and the abstract. The actual Biblical phases (two and four) are set apart from the noncanonical portions of the story. The cast is accordingly divided between historical and moral. Except for Infidelity the Vice and Malicious Judgment, no allegorized personifications take part in the two central Biblical episodes. The progressive moral figures such as Pride of Life, Repentance, Faith, and Love move in their own world, in alternating scenes that provide a homiletic background for the Scriptural incident. Phases two and four dramatize the Biblical narrative, whereas phases one, three, and five are the moral exposition of Mary's inner spiritual conflict.

	Phase 1 *1–825*	*Phase 2* *826–971*	*Phase 3* *972–1461*	*Phase 4* *1462–1945*	*Phase 5* *1946–2035*
Forces *of* *Good*			Repentance Faith Knowledge of Sin Law of God Christ	Christ	Love Justification
Heroine	Mary Magdalen		Mary Magdalen	Mary Magdalen	Mary Magdalen
Forces *of* *Evil*	Infidelity Pride of Life Cupidity Carnal Concupiscence	Infidelity Simon Malicious Judgment	Infidelity	Infidelity Simon Malicious Judgment	

The traditional movement of the cast from one side of the Psychomachia to the other now parallels an important alternation from scenes of chronicle to scenes of abstraction. The supporting actors shift sides as they have always done, but now they shift from Biblical episode to allegory.[4] Mary and Infidelity probably demanded the undivided attention of two leading actors; the third actor might have presented Pride of Life, Christ, and Justification, the fourth Cupidity, Simon, Law of God, Faith, and Love, and the fifth Carnal Concupiscence, Malicious Judgment, Knowledge of Sin, and Repentance. Wager's method of doubling in the dual world of the hybrid chronicle thus resembles that of the intermediate playwrights.

Indeed, the technical traditions of the Psychomachia contribute extensively to this new hybrid pattern. Conventional structure prevails, naturally, in the scenes of allegory rather than in those of Biblical story. For example, Wager's method of compressing homiletic character recalls the earliest days of the moral drama. In the first scene, Mary's encounter with the seven Deadly Sins must somehow be conveyed by a troupe of five actors. Since one actor takes the part of Mary in this scene, only four actors remain to portray the qualities of her sinfulness:

In vs foure without faile be contained
As many vices as euer in this world raigned.   [ll. 291–292]

Wager utilizes a scheme like that in *Wisdom Who Is Christ*, of grouping the seven Deadly Sins into three categories of World, Flesh, and Devil. Carnal Concupiscence introduces himself as the embodiment of lust, sloth, and gluttony (ll. 295–312), Cupidity ("the roote of all iniquitie") as the source of theft, penury, inhumanity, unquiet mind, avarice, and other sins (ll. 315–334), and Pride as the foremost of the sins of the spirit (ll. 335–358). Infidelity the Vice is the Devil's agent on earth and is the epitome of all evil.

In scene three when Christ cleanses Mary of her sins, however, He exorcises not the four who previously appeared on stage but the full seven who compose the usual listing of the Deadly Sins:

Auoide out of this woman, thou Infidelitie,
    With the .vii. diuels which haue hir possessed.

. . . .

[stage direction:] *Infidelitie* runeth away. *Mary*
falleth flat downe. Cry all thus without the doore,
and roare terribly.   [ll. 1282–1285]

Christ, by expelling Infidelity alone from the stage, symbolizes the
expulsion of all the Deadly Sins at once. Pride, Cupidity, and
Carnal Concupiscence have not reappeared since the first scene,
but three actors "roare terribly" from off stage ("without the doore")
to indicate the seven devils cast out of Mary's soul.[5] The impression
is created of seven sins, even though Infidelity's henchmen were
suppressed permanently after the first scene.

In their separate world of homiletic abstraction, the personifications
lead a timeless existence virtually untouched by the specific Scriptural
events of phases two and four. At the end of the play Wager renames
in order the allegorized personalities who have illustrated the
steps in Mary's spiritual pilgrimage:

Fyrst, the lawe [of God] made a playne declaration,
That she was a chylde of eternall damnation:
By hearyng of the law came knowledge of synne;
Then for to lament truely she dyd begynne.

Then came Christ, with his gospel of hope:

By the word came faith; Faith brought penitence;
. . . .
From thens came loue, as a testification
Of God's mercy and her iustification.   [ll. 2016–2031]

These abstractions delineate Mary's progress from sin to salvation
as though she were another mankind figure. They describe a universal battle against evil of which the Biblical account is only an
isolated example. They direct attention toward the generic, whereas
the Biblical scenes dramatize religious emotion in historical terms.

This dualism of the abstract and the concrete, so essential to a
hybrid play, removes the allegory from its former centrality in
moral drama. If read independently, phases one, three, and five of
Mary Magdalen are as conventional in form as the Psychomachia
in a play like *Juventus*. But these scenes have now only a secondary
function, of explicating an event taking place in the realm of Scriptural chronicle.

With two nearly segregated casts of characters, Wager tells a single story from two points of view that are no longer homogeneous. The strands run concurrently and alternately, but each is structurally independent. They are still related by theme, for the abstract figures explain the spiritual significance of the Scriptural incident. Nevertheless *Mary Magdalen* constitutes an important first step in separating the personified abstractions from the arena of historical event newly introduced into the homiletic drama. The Vice is the exception to the rule. In the ensuing plays, it is he alone who is able to bridge the gap between chronicle and abstraction. Apart from him, it will be seen that in the hybrid morality secular and allegorical figures never exist "side by side" in the fullest sense of sharing the same world.

In the comparative orthodoxy of its Psychomachia plot, *Mary Magdalen* contrasts with the anonymous interlude of *King Darius,* "Beinge taken out of the third and forth Chapter of the thyrd booke of Esdras." This relatively early Biblical chronicle (published in 1565) contains much dull poetry, but structurally it is an important link in the transition from intermediate morality to Elizabethan chronicle play. *King Darius* goes much further in the segregation of its two hybrid elements than did *Mary Magdalen*.[6] Whereas Knowledge of Sin, Faith, and Repentance contributed directly to Mary's spiritual biography even though dwelling apart, the allegorized figures in *King Darius* have no such necessary function. Their story echoes that of King Darius in a tenuous way, but they never meet him or his courtiers and never contribute even indirectly to the conduct of affairs in the Biblical scenes. *King Darius* has in fact a dual plot, evolved from the alternating pattern of the intermediate morality.

The Scriptural story is a simple one. It records two virtuous acts of its title figure. In the first Biblical incident (scene two of the play) he entertains the monarchs of Ethiopia, Persia, Judah, and Media. He is hospitable and bounteous to his guests, and allows them to return amicably to their own lands. In the second Biblical incident (scene four) Darius judges a debate by three courtiers on the subject of the strongest force in the world. The two flattering courtiers (labeled only as Stipator Primus and Secundus) urge the power of wine and regal authority. The honest courtier, Zorobabell, praises the power of love both earthly and divine. Darius rewards Zorobabell generously for his virtuous answer. The King thus demonstrates the impartiality of a true prince, and Zorobabell the sincerity of a loyal courtier. Significantly, these episodes have been chosen to illustrate a secular lesson rather than a spiritual one, even though they are Biblical in source. Neither provides theme for an adaptation of the Psychomachia, as in *Mary Magdalen*.[7]

The other three scenes, that alternate with the Biblical episodes, are peopled by three virtuous personifications and three vice figures continually disputing with each other: Charity, Equity, and Constancy opposed to Partiality, Inequity, and Importunity. The vice figures carouse as old friends in villainy, rail at the virtuous and their sermonizing, but are eventually driven off to perpetual damnation. This controversy, as in many such scenes of the intermediate moralities, is a polemical allegory of England's religious struggle. The antics of the vice figures satirize Papist corruption and hypocrisy, and the discomfiting of these villains is a victory for the Reformation.

The relationship between the two plots escapes the reader at first, though a connection does exist. The virtuous characters of the main plot embody the very qualities that are personified in the scenes of allegory. Zorobabell's great virtue is constancy; the virtues of Darius are charity (in the banqueting scene) and equity (in the trial scene).[8] The King proclaims himself an enemy to partiality and importunity, and he rebuffs his courtiers who try to succeed by these policies. Constancy, acting as epilogue, establishes the thematic link:

> The thyrde, Zorobabell by name,
> Dyd remayne in constancye and kepe the same.   [ll. 1556–1557]

In both plots the virtues of constancy, equity, and charity receive their reward. The allegory therefore relates the story of Darius to contemporary England and the Reformation. Darius' conduct becomes a mirror for Christian princes, and that of Zorobabell an edifying example for all who serve such a king.

The segregation of the two plots into alternate scenes and alternate casts is complete. As in *Mary Magdalen*, scenes two and four are Biblical whereas one, three, and five are allegorical. This divided plot alternates from moral allegory to Biblical chronicle just as the intermediate morality alternated from comic depravity to edification. *Darius* shifts from negative to positive example,

	Scene 1 35–610	Scene 2 611–738	Scene 3 739–1226	Scene 4 1227–1547	Scene 5 1548–1605
				Agnostes	
				Optimates	
				Stipator Primus	
				Stipator Secundus	
				Zorobabell	
Biblical		King Darius		King Darius	
Chronicle		Agreeable		Agreeable	
		Preparatus		Preparatus	
		Perplexity			
		Curiosity			
		Ethiopia			
		Persia			
		Judah			
		Media			
	Charity		Charity		Charity
	Equity		Equity		Equity
Allegory			Constancy		Constancy
	Inequity		Inequity		
	Importunity		Importunity		
	Partiality		Partiality		

from laughter to pious instruction. Obviously the cast changes from straight to character parts in adjoining scenes. The casting of *Darius* is not worked out in detail ("syxe persons may easely play it"), but the diagram makes it clear enough that the entire cast, including the leading actor, has to change sides with each scene. Yet the alternation in *Darius*, so traditional as a means of doubling, results in a new structural phenomenon.

How then did the alternation of the Psychomachia become transformed into the alternation of a divided plot? Basically it was accomplished by the preservation of a stage convention after it had outgrown its original function. Vice comedy was essential to the Psychomachia plot of tempting the hero to sin. It functioned as an analysis of the nature of evil, showing the brief prosperity of evil in the world and its final punishment by the forces of good. Yet vice comedy was evidently important also as entertainment for popular audiences, since it lived on in plays like *Darius* where it was no longer necessary. Its scenes of carousing and scurrilous joking had become a stock in trade which the troupe theater could not simply abandon when it turned from Psychomachia drama to chronicles of actual persons and events. Accordingly, playwrights had to find new justification for the inclusion of vice comedy in hybrid drama.

The author of *Mary Magdalen* avoided the problem by choosing a figure whose story conformed to the conventional pattern of spiritual struggle and ultimate victory. The story of *King Darius*, however, does not so conform. It narrates two unrelated incidents in the life of a worthy king and a loyal courtier, as examples of virtuous behavior. Where are the comedy routines of the vice figures to be fitted into this outline? The author of *King Darius* chose to present them in a plot that is separated in cast and in incident, and yet occupies the alternating scenes in which an audience would expect comedy. The first comic scene, with its intrigue, conflicts, threats, and struggles for supremacy, is typical of any moral play. The phase of degeneracy in scene three is in its expected position. Yet the functional relationship of this comic villainy to the main figure has been altered. Since it no longer has any bearing on the protagonist's history, it creates a relevancy by a thematic echoing of that history.

The minor historical figures in *King Darius* also derive structural attributes from the homiletic drama. Between the two separated Scriptural incidents of banquet and trial, Darius and his two servants provide the only continuity in *dramatis personae*. All others appear only once. The foreign princes, who exist only to demonstrate Darius' generosity, are superseded by courtiers who demonstrate his judicial wisdom. The use of secular names such as the King of Persia or Zorobabell is only a disguise for their traditional function in a linear sequence. Thus, in this Biblical hybrid, the alternating struggle between good and evil disappears and leaves behind the familiar alternation of comic and serious scenes, the episodic plot, the series of minor figures. Both comic and serious figures find new justification for existing in a secular play, but the structure of their alternating and sequential appearance remains unchanged.[9]

The shift from Biblical story to classical chronicle represents another departure from the subject and intent of the standard morality. In the early hybrid chronicle plays taken from ancient legend or history, Pickering's *Horestes* and Preston's *Cambises*, the moral personifications are drawn even further out of their native element than heretofore. The adaptations and transmutations are accordingly more pronounced. Yet a continuity in tradition of doubling and a resulting continuity in structure are equally discernible, and emphasize once again the debt of popular Elizabethan secular drama to its religious ancestor.

J. Pickering's *Horestes* (ca. 1567) contains an abundance of vivid incident, since it incorporates all the ancient legend of Orestes into one continuous, sprawling entertainment. Æschylus' *Oresteia* trilogy was not Pickering's source, however. *Horestes* is based upon Caxton's *Recuyell of the Historyes of Troye*, translated from the French of Raoul Lefevre, and is accordingly far more medieval than classical in theme and structure.[10] Disparaging comparison with Æschylus has led inevitably to charges of "utter formlessness," "no art," and "little dramatic skill" in Pickering's work,[11] but the author's grasp of structural principles cannot be comprehended in classical terms. Pickering's plan is naturally inclusive. It extends from Horestes' revenge upon his mother and her lover for the murder of Agamemnon, to his public exoneration at Athens and his marriage to Menelaus' daughter, Hermione. Violent action fills the stage: armies mill about and beseige walled cities, trumpets "exault your tubal sound" (l. 722), soldiers chase after women, and a hanging takes place in view of the audience ("flyng him of ye lader and then let on bringe in his mother Clytemnestra; but let her loke wher Egistus hangeth," l. 790).

In such surroundings, the moral personifications are few and have only peripheral significance. An important exception is the Vice, variously named Courage and Revenge, who counsels Horestes to seek vengeance "vpon his one [own] naturtll Mother" and accordingly suffers the fate of exile for his heinous crime while Horestes is exonerated. The hero's character is cleansed by the transfer of his avenging nature to an allegorical abstraction.[12] The Vice's moral opponent, Nature, urges forgiveness toward one's own flesh and blood. These two contenders are vestiges of spiritual conflict from the moral drama. Even in them the Psychomachia is only ambiguously operative, for no simple equation of right and wrong differentiates the rival counsels of Revenge and Nature. Horestes follows the suggestion of the Vice, and yet is fully and publicly justified in doing so.

The remaining abstractions in *Horestes* are not allegorized figures at all, but general types who could have been given specific names if the author had so wished. Counsel is merely a loyal counselor in the court of Idumeus. Commonalty expresses the people's loyalty to Horestes, and Nobility expresses that of the ruling class. Fame (ll. 838f) is little more than a messenger to tell us of Horestes' journey to Athens. Provision acts as usher for the trial scene (ll. 926–1037). Even Truth and Duty do little more than bestow a final blessing on the victorious hero in behalf of his people. In *Horestes* the debt to homiletic character is slight. Spivack has noted this declining function of personifications in the hybrid morality, observing that "the compact interplay of human relationships inside a literal story robs them of their previous force and function, and they survive merely as homiletic embroidery around its edges." [13]

The structure of *Horestes*, on the other hand, owes a great deal to the moral tradition. The alternating pattern of the first few scenes is clear in the following outline, which pays particular attention to the characters and incidents that Pickering has added for diversion. *Lines 1–170:* The Vice appears with two country clowns, Rusticus and Hodge. They have heard it rumored that Horestes is coming home to avenge his father's death. Even these simple folk suspect that Clytemnestra and Egistus are guilty of adultery and murder. The Vice promotes an altercation between Rusticus and Hodge over a hog and a dog. They fall to blows; the Vice thwacks them and runs out. They patch up their quarrel and depart amicably. *Lines 171–305:* Horestes marches in, resolves upon revenge (egged on by the Vice), and receives promise of aid from Idumeus. *Lines 306–399:* Haltersick and Hempstring, two depraved soldiers serving Horestes, discuss the worldly pleasures of the military life. They sing warlike tunes, and swear military oaths. Hempstring proposes that they hire a pretty wench to do their laundry and perform (like Mademoiselle from Armentières) other campfollowing services. His fellow scoffs at dallying with a "jenny" in the heat of battle, and they "fyght at bofites with fystes." They part enemies. *Lines 400–625:* In three scenes Horestes prepares for war while Clytemnestra and Egistus fortify their city. *Lines 626–647:* A widow enters, running before the soldier who has killed her husband. She begs vainly for mercy. Suddenly the tables are turned: "Go a fore her, and let her fal downe upon the [soldier] and al to be beate him." When he yields, she returns his weapon and peace is made between them.

What has happened, clearly, is that Rusticus, Hodge, Haltersick, and their fellows have taken over the structural position of the old vice characters. They appear alternately with the "straight" characters in scenes of comic degeneracy. They quarrel, swear, make plots, struggle for supremacy, and jest endlessly of taverns, women, and hanging. As in the older moral plays, the actors shift back and forth from comic to serious parts. Traditions of casting sequence and suppression create the need for alternate scenes of comedy and serious drama, so that the two groups never meet each other except for the ubiquitous Vice. Player two shifts from Rusticus to Idumeus, then to the soldier. Haltersick and Hempstring disappear as a team only to reemerge as Egistus and Clytemnestra. Hodge becomes Counsel. Horestes himself plays the woman in the seventh scene. Similar comic respites are provided throughout, mainly by the Vice (ll. 648–679, 849–916, and 1038–1121).

	Scene 1	Scene 2	Scene 3	Scene 4	Scene 5	Scene 6	Scene 7
						Egistus Clytemnestra Messenger	
Classical Chronicle				Drum Men Nature	Drum Men		
		Counsel Idumeus Horestes		Horestes	Counsel Idumeus Horestes		[etc.]
Vice Comedy	Vice	Vice Rusticus Hodge	Vice				
				Haltersick Hempstring			
							Soldier Woman

The important fact is that these comic figures are not obsolescent moral personifications, strange vestiges in an alien environment, exiled to a separate realm of existence like Charity and Constancy in *King Darius*. The vicious characters in *Horestes*, apart from the Vice himself, are flesh-and-blood realities, countrymen in Argos or soldiers in the employment of the King. The vice figures have been secularized along with the figures of the main plot. Although they behave as vice lieutenants should, and occupy alternating scenes of comedy, these characters have historical substance in a chronicle play.

Even this secularization is less radical a change than one might suppose at first. We have seen that the vice comedians in the late intermediate moralities were becoming increasingly social in aspect, and were losing their generalized homiletic attributes. What is there, for example, to distinguish Tom Collier, Philip Fleming, and Cuthbert Cutpurse in *Like Will to Like* from Hodge, Rusticus, and Haltersick in *Horestes?* Merely that the former are satiric social types in sixteenth-century England, whereas the latter are purportedly citizens of ancient Greece, and yet are patently anachronistic.

It is the structural relationship of these personages to the main narrative of *Horestes* that has changed, not the stuff of the comedy or the mode of behavior. Since the "vice figures" no longer engage in a moral battle for the hero's soul, and hence are not central to the plot, the author invents historical motivations in order to preserve their captivating brand of comedy. He makes his "vice figures" rustic countrymen or soldiers, thereby accounting for their appearance in a chronicle play. The device points forward strikingly to the relationship of Falstaff, Peto, Bardolph, Nym, and company to the main plots of Shakespeare's *Henry IV*, Parts I and II, and *Henry V*. In *Horestes* the comedy is not nearly so well developed as in Shakespeare, but its structural source in moral drama shows it to be an important link in the gradual secularization of the Psychomachia.

A secular transformation also accounts for Pickering's handling of minor sequential figures in the serious scenes of the main narrative. *Horestes* contains few actual personifications in such scenes, just as it contains few actual vice figures, because the hero's spiritual struggle is not integral to the action. Yet the serious action teems with minor figures. Of twenty-seven roles and unspecified extras, only five — Horestes, Clytemnestra, Egistus, Idumeus, and the Vice — have any centrality or permanence. The others make one, at most two, appearances. With only six professional actors at his disposal, Pickering needed to rely on progressive suppression in arranging his minor personages.

Accordingly, his lesser historical figures replace the serious personifications of the moral drama. In that drama, such figures marked the phases of the Psychomachia from downfall to recovery. They bolstered the hero and taught him repentance, or punished the wayward. Similarly in *Horestes* the lesser figures mark episodes in the life of the hero. The early scenes of the main plot emphasize

Horestes' choice of a plan of action and his need for good advice. Accordingly the supporting actors appear as Counsel, Idumeus, and Nature, the counterparts of Knowledge, Conscience, and Good Counsel in earlier plays who defended the morality hero in his primal innocence. The center of the play is a story of civil war, and so we see soldiers, drums and trumpet, messengers, and heralds. The trial in Athens calls forth a new grouping: Fame, Provision, Nestor, Menelaus, and Hermione, who replace the figures of judgment and retribution commonly associated with the penultimate phase of the earlier morality. The final blessing bestowed upon Horestes by Nobles, Commons, Duty, and Truth corresponds to the familiar benediction by such "reward" figures as God's Felicity, Assurance, and Contentation. As in the conventional moral formula these personages are introduced solely to illustrate the progress of the hero, and are suppressed when no longer needed.

Allegorized types like Nature and Duty are a dying breed in the hybrid chronicle. The personifications of virtue certainly "lose their functional integrity and become one-speech supernumeraries," limited to "a single appearance in a sequence." [14] Whereas the disappearing of such homiletic names from *Horestes* is important, it does not, however, indicate a sharp break with the moral tradition. In the intermediate morality, many personifications were already "one-speech supernumeraries" appearing briefly in a linear plot. The personifications of virtue, especially, were often robbed of their "functional integrity" in homiletic tragedies like *The Longer Thou Livest* that provided no wavering hero to be reclaimed. *Horestes* represents a transition, but not a sudden one. In place of comic vice lieutenants alternating with a progression of minor allegorical figures, it offers soldiers and rustics alternating with a progression of courtiers and statesmen. Accordingly, the sense of unity in *Horestes* still depends upon the relationship of many episodes to a single theme. By examining the lives of private citizens and public men, of rowdy soldiers, widows, and Greek chieftains, *Horestes* explores many sides of a central political issue — the evil fruits of regicide and unlawful lust, and the unnaturalness of civil strife. [15]

Thomas Preston's *Cambises* is the best known of the hybrid moralities, with its lively mixture of farce and tragic chronicle in disjointed linear sequence. Critical attitude toward the episodic structure of *Cambises,* as of *Horestes,* has tended to be deprecatory rather than understanding. Willard Farnham, for example, criticizes the "disconnected anecdotal structure" of *Cambises*, blaming Preston's too easy acceptance of the pattern of his source, Richard Taverner's *The Garden of Wisdom*. As Farnham has shown, Preston retained Taverner's order in portraying Cambises' one good and three bad deeds; all are present in Herodotus, but are told there in a different sequence. "The play might have been far better if Preston had not found it so easy to let Taverner's arrangement of anecdotes take on dramatic meaning and be sufficient in themselves for the main business of the action." [16] Irving Ribner also maintains that "there is no overall integrating structural pattern, and little principle of relationship other than the chronological." [17]

Taverner's order of incident, as it happened, fitted with remarkable convenience into Preston's theatrical preconception of what was needed for his limited troupe. He evidently chose this particular source because it was so readily adaptable to a pattern of moral chronicle. As a result, the structure of *Cambises* bears numerous important similarities to that of *Horestes*.

Cambises' one good deed is to punish the wicked judge Sisamnes; his three evil deeds are (1) to shoot Praxaspes' son with bow and arrow in order to prove his steadiness of hand after drinking, (2) to murder his younger brother Smirdis, and (3) to marry his kinswoman and then execute her for daring to remind him of his brother's death. Cambises himself ultimately dies for his crimes, completing a progression, typical of homiletic tragedy, from virtuous beginning to depravity and thence to retribution. The dramatic convenience of relating these famous incidents one after the other is obvious. Each is a separate phase, containing a cast that is largely isolated from the rest of the play. Sisamnes' execution clears the way for new figures to participate in the episodes of Praxaspes and Smirdis. Cambises' unfortunate Queen does not appear until the fourth episode. (The accompanying diagram omits the comic material, to be discussed later.)

The minor characters, like those of earlier moralities, group themselves in sequence about the major figures and events. Small Ability exists only as a humble petitioner whose honest suit is spurned by the corrupt Sisamnes. Commons' Cry and Commons' Complaint accuse Sisamnes before the King in order that Proof and Trial may bring him to justice. The unhappy Otian witnesses the flaying of his father by Execution. All these figures become superfluous with the disappearance of Sisamnes. Similarly, in phase three Attendance and Diligence are merely the loyal followers of Smirdis, and Cruelty and Murder are the suborned henchmen who murder him for Cambises.

In this play, as in the moralities, the need for suppression in groups arises from the desire to crowd the stage with incident and spectacle, under the limiting conditions of troupe presentation. Minor Psychomachia figures have merely been replaced by minor historical figures. They are treated in the same way: developed only to illustrate a theme in the life of the protagonist, and then dis-

Phase 1: Good deed	Phase 2: First evil deed	Phase 3: Second evil deed	Phase 4: Third evil deed
Cambises	Cambises	Cambises	Cambises
Ambidexter		Ambidexter	Ambidexter
Counsel			
Lord	Lord		
Knight	Knight		Knight
Sisamnes			
Small Ability			
Shame			
Commons' Cry			
Commons' Complaint			
Proof			
Trial			
Execution			
Otian			
Praxaspes	*Praxaspes*		
	Child		
	Mother		
		Smirdis	
		Attendance	
		Diligence	
		3rd Lord (?)	3rd Lord (?)
		Cruelty	Cruelty
		Murder	Murder
			Venus
			Cupid
			1st Lord
			2nd Lord
			Lady
			waiting-maid

carded. Unity in *Cambises* derives from theme, elaborated through a variety of incidents, all showing the corruption of civil power in the hands of a temperamental and worldly king. The theme, implying a doctrine of passive obedience to an evil ruler whom God would surely punish,[18] had contemporary political significance for an age still sensitive to the potential disaster of capricious and strife-torn government. All the episodes lead inevitably toward divine retribution for Cambises' wicked life. Even though no personifications such as God's Visitation signal the last stage of the progression, a popular audience would not have failed to recognize the causal link between Cambises' iniquitous doings and his "accidental" death. The prologue promises:

> Then mighty Jove would not permit to prosecute offense;
> But, what measure the king did mete, the same did Jove commence,
> To bring to end with shame his race — two years he did not reign.
>   [ll. 31–33]

And Cambises' own last words confess the appropriateness of his untimely death: "A just reward for my misdeeds my death doth plain declare" (l. 1165). The episodes grow toward a single point, and are interrelated thematically in the manner of the Psychomachia.

As in *Horestes*, it would be a mistake in *Cambises* to overemphasize the disappearance or peripheral function of the genuinely allegorical personifications.[19] It is true that few remain, and that excepting the Vice few are vital. Shame appears "with a trump, black," like Fame in *Horestes*, to express public attitude toward the protagonist. Such figures, later exemplified by "Rumour, painted full of tongues" in *2 Henry IV*, are out of context in secular chronicle, and act only in separate scenes as choral spokesmen. Increasingly they are exiled to prologue and epilogue, like Comedy and Envy in *Mucedorus*, or History, Tragedy, and Comedy in *A Warning for Fair Women*.[20] Even in the intermediate moral drama, however, such personifications were usually incidental walk-ons. They live on in the hybrid plays as secular figures marking the stages of episodic sequence. Most of the personifications in *Cambises*, as in *Horestes*, are not true allegorizations at all but generalized types set in historical context. They might have been named specifically had the author so wished.[21] Execution, for example, is merely an executioner, using the language of such men in contemporary England:

Come M[aster] Sisamnes, come on your way.
My office I must pay; forgive therefore my deed.   [ll. 458–459]

Execution is actually referred to as "the execution man" (l. 411). Cruelty and Murder are in effect that pair so familiar in Shakespeare's chronicles and tragedies, signaled by the stage direction "Enter two murderers." Small Ability, Commons' Cry, and Commons' Complaint are only humble citizens who testify against Sisamnes. Naming these figures generically should not obscure their specific purpose in a chronicle. Yet their limited and sequential contribution to the episodic plot is derived from the progressive allegory of the moral drama.

The shift from Psychomachia to historical sequence brings with it more specific motivation for entrances and exits. Whereas in the moral drama such figures as Repentance or Confusion might be dismissed without explanation once their homiletic functions were discharged, in *Cambises* the actual disposition of the characters becomes a matter of factual consequence. At Sisamnes' trial, for example, after Proof, Trial, and Commons' Complaint have given their adverse testimony and opinion, they are sent away to find "the execution man." The suppression is important, for all six adult players in the troupe are on stage, and Proof has to prepare quickly for the very Execution whom he was supposed to find. Later, when Sisamnes has been executed, his son is ordered to dispose of the body:

Otian, convey your father hence to tomb where he shall lie.   [l. 471]

Otian needs help with the heavy body, and accordingly asks:

Good execution man, for need, help me with him away.   [l. 473]

By this means Preston motivates the exit of Execution, who after a fifteen-line interval reappears as the Knight. Otian too must change quickly for the part of Praxaspes' wife. Clearly, by Preston's time the popular theater had greatly increased its skill in doubling such busy scenes with a minimum of false contrivance.

The comedy of *Cambises* is Preston's own addition, and, as in *Horestes,* it is a secular adaptation of vicious intrigue in the Psychomachia. The comic figures, who are nominally a part of the historical setting, dwell in alternate scenes that comment satirically upon the main action. Although this comedy lacks sufficient continuity to form a proper subplot, it anticipates by its quasi-historical nature the structural function of comic subplots in later popular plays.

Preston motivates the appearance of "vice figures" in a secular chronicle just as Pickering did. The humorous characters in *Cambises* are soldiers in the service of the King, and country rustics of his domain who have heard rumors of the goings-on at court. In the first comic scene (ll. 126–291), even Ambidexter the Vice is a soldier, though attired in an outlandish uniform. He has a series of contests with Huf, Ruf, and Snuf, three regular soldiers, whose talk is full of oaths, scurrility, and boasts of their derring-do. Their cowardly skirmishes end in truce, only to be inflamed again by the appearance of Mistress Meretrix, who sets them to bidding for the price of her sweet favors. In the second battle Meretrix bests them all and takes Ruf into captivity as her servant.

The next comic interlude (ll. 732–842) follows the murder of Smirdis, thereby marking the interval between the third and fourth phases of the main plot. Ambidexter meets two Cotswold-speaking rustics, Hob and Lob, on their way to market. They have heard reports of the King's unnatural cruelty, and the perverse Vice encourages their criticism of Cambises only to denounce them finally as traitors. The rustics fight with each other until Marian, Hob's shrewish wife, effects a reconciliation and beats Ambidexter soundly. In a third comic incident (ll. 965–993), the Vice picks a quarrel with Preparation, the servant who is arranging the King's wedding banquet. After teaching Preparation a lesson in proper respect, Ambidexter helps to set the banquet, and drops his dish of nuts all over the stage.

The materials for comedy, then, are the familiar "vice" fare of ludicrous quarrels, boasts, profanity, scatological humor, physical violence, cowardice, tavern talk, and wenching. The comedy is not without its homiletic lesson in the framework of the play. Since the main plot teaches the danger of a quarrelsome, vain, and pleasure-loving King, the comic scenes should be regarded as the below-stairs view of this serious moral. The "vice lieutenants" indulge in Cambises' depravities, making them preposterous by exaggeration, holding up to ridicule the same viciousness that is presented as direful in the main plot. Nevertheless, the conventional homiletic justification has disappeared, for these comic figures (excluding the Vice) do not participate as tempters in Cambises' own story. What is important is that they have found a naturally motivated place in serious chronicle, while retaining their comic mode of behavior. They no longer cling, like the outmoded vice comedians of *Darius*, to a precarious exile. Instead, they have bridged the transition to secular drama. Far from being obsolescent remnants of a fading theatrical convention, they are the forerunners of comic soldiers and tavern-frequenters on the late Elizabethan stage. *Henry IV*, despite its incomparable superiority as a play, owes much to the structural tradition of *Horestes* and *Cambises*.

XIII   The Transition to Romance

The search for new secular material in the popular drama of the 1570's and 1580's led to extensive borrowings from the storehouse of narrative romance. Stephen Gosson charged popular dramatists with pilfering their plots from collections and individual romances such as *The Palace of Pleasure,* the *Golden Ass* of Apuleius, the *Aethiopian History* of Heliodorus, *Amadis,* the romances of the round table, and bawdy comedies in French, Italian, and Spanish.[1] The problem of shaping these sprawling narratives into a theatrical discipline was vast, but for the troupes such generous dimensions in scope were familiar and welcome. Gosson, with his classical training, naturally found the structural solution in these plays to be no more than a surrender to discursiveness:

Sometime you shall see nothing but the aduentures of an amorous knight, passing from countrie to countrie for the loue of his lady, encountring many a terible monster made of broune paper, & at his retorne, is so wonderfully changed, that he can not be knowne but by some posie in his tablet, or by a broken ring, or a handkircher, or a piece of cockle shell, what learne you by that?[2]

In their own terms, however, popular dramatists made sense of such a narrative progression by adapting it to the capabilities and practices of the troupes, as their predecessors had done with the equally formidable panorama of medieval religious spectacle. From the romantic saga of separation, wandering, and reunion they extracted a formula similar to the moral theme of fall from grace, temporary prosperity of evil, and divine reconciliation. The pattern continued because the deployment of actors in alternate, symmetrical, and sequential configuration remained substantially unchanged by the secularization of their material.

From the sizable group of romance plays existing for the most part in name only,[3] two anonymous plays have survived, *Common Conditions* and *Clyomon and Clamydes*. Both are hybrids of romantic and allegorical figures, suggesting that many of the lost plays also contained this characteristic of transition from the moral to the high Renaissance drama. *Common Conditions* is offered for acting ("Six may play this Comedie"), a fact that helps to place this drama in the main line of the popular acting tradition from *Mankind* to *Tamburlaine*. A plausible suggestion that Thomas Preston may have written *Clyomon and Clamydes*[4] argues a continuity in authorship and dramatic method. These romances were presented under the auspices of the troupes, only slightly expanded in size from their mid-century strength.

Common Conditions contains even fewer allegorical figures than *Horestes* or *Cambises*. In fact only the Vice, Common Conditions, remains as an abstract personification. The comic figures are secular, and the author justifies their presence with factual explanation, as Pickering did with Rusticus and Hodge, and Preston with Huf, Ruf, and Snuf. Nevertheless, their comic routines have the sanction of an old tradition. Spivack is overzealous for the claims of his Vice when he insists that "almost the only vestiges of the morality convention surviving in *Common Conditions*, licensed in 1576, are the title and the Vice." [5]

The first comic episode occurs in its customary place, after the opening scene of the main plot. In that opening scene, an old courtier named Galiarbus learns he must flee from Arabia to escape the King's wrath. Galiarbus' two children, Sedmond and Clarisia, also escape in the company of Common Conditions, their "faithful" servant and double-dealing Vice who actually poisoned the King's mind against their father merely for the joy of sowing discord. Their departure sets in motion an involved plot of love and adventure.

The second scene opens with the stage direction, "Here enter. 3. Tinkers, Shifte, Drifte, and Vnthrifte, Singinge." They are wags and roisterers, tinkers by trade but thieves by avocation. Their song is an exuberant celebration of women, dice, and drink. They swear at each other, compete for precedence, and end up in the inevitable scuffle having no other point than to provide a comic battle on stage. It is the old vice lieutenants' quarrel. Soon this trio waylays Sedmond, Clarisia, and Common Conditions. Sedmond

flees and Clarisia is bound to a tree, but the Vice outwits his captors. He asks their help to climb a tree in order that he may hang
himself, from whence he proceeds instead to haloo for help. The
cowardly highwaymen take to their heels, leaving Common Conditions to unbind the lady.

The author presents this episode for its traditional comic appeal,
but transforms his vice lieutenants into tinkers and robbers. The
episode has potential as subplot: these pillaging escapades more substantially resemble those of Shakespeare's Gadshill highwaymen than
do those of Haltersick and Hempstring, or Huf, Ruf, and Snuf.
Furthermore, the comedy has a closer relationship to the main plot
than that of *Horestes* and *Cambises*. These "vice lieutenants" actually enter into the action of the story. It is their attack that
separates Sedmond from Clarisia, producing two strands to the
main plot. At the same time the scene serves as comic diversion in
a romantic story, occupying the dramatically potent second scene.
The troupe alternates accordingly in the established pattern between "straight" and "character" parts. Since all six players are on
stage in this robbing scene, it is obvious (although the play lacks a
specific casting chart) that one of the tinkers must have played
Galiarbus in the first scene, and that all of them soon afterwards
will be engaged in other romantic parts.

Common Conditions appears in later scenes (ll. 983-1047, 1125-
1194) with another group of carousing villains who derive their
quality from the comedy of vice: the mariners, consisting of Master,
Mate, Bosun, and Boy. As one would expect, they are pirates, essentially the salt-water equivalents of Shift, Drift, and Unthrift. Their
speech is racy and colloquial, containing marine terminology. They
enter twice with brave sea chanties and other entertaining songs,
and naturally they quarrel. In one sequence Common Conditions
pretends to be ready to fight with them until he discovers they are
seamen, whom he makes a policy of befriending; if they had been
soldiers, he claims, he would have fought any number of them. He
passes himself off as a former pirate, and after some discussion they
elect him their captain. The conclusion seems utterly pointless until
it is viewed as a secularized version of the usual contest for supremacy between the Vice and his henchmen, and the final acknowledgment of the Vice as master. Pirates as well as highwaymen fit
neatly into a tale of romance, and the mariners' episode contributes

to the plot by again separating Clarisia from a loved one, this time from her betrothed Lamphedon. The comic material thus blends into the story, but still occurs as episode with a basically separate cast.

In the main plot, as in the scenes of comic counterpoint, this romantic play freely employs casting patterns of the popular morality by substituting a pilgrimage of adventure for a pilgrimage of spiritual conflict. Romantic adventure dispatches its heroes and heroines through several far-off lands, in which they meet a series of formidable opponents and obstacles that appear only as phases in the journey. Romance tends also to separate its central figures, sending them in different directions, and revealing their parallel careers of adventure in alternate glimpses as the narrative moves from one protagonist to the other. Both of these techniques — progressive suppression of incident and alternating narrative — appear to have grown from extensive experimentation in the intermediate morality.

Accordingly, in *Common Conditions* the central figures are few: Sedmond and Clarisia from Arabia, Clarisia's beloved Lamphedon (son of the Duke of Phrygia), and Common Conditions. The remaining fifteen characters, with the prologue and epilogue, appear only in episodes as the story moves rapidly from Arabia to Phrygia and thence to Marofus Isle and the country of Leostines. Galiarbus disappears after having left his children and found refuge in Phrygia. The maid Sabia appears later with her Spanish father Mountagos (ll. 732–893, 1048–1101) to complicate matters by falling in love with "Nomides" (Sedmond's disguise-name) who himself falls in love instead with "Metrea" (disguise-name for his sister, Clarisia). Lamphedon becomes separated from his Clarisia and in searching for her accosts an ogre named Cardolus, in a single encounter on Marofus Isle (ll. 1293–1350). Various highwaymen and robbers briefly enliven this saga with their ludicrous exploits. The story ends in the domain of Leostines, a prince who presses his unwelcome attentions on "Metrea" (Clarisia) and ultimately forces Metrea and her lover Lamphedon to end their lives. This episode brings with it a whole new cast of secondary characters, none of whom appears before line 1379: Leostines, the "natural fool" Lomia, who betrays the lovers unwittingly, two lords, and "a lorde or two more."

Thus the cast of *Common Conditions*, like its locale, is sequential. The minor romantic figures are treated sequentially in a progression of adventurous travel, just as the minor homiletic figures of moral drama were used to mark stages of a spiritual odyssey. A casting list for six actors might be constructed as follows: (1) Sedmond, Bosun, Leostines (2) Clarisia, Boy, Sabia (3) Prologue, Common Conditions, Epilogue (4) Galiarbus, Shift, Master, Cardolus, Lomia (5) Drift, Lamphedon, Mountagos (6) Unthrift, Mate, Lord. The shift from comic to romantic parts is inevitable and desirable. The chief characters move through a variety of experience, some of it exciting, some amusing, and some tender. The play's varied appeal and fulness of incident are derived from the moral structure. Of course this episodic structure was not the exclusive discovery of the popular stage. Non-dramatic romance was itself markedly linear; but its form was congenial to popular drama in the same way that Taverner's sequential account of Cambises was congenial to Preston's dramaturgic aims and limitations.

The other extant example of the romantic school of the 1570's and 1580's is *The Historie of the two valiant Knights, Sir Clyomon Knight of the Golden Sheeld, sonne to the King of Denmarke: And Clamydes the white Knight, sonne to the King of Suauia.* Printed in 1599 "as it hath bene sundry times Acted by her Maiesties Players," *Clyomon and Clamydes* unmistakably belongs to the romantic drama that Sidney and Gosson so ridiculed. Like *Common Conditions* its adventures extend through several distant or fanciful territories. Although lacking "vice" comedy like that of Shift, Drift, and Unthrift (except for the brilliant performance of the Vice, Subtle Shift), *Clyomon and Clamydes* employs the linear and episodic form by which the typical romance was adapted for the troupes. The play has a cast even larger than that of *Cambises*, with thirty-seven roles plus drums and trumpets and an unspecified number of soldiers. It is not offered for acting and has no casting chart, but the phrasing of stage directions like "as many souldiers as can" (l. 359) certainly implies limitation in acting resources. Internal evidence, by analogy with *Common Conditions* and other popular plays, suggests a company of ten players, three of them probably boys.

Like *Common Conditions*, this play diverges into two narrative strands, making possible a structure of alternation as well as of progressive incident. Commencing successively in the two kingdoms of Denmark and Suavia, the tale introduces a chivalric rivalry between its title figures and sends them far afield on acts of valor. They ultimately come together at a tournament in the kingdom of the Strange Marshes and are cannily reconciled by King Alexander, but not before each has traversed strange lands like the Forest of Marvels, coping with wizards, abductors, and usurpers such as Brian Sans Foy, Thrasellus King of Norway, and Mustantius.

Of the thirty-seven characters plus extras in the play, only five are central: Clyomon, Clamydes, Subtle Shift, Neronis (Clyomon's beloved), and perhaps Brian Sans Foy. Even Clamydes' betrothed Juliana, one of the female leads, appears only in the first and final scenes of the total twenty-three. Other personalities are restricted to specific phases and locales. At each royal court we meet a new retinue of officials and advisers — at Denmark, Suavia, Macedonia, and the Strange Marshes. Each of the forests has its special inhabitants. The linear suppression of groups of characters corresponds to the movement from locale to locale in the following manner (omitting the names of the five permanently central figures). (1) Denmark: Princess Juliana. (2) Suavia: the King of Suavia, Herald, three Lords. (3) Macedonia: Alexander the Great, Lords, "as many souldiers as can," drums and trumpets. (4) Forest of Marvels: two servants to Brian Sans Foy, three Knights, Rumor. (5) Strange Marshes: Boatswain, two Lords and two Ladies attendant on Neronis. (6) The forest: Thrasellus, his two Lords, Corin the Shepherd, Corin's dog, Providence. (7) Return to the court of Strange Marshes: Alexander the Great (reappearing), Queen of Strange Marshes, Mustantius, two Lords. (8) Return to Denmark: Juliana (reappearing), the King of Denmark and his Queen, and two Lords attendant. Of all these minor sequential figures only two make reappearances, Juliana and Alexander the Great. At the same time, the action sometimes weaves back and forth between two locations and hence two sets of characters, employing the alternation of cast with which we are familiar in intermediate moralities with two protagonists.

The minor romantic figures, then, are treated in sequence or in alternate episode as were their universalized counterparts in the progression of the earlier Psychomachia. The pattern of wandering, confusion, separation, and loss leads ultimately to rediscovery and reunion, a linear process not unlike the fall from grace leading to regeneration in the moral play. The sequence that results for the supporting players is indicated by a conjectural casting for ten actors, the last three of them boys: (1) Clyomon, (2) Clamydes, (3) Prologue, Subtle Shift, (4) Herald, King Alexander, Lord, Knight, Rumor, Corin, King of Denmark, (5) King of Suavia, Brian Sans Foy, Thrasellus, Providence, Mustantius, (6) Lord, Servant, Boatswain, Soldier, Knight, (7) Lord, Servant, Knight, Soldier, (8) Neronis, (9) Juliana, Lady-in-waiting, Queen of the Strange Marshes, and (10) Lady-in-waiting, Queen of Denmark, Lord. The whole constituted a range of display notable for a relatively small company, and gave English viewers what they had long appreciated: variety of incident, a mixture of the light-hearted and the serious, and visual spectacle on a crowded stage — all expressing through repeated and cumulative effect the tribulations and happy resolutions of romantic adventure and love.

With *Clyomon and Clamydes* we have arrived at the threshold of a semipermanent London theater, and thereby bring to a close an era in which the itinerant troupes were the dominant professional caterers to a national popular audience. Before moving on to Marlowe and his debt to the troupe tradition, it will be well to summarize the over-all pattern of dramatic development in the popular theater prior to 1576.

The fundamental materials out of which the early troupes had to create a dramatic structure were the medieval legacy of inclusive panoramic spectacle and burlesque comic routines, combined with the limitation imposed by economic necessity upon a small and itinerant troupe. Early experiments in employment of locally hired extras and restriction of *dramatis personae* were soon discarded in favor of doubling as the most versatile solution.

The technique of doubling, fitted to the outline of the popular Psychomachia plot, established in the early years of the intermediate morality a workable formula for popular entertainment. This formula expounded the spiritual odyssey of the mankind hero through a series of episodes from innocence to degeneracy and eventually to regeneration. This hero was invariably introduced to a succession of acquaintances, both good and bad, his tempters and supporters in his wavering quest for salvation. The total number of roles thus presented grew to considerable size. The actors were able to portray numerous roles by shifting rapidly from scenes of comic degradation to scenes of moral edification, with one group of actors filling both types of roles; or by discarding permanently the tempters or guides who were superseded by the linear movement of the plot from temptation to spiritual recovery. The alternation between good and evil often adopted the symmetry of form inherent in much late medieval art and in the Psychomachia. Compression of allegorical character was also common, and was an element in the creation of the Vice himself. The practice of alternation led to a structural separation in the morality between serious and comic action, and created in the scenes of vice comedy a routine of burlesque viciousness that was to persist in popular drama, because of its widespread appeal, beyond the days of the conventional morality.

As the intermediate morality in the 1560's and 1570's became increasingly secular with the introduction of more and more social types (such as Philip Fleming and Tom Tosspot) to replace the allegorized abstractions, it evolved a formula of spiritual defeat rather than spiritual victory. Such a change was of great importance to subsequent homiletic tragedies like *Conflict of Conscience* and *Doctor Faustus*. Defeat was the natural outcome of vice comedy; increasingly the comedy dominated the action of the moral drama until it ultimately created out of its inherent viciousness a declining pattern of failure and damnation. At first, the Psychomachia hero was matched by an evil protagonist (as, for example, Just and Lust) whose dissolution reversed the spiritual success of his counterpart. Subsequently the unregenerate protagonist reigned supreme (like Moros and Worldly Man); the figures of virtue retreated to a choral function of defining the norm of moral behavior without participating in the action of the plot. Progressive suppression, still vital as a method of doubling, was applied to the sequence of vicious decline rather than of regeneration. The tragic pattern thus formulated was in effect a reversal of the Psychomachia, and employed satiric comedy as the basic expression of its negative message. The grotesquely amusing led to the frightening consequence of spiritual destruction.

Another development in the 1560's and 1570's was the transition to hybrid chronicle and romance. Here the figures of allegory found themselves in an uncongenial world of historical persons and human adventures. After clinging for a while to a separate and abstract existence in which they could relate historical phenomena to sixteenth-century England, they were inevitably transformed into social types with believable and specific reasons for appearing in an historical or romantic context. Yet the structural methods of alternation and suppression lived on in these late troupe plays, producing the characteristic separation into alternate scenes of chronicle (or romance) and vicious comedy. The vice lieutenants became soldiers, rustics, highwaymen, or mariners, but their comic behavior and quarrels for supremacy with the Vice lasted on in the structural position of alternating comic relief. No longer integral to an account of spiritual conflict, this comic legacy nevertheless found a vital place in chronicle and romance. By suggesting a new relationship of the degenerate comedians to the protagonist of the main plot, this hybrid comedy offered a pattern for a coherent subplot in later Elizabethan plays. Progressive suppression, previously used with the allegorized personages of the Psychomachia, found its way into the hybrid chronicle or romance in the succession of minor historical figures surrounding the episodic career of the protagonist.

Marlowe's legacy in the moral tradition was thus, broadly speaking, twofold. From it he was able to discover a formula for Christian tragedy based on the unrepentant decline of comic vice, and a formula for vivid chronicle (or romance) portraying a succession of stage-filling episodes in the life of a secular hero, often mixed with humorous scenes involving historically related figures of low comedy. His indebtedness to classical learning and to his reading in various subjects was of course considerable, but the native tradition became vital in the structure of his plays written for a popular London company.

XIV *Tamburlaine the Great*

In Chapter VII, after a discussion of the composition of popular troupes in England before 1576, our study concluded with an analysis of the composition of the companies of Marlowe's and Shakespeare's stage during the late 1580's and the 1590's, showing the essential similarities in organization that had persisted despite major changes in the fortunes of these players. We saw that throughout this period of growth the companies retained their traditional hierarchy, their practice of doubling, their impulse toward inclusiveness rather than selection, and their flexibility of acting styles. The purpose of observing this continuity was to prepare the way for the study of a similar and resultant continuity in the dramatic structure of the great Elizabethan popular drama, which in many ways had outgrown its original homiletic frame.

The manner in which an indigenous structural heritage was employed and transformed by Marlowe, Greene, Dekker, Shakespeare, and their contemporaries is a question of far greater importance to critical understanding than the bare fact of its existence. Nevertheless the quantity of available material requires that such an investigation be indicative rather than exhaustive. Marlowe's drama provides a useful example because the plays are few in number, and because in them popular structure contributes an important element too often neglected in evaluating the author's achievement. All of Marlowe's plays will be considered in chronological order excepting *The Tragedy of Dido*, since it was written for a select repertory rather than for the popular theater, and *The Massacre at Paris*, since its text represents a particularly unreliable memorial transmission in which the elements of structure cannot be studied with any certainty.

Marlowe's first great stage success, *Tamburlaine the Great*, is a chronicle that owes much to its English predecessors such as *Horestes* and *Cambises*, despite Marlowe's university training and his ardent espousal of classical learning, and despite his scornful declaration of independence

> From jigging veins of riming mother wits,
> And such conceits as clownage keeps in pay.
>
> [The Prologue to Part I]

His impatience with mid-century playwriting, however strongly felt, is more concerned with sterility of poetic idiom and stereotyped characters than with popular conceptions of dramatic structure. Shakespeare too has his joke at the expense of "King Cambises' vein"; in both poets the satire is aimed primarily at the appalling rigidity of septenary couplets and Poulter's measures, the overdone rhetoric of alliterative bombast, and all the poetic failures that were characteristic of much mid-century lyric and narrative poetry — Googe, Turbervile, Tusser — as well as the popular drama. Yet Marlowe's greatness in rising above such mediocrity, and his psychological astuteness in portraying complex human emotion, should not obscure the tradition of popular form so strongly implicit in the theater for which he wrote.

The original performances of *Tamburlaine*, Parts I and II, evidently contained comic material which was omitted from the edition of 1590 by the printer, Richard Jones. He explains in a preface "To the Gentlemen Readers and Others that Take Pleasure in Reading Histories":

I have (purposely) omitted and left out some fond and frivolous gestures, digressing (and in my poor opinion) far unmeet for the matter, which I thought might seem more tedious unto the wise than any way else to be regarded, though (haply) they have been of some vain, conceited fondlings greatly gaped at, what times they were showed upon the stage in their graced deformities. Nevertheless now to be mixtured in print with such matter of worth, it would prove a great disgrace to so honourable and stately a history.

One may well wonder if the comic characters who indulged in these lost "fond and frivolous gestures" were not the theatrical descendants of Huf, Ruf, and Snuf, or Hempstring and Haltersick: some cowardly and depraved villains in the camp of Tamburlaine or of his enemies, whose antics showed the satiric obverse of Tamburlaine's grandiloquent bravado. Conceivably the comedy was the work of a collaborator rather than of Marlowe. If so, Marlowe (who may have had a hand in the publication of these unusually good texts) might well have encouraged Richard Jones's plan to excise the coarse and "popular" comic routines of some other dramatist.[1] One cannot be certain, and this lack of information is unfortunate. Despite the loss, however, Richard Jones's comments provide valuable clues as to the nature of the missing comedy. He sees it as a concession to popular taste, "digressing," and "greatly gaped at." It was evidently irrelevant to the main plot, like the burlesque routines of Rusticus and Hodge. Jones considers it as "far unmeet for the matter" in the context of two plays which he views as "tragical discourses"; he is deploring the mixture of comedy and tragedy as improper for fashionable readers. The original play was apparently a mixture, unlike the extant version, and its comic material was to some extent separate both in plot and in tone.

F. P. Wilson has argued that these excised "fond and frivolous gestures" could scarcely have incorporated the broad indecencies of comic villainy, since Marlowe rejects "such conceits as clownage keeps in pay" in his manifesto-like prologue. Wilson conjectures instead that the unprinted material was a more elevated, scornful comedy such as the taunts addressed to Mycetes or Bajazeth in Part I.[2] In rebuttal to this plausible inference, it may be pointed out that Wilson himself admits the likely existence of "clownage" in the original performances of *Doctor Faustus*. Following W. W. Greg's careful textual analysis, Wilson agrees that the extant texts of *Faustus*, bad as they are, include genuine comic material from early commercial presentations.[3] The argument that this material may have been from a collaborator's hand is beside the point here. If the first staging of *Faustus* contained buffoonish comedy, so may that of *Tamburlaine*. Marlowe's company would hardly have countenanced a public renunciation of its popular vice comedy in *Tamburlaine*, only to return to it in *Faustus*. Besides, Jones's satiric denunciation of passages that "have been of some vain, conceited fondlings greatly gaped at" suggests something more offensive to literary taste than the subtle witticisms directed against the cowardly Mycetes. In the light of this argument, Marlowe's disavowal of "such conceits as clownage keeps in pay" may imply reform of the stylistic abuses of his predecessors, since this second line of the prologue continues and amplifies the thought in line one. An alternate possibility is that the ambitious young Marlowe devised or rewrote the prologue especially for the printed edition, deliberately catering to those who would welcome a sneer at lowbrow conventions. If Marlowe in fact endorsed Jones's excision of the comic scenes, his own prefatory self-congratulation might well disavow the humor that had delighted popular audiences.

Whether or not we are dealing with the main plot bereft of its comic diversion, we nevertheless find in both parts of *Tamburlaine* a sequence of episodes strikingly reminiscent of the moral play and the mid-century hybrid chronicle. It is hardly necessary to point out that *Tamburlaine* has an episodic linear structure, for the fact has long been known and almost universally deplored. John Bakeless speaks of the play's "faulty structure" in characterizing Marlowe's early manner: "his rant, his purple patches, his exquisite verse, his faulty structure, his lack of all humor save his own grim kind. . . ."[4] A study of *Tamburlaine*'s structure in relation to that of its homiletic predecessors, however, reveals the inner logic and consistency of its "primitive" form.

Marlowe was writing for a company that could hardly have exceeded eight or ten regular players, some hired assistants and extras, and perhaps four boys. This we know from plots of analogous contemporary plays rather than from a casting list for *Tamburlaine*, but the information is nonetheless reliable. The size of the company was only slightly larger than that which had produced *Cambises*, and accordingly Marlowe was bound, though to a lesser extent than was Preston, by the casting limitations of the organization. Had he wished to create a tragic history on the model of the ancient dramatists, involving the interrelated fate of a few personages, Marlowe could have avoided doubling entirely by limiting the cast of characters. Significantly he chose instead to follow the example of Preston and of popular writers like him, even though the two parts of *Tamburlaine* were ostensibly divided into the five acts of classical structure in the original edition of 1590. Like Preston, Marlowe dramatized the life of a towering hero from the past, drawing his material largely from prose accounts, and following (in Part I, at least) the order of incident found in the chief of those accounts.

Most critics and editors of *Tamburlaine* have concluded that Marlowe followed two main sources: the life of Tamburlaine in

Pedro Mexia's *Silva de varia lección* (Seville, 1544), redacted in English by Thomas Fortescue in *The Foreste*, 1576; and Petrus Perondinus' *Vita magni Tamerlanis* (Florence, 1551). Marlowe could have found most of the material of *The Foreste* in George Whetstone's *The English Mirror*, 1586, and most of Perondinus in the *Beautiful Blossoms Gathered by John Bysshup*.[5] C. H. Herford and A. Wagner were the first scholars to observe that Mexia and Perondinus follow practically the same order of events, and that since the order is partly unhistorical, Marlowe's use of it demonstrates an acquaintance with the two sources.[6] Bakeless, who has since reviewed these commonly accepted findings, disputes the extent of the acquaintance. He argues convincingly that Marlowe relied considerably on material not found in Mexia or Perondinus, and had access to sources that could have provided him with everything found in Perondinus. Nevertheless, Bakeless readily concedes that Marlowe consulted Mexia's bibliography, and used it as a basis for his further inquiry into Tamburlaine's history.[7] In any case Mexia's work provided the outline, especially for the order of incident in Tamburlaine's military exploits. Like Preston before him, Marlowe found the successive arrangement of episode inherent in the prose chronicles of his day congenial to his structural aim of achieving maximum dramatic impression with a limited cast. He freely added details to Mexia's plan, aiming at inclusiveness rather than rigorous selection.

Accordingly, with each new incident in the life of his hero Marlowe suppresses one group of supporting roles in order to introduce another. In addition, following the model of *Cambises* and plays of its type, Marlowe retains a few central characters throughout the work in order to provide continuity of narrative. The number of these central figures is small in comparison to the total cast: Tamburlaine, his beloved Zenocrate, and his three lieutenants Techelles, Usumcasane, and Theridamas. This central core of personnel is common to both parts of the two-play sequence, so that in structure the two parts are homogeneous.

As in *Clyomon and Clamydes*, the change in cast corresponds to a shift in locale, following the geographical progression of Tamburlaine's rise to glory. His Persian campaign occupies the first two acts of Part I, and introduces in addition to the five central characters a host of princes who belong to the Persian court and are permanently discarded when Tamburlaine moves on to new exploits. The third act chronicles the overthrow of Bajazeth, with his three contributory Kings of Fez, Morocco, and Argier, his wife Zabina, and her maid Ebea. By the end of Act III, Bajazeth and his wife are in captivity, and the three deputy Kings and Ebea disappear from the scene. The sack of Damascus in Acts IV and V introduces the Soldan of Egypt, his supporters, Capolin, the King of Arabia, the Governor of Damascus, and the four pitiable Virgins of the city.[8]

Acts I and II *Persia*	*Act III* *Turkish Empire*	*Acts IV and V* *Damascus*
Tamburlaine	Tamburlaine	Tamburlaine
Zenocrate	Zenocrate	Zenocrate
Theridamas	Theridamas	Theridamas
Techelles	Techelles	Techelles
Usumcasane	Usumcasane	Usumcasane
Mycetes		
Cosroe		
Meander		
Ceneus		
Menaphon		
Ortygius		
Magnetes		
Agydas	Agydas	
	Bajazeth	Bajazeth
	Zabina	Zabina
	Anippe	Anippe
	Ebea	
	Fez	
	Morocco	
	Argier	
		Soldan of Egypt
		Capolin
		King of Arabia
		Governor of Damascus
		Virgins of Damascus

The supernumeraries amplify the effect of suppressed episodic progression, for they are lords and soldiers of one emperor and then another, spies, messengers, Moors, Bassoes, citizens, and attendants as occasion demands.

The speaking roles in Part I could be performed easily by eleven men and four boys, a total that corresponds closely to average company strength in the late 1580's.[9] Any feasible doubling plan emphasizes the advantage and necessity of the episodic pattern that Marlowe has adopted; for example, (1) Tamburlaine (2) Theridamas (3) Techelles (4) Usumcasane (5) Cosroe, Bajazeth (6) Mycetes, Fez, Soldan (7) Meander, Morocco, Arabia (8) Menaphon, Argier, Capolin (9) Ortygius, Governor of Damascus (10) Agydas, Messenger (11) Magnetes, Spy, Basso.

The four boys all appear in two scenes (III, iii and V, i), and therefore could double only the four Virgins of Damascus together with their primary roles: Zenocrate and her maid Anippe, and Zabina and her maid Ebea. The relative importance of these four boy players is apparent in the script. Two of them, playing Zenocrate and Zabina, are qualified for fully developed dramatic roles, and the player of Zenocrate is probably the more experienced of the two. Anippe and Ebea, on the other hand, are almost silent on stage. Ebea speaks but once, and is entrusted with only three lines of blank verse. In Act V, two of the four Virgins speak, and of these the first plays the larger part. This striking differentiation between experienced boys and beginners is like that of *Anthony and Cleopatra*, in which Cleopatra's role is enormously demanding, Octavia's and Charmian's less so but still substantial, while Iras, the second lady-in-waiting, has practically nothing to say other than "Royal Queen!" or "The Gods forbid!" and even dies without explanation or farewell. *Cambises* employed the services of two boys, one with experience. Marlowe's company has only doubled the figure, and Shakespeare's seldom goes far beyond that mark.

Part II of *Tamburlaine* represents a continuation of the structural plan found in Part I. No source has been discovered, however, for the order of incident found in this sequel. Marlowe had used up his primary sources in Part I, and had very little connected narrative left for Part II.[10] As F. S. Boas justly remarks, invention of original plot material was never Marlowe's forte, and consequently the poet appears to have gleaned episodes from various sources. "Instead of following more or less closely in the track of Fortescue and Perondinus, Marlowe now borrows in turn from Lonicerus and Bonifinius, from Belleforest and Ariosto, and welds them together for his purposes."[11] Yet for the order of incident, which constitutes the basis of dramatic structure, Marlowe followed no specific source.

Rather than invent a structure or follow classical precept in his second play, Marlowe contented himself with what he had used before, a popular theatrical formula based on the practical necessities of troupe production. Part II retains the tripartite construction of the earlier play,[12] upon which is superimposed the nominal division of the text into five acts. Its casting solution combines the two elements of a small and permanent central cast together with a constantly shifting progression of secondary figures. The permanent cast is slightly enlarged, since Tamburlaine's three sons, Calyphas, Amyras, and Celebinus, are present through most of the play. In addition, Tamburlaine's two chief antagonists, Callapine the son of Bajazeth and Orcanes King of Natolia, make several reappearances and are not limited strictly to one phase. At the same time, the scene of the action shifts from one military arena to another as in the earlier play, and brings new groups of personalities following one upon the other. The first two acts portray concurrently the death of Zenocrate and the strife between the Turks under Orcanes and the Christians under Sigismund, King of Hungary. Act III replaces these hosts with three more kings, Trebizon, Soria, and Jerusalem, who make alliance with Callapine and suffer the humiliation of capture with him in the last acts. The structural imitation of Part I is complete to the point of symmetry. Callapine relies on the assistance of three princes, just as his father Bajazeth had commanded the allegiance of his three contributory Kings of Fez, Morocco, and Argier. Act V concludes for Tamburlaine "the progress of his pomp" with the last siege of the city of Babylon, introducing the Governor of the city, a follower named Maximus, various citizens, and the King of Amasia who plans with Callapine to avenge the sack of Babylon.

Casting requirements and doubling patterns reinforce the impression that Part II is modeled structurally upon the formula of Part I. In each play the minimum size of the cast may be determined by a central panoramic scene, evidently demanding the participation of the entire company, including the extras. In Part I the scene is the confrontation between the forces of Tamburlaine and those of Bajazeth (III, iii), presenting a cast of thirteen speaking roles. In Part II there is a strikingly similar confrontation between Tamburlaine and Callapine, also in the third act (III, v), in which thirteen named roles participate. The speaking characters in all of Part II could be handled easily by these thirteen players, together with one or two boys: (1) Tamburlaine (2) Theridamas (3) Orcanes (4) Callapine, Percidas (5) Frederick, Techelles (6) Baldwin, Usumcasane (7) Gazellus, Trebizon (8) Uribassa, Soria (9) Sigismund, Jerusalem (10) Almeda, Captain of Balsera, Governor of Babylon (11) Calyphas, Maximus, King of Amasia (12) Amyras (13) Celebinus. Perhaps boy actors could undertake the roles of Tamburlaine's sons. In any case, an experienced boy actor is required for the two roles of Zenocrate and Olympia, and a beginner is required for Olympia's son who speaks only five lines. It is clear that the total company strength in Part II, and the method of assigning roles, closely parallel Part I.

The sense of form achieved in both parts of *Tamburlaine* through episodic progression is derived from the moral play and the hybrid chronicle. Marlowe chooses an enormously varied number of in-

Acts I and II *Turk versus Christian*	Acts III and IV *The Battle at Aleppo*	Act V *Siege of Babylon*

Tamburlaine,
  his three lieutenants
  and three sons
	Tamburlaine,
	  lieutenants, and sons
		Tamburlaine,
		  lieutenants, and sons
		  (excepting Calyphas)

Zenocrate		
Callapine	Callapine	Callapine
Orcanes	Orcanes	Orcanes
Gazellus		
Uribassa		
Sigismund		
Frederick		
Baldwin		
Almeda	Almeda	
	Captain of Balsera	
	Olympia, his wife	
	their son	
	Percidas	
	Trebizon	Trebizon
	Soria	Soria
	Jerusalem	Jerusalem
		Governor of Babylon
		Maximus
		King of Amasia

cidents and unifies them by thematic treatment. The secondary
figures exist only to illustrate a phase of the protagonist's career,
and are dismissed when they have fulfilled this function. The lack
of three-dimensional characterization, so often noted of all the
figures in the play except Tamburlaine himself, is entirely characteristic of Psychomachia drama. Depth and subtlety of character
were never the intent of the homiletic playwright. Similarly the
incidents in the life of Tamburlaine, both admirable and deplorable,
are chosen with care to represent from many points of view, and
through successive iteration, the greatness of Tamburlaine's character. The episodes reveal his capacity in love for generosity, loyalty,
and a sense of justice, his capacity in war for impassive cruelty,
treachery, endurance of hardship and pain, invincible resolution,
and ruthless lust for dominion. As in *Cambises* the repetition of
events, with its variety of incident and character, builds in crescendo,
and establishes its message through the very fact of repetition. The
relation of parts to whole lies in the cumulative effect. The form of
Tamburlaine has a grand simplicity about it, but this simplicity is
not a lack of structural sophistication on the part of its creator.

One digressive episode in *Tamburlaine* bears resemblance to a
scene in *Horestes*, and the scene is repeated often enough in late
Tudor chronicle plays that it might be called generically "the
soldier and the lady." In *Tamburlaine* the story is that of Theridamas and Olympia, widow of the Captain of Balsera. Olympia
prefers death to dishonoring her husband's memory, and consequently the episode ends unhappily; but it reiterates the motif in
Horestes of the widow running before the soldier and then turning
bravely on him. The theme in such incidents, bearing only an
indirect relation to the main plot, is the effect of the ravages of war
on the personal lives of private citizens caught in the arena of
conflict. Whether treated comically or pathetically, these scenes emphasize the dislocation of the victims of war. The plight of Lady
MacDuff in *Macbeth* comes to mind as a well-known example of
the convention. Other examples, involving children rather than
women, are to be found in the pointless slaying of the Earl of
Rutland (*3 Henry VI*, Act I), or the son who has killed his father
and the father who has killed his son (*3 Henry VI*, Act II).

Tamburlaine borrows other aspects of structure from the moral
drama besides the episodic, sequential plot. An element of sym-

metry is noteworthy in the casting. Since the alternating Psychomachia with its opposed legions of virtue and vice plays no important part in the casting formula of *Tamburlaine*, the symmetry contained in the play is of a residual nature, existing like vice comedy in the hybrid morality after the specific motive for its creation has disappeared. The impulse toward symmetry is particularly marked in Part I, III, iii, when the forces of Tamburlaine confront those of Bajazeth. Despite a thoroughly secular frame of values, the scene is staged in a way that recalls the full panoply of contending spiritual forces in early moralities like *The Castle of Perseverance*. Apparently Marlowe employed the entire strength of his company in creating this climactic confrontation. Tamburlaine enters with Techelles, Usumcasane, Theridamas, a Basso, Zenocrate, and Anippe, "with others" — as many extras as the company was able to supply. Soon Bajazeth arrives at the parley (doubtless from an opposite entrance way) with his Bassoes, the Kings of Fez, Morocco, and Argier, Zabina, and Ebea. The stage thereupon mirrors the rivalry of the two warlords, each with three contributory kings and attendant lords, and each with his consort and her lady-in-waiting. The four boy actors are balanced symmetrically, with one experienced actor and one beginner on each side. The business of the meeting is to exchange proud boasts and threats. Just as in *Perseverance* the seven Deadly Sins and their leader, the Bad Angel, step forward one at a time to challenge and denounce their opposites in the ranks of the seven Cardinal Virtues led by the Good Angel, and are answered in kind, so in *Tamburlaine* the warriors exchange hard words in ordered succession and in nearly equal numbers of lines:

> *Fez.* What means the mighty Turkish emperor,
>   To talk with one so base as Tamburlaine?
> *Morocco.* Ye Moors and valiant men of Barbary,
>   How can ye suffer these indignities?
> *Argier.* Leave words, and let them feel your lances' points,
>   Which glided through the bowels of the Greeks.
> *Bajazeth.* Well said, my stout contributory kings!
>   Your threefold army and my hugy host
>   Shall swallow up these base born Persians.
> *Techelles.* Puissant, renowned, and mighty Tamburlaine,
>   Why stay we thus prolonging all their lives?

Theridamas. I long to see those crowns won by our swords,
    That we may reign as kings of Africa.
Usumcasane. What coward would not fight for such a prize?
Tamburlaine. Fight all courageously, and be you kings:
    I speak it, and my words are oracles.   [III, iii, 87-102]

Having presented their six contributory kings or military chieftains, Bajazeth and Tamburlaine address in turn the fair ladies and receive their best wishes for success. Then, after the exit of the two armies, Ebea and Anippe engage one another in a combat of wit that extends the symmetry of the design. During the battle, which is conducted off stage, the two aspiring queens occupy facing chairs, holding the crowns at issue in the conflict, and contending in balanced verbal sparring until the end of the action. After the battle, Tamburlaine assigns to Theridamas the crown of Argier, to Techelles that of Fez, and to Usumcasane that of Morocco. Tamburlaine's three lords thereby absorb the positions and qualities of their three military counterparts, much as Mind, Will, and Understanding had been transformed into Maintenance, Lechery, and Perjury in *Wisdom Who Is Christ,* or as Idleness, Wrath, and Incontinency had expelled Exercitation, Discipline, and Piety from the presence of Moros in *The Longer Thou Livest.*

Marlowe's predilection here for the configuration of three (suggestive of Bale's *Three Laws*) appears also in Zenocrate's death scene, Part II, II, iv. Around her bed are three physicians, Tamburlaine's three captains, and his three sons. Only one physician speaks; Marlowe provides three for visual balance. This elaboration of three is continued in the tripartite division of both plays, already discussed, and in the three contributory chieftains in the camp of Callapine. Throughout, the symmetry of balanced numbers appears to be related to casting methods and to traditional formulas of the homiletic stage.

Act III scene iii of Part I illustrates the use of another structural technique developed in the limited-troupe drama of the popular Tudor stage: the expansion of the apparent cast by reference to invisible presences, to persons who cannot appear because of the size of the troupe and hence are evoked by the magic of words. The Basso, for example, in describing the size of Bajazeth's forces, refers to "fifteen contributory kings" (l. 14), after which, with the acting company seemingly all present on stage, only three kings appear. The references to "ten thousand janizaries," "Two hundred thousand footmen," and the like, are as familiar in Marlowe as is Shakespeare's appeal to our "imaginary forces" to provide him with soldiers, horses, fields, and kingdoms. The phenomenon is well known in the late Elizabethan drama, and it is worth noting that the impulse toward this scenic shorthand, of suggesting the presence of many through the presence of a few ("since a crooked figure may / Attest in little place a million"),[18] may be traced to the compression of medieval guild pageantry into the limitations of an itinerant commercial troupe drama.

Of the four elements of structure — suppression, alternation, symmetry, and compression — which were classified in many of the very earliest of the troupe plays, all but alternation play a prominent role in the structure of *Tamburlaine*; that is to say, in the play as it issued from the press of Richard Jones. With the inclusion of "some fond and frivolous gestures, digressing (and in my poor opinion) far unmeet for the matter," we might expect to find alternation alive, as well.

The foregoing analysis of structural tradition in *Tamburlaine* will be of value only if seen in relation to the play's larger achievement as a work of art. No implication could be more unfortunate than that *Tamburlaine* is merely an oversized outgrowth of the transitional morality. Marlowe had greater things in mind, and the moral formula of the hybrid chronicle probably represented for him little more than a matter of convenience in adapting his themes to the concerns of commercial theater. The glorious fact of his hero's life was what Marlowe had to tell, and for such a secular aim he turned not to the moral drama but to his reading and his imagination. At the same time he did choose to employ a traditional structure. The ironic result was that the more he dared to experiment in subject and theme, the more he came into conflict with inherited structure without actually discarding it. The conservative influence of this structure was thus exaggerated by Marlowe's radicalism as a playwright. This dilemma may best be illustrated by a comparison of *Tamburlaine* with *Cambises,* a transitional chronicle involved in a lesser but similar conflict.

A curious structural correspondence exists between *Tamburlaine* and *Cambises* in the presentation of moral lesson. Both tell of men who are at once vicious and admirable, and both relate their good

as well as their bad deeds. Cambises' handling of the wicked judge
Sisamnes is a virtuous act; so is Tamburlaine's loyal devotion to his
followers and to Zenocrate, his fierce defense of the ideals of
chastity, and his scorn of the Turkish concubines. Even in the
evil deeds of both kings there is much to applaud. When Cambises
shoots an arrow into the heart of Praxaspes' son, the reaction of an
audience is mixed: that was an act of needless cruelty — but what
superb shooting! [14] At least two incidents in *Tamburlaine* provoke
similar contradictory emotions. When the monarch stabs his own
son, Calyphas, for cowardice in time of battle (Part II, IV, i), we
flinch at the unnatural violence of the act and yet cannot help
admiring Tamburlaine's consistent adherence to his self-defined
values. In the same way Marlowe's audience must have watched
with fascination the archery at Babylon, with the governor of that
city as its pitiable target (Part II, V, i). The incredible daring of
Tamburlaine's drive for power enlists our imaginative sympathy in
the aspiration of humanity for greatness. Both Cambises and Tamburlaine offer in some ways a positive moral example, and yet at
the same time the sum of their deeds must be denounced and ab-
horred. We cannot countenance the slaughter of the Virgins of
Damascus nor the murder of Smirdis, no matter how command-
ingly performed. Ultimately we sympathize most with the victims
and wish for the downfall and punishment of their persecutors.
Even the argument that Tamburlaine's victims are all unworthy
pagans, and that he is the scourge of God cleansing the moral
decay of a godless wilderness (as he is interpreted in George
Whetstone's *English Mirror*),[15] fails to account sufficiently for the
hideousness of his worst acts.

   The ambiguity of moral impact in *Tamburlaine* has led to widely
varying interpretations. The suggested solutions have ranged on the
one hand from identifying the hero's aspirations to power with
Marlowe's own supposed Daedalian impulses, by which token the
play becomes a subversive attack on order and degree;[16] and on
the other hand to a portrayal of Tamburlaine as a wicked man
employed unwittingly for a time to subdue God's enemies, who
earns by his own proud atheism a dire and inescapable retribution.[17]
In one view *Tamburlaine* is a calculatedly amoral drama, and in
the other it is an edifying example of the inevitable downfall
awaiting all ruthless villains. The second of these readings postulates

a close connection between the two parts of *Tamburlaine*. It presupposes a causal link between Tamburlaine's death and the earliest of his evil deeds. If Marlowe conceived of Part I as complete in itself — and his audience, at any rate, could hardly have done otherwise — the causal link is broken.

The argument that Marlowe originally planned *Tamburlaine* as a single work of two parts has serious flaws, and most critics have wisely rejected the proposition as unsound. It fails to account for Marlowe's squandering all his primary source material on the first part alone. F. P. Wilson, who finds the ten-act idea "a desperate argument," points to the prologue of Part II which offers a continuation in answer to popular demand:

> The general welcomes Tamburlaine receiv'd,
> When he arrived last upon our stage,
> Hath made our poet pen his second part.

Even if conceived in ten acts, Wilson continues, the first five acts stand alone in dramatic presentation: "There is no epilogue warning the audience that ambition does not triumph in the end." [18]

The homogeneous structure of the two plays, however, inevitably suggests an entity of ten acts. The whole is plausible as a single linear narrative. Part II continues with essentially the same central cast as that of Part I, and proceeds episodically to further exploits in the life of the hero. The separation of cast between the two plays is hardly more distinct than the separation of cast between the various phases in each part. It is this structure, therefore, that implies moral causality in the progressive order of Tamburlaine's good and bad deeds.

Such implied causality is clearly present in the structure of both *Cambises* and *Tamburlaine*, and it creates an ambiguous effect in the context of secular chronicle. This kind of structure developed in Psychomachia drama, and adapted its form to the aims of moral expression in that drama. The sequence of innocence, plotting, downfall, retribution, and recovery always led through episodic incident and suppression of character to a conclusion. It was the conclusion that justified the linear form of the spiritual journey from damnation to salvation, or, in homiletic tragedies, from innocence to damnation. In *Cambises* and *Tamburlaine*, however, the episodic sequence lives on as a theatrical method in secular drama, deprived of its original homiletic justification. Preston and Marlowe are therefore faced with the problem of establishing a new rationale for the existence of an episodic plot, in terms of the message and moral direction of their plays. Are their episodes to lead toward a moral conclusion?

Preston avoids the problem in large part by adapting the moral convention of homiletic tragedies such as *The Longer Thou Livest.* As we have seen in studying *Cambises,* the author gives credence, or lip-service at least, to the notion that Cambises' death is a just and inevitable punishment for his three great deeds of evil. The prologue promises as much, and Cambises dies with words of contrition and self-accusation for a life ill-spent. Farnham in fact interprets *Cambises* as a study in retribution, which leaves the guilty protagonist "with the utmost lack of hesitancy to the wages of sin which his acts might be expected to gather in this world." [19] Nevertheless an ambiguity exists, because the death of Cambises is sudden and accidental. It comes only in the last few lines of the action, and its moral function is underplayed. The retribution does not compensate sufficiently for the grossness of the crimes. Cambises would have died in any event; he happens to die at a particular time and in a particular manner. The lesson suggested is that every life must end, even a king's. The wheel of fortune ultimately turns, and he is cast down. In this concept there is little direct invocation of a vengeful Providence exacting punishment for sin. The conflict, then, lies between a chronicle of life that exalts great deeds and presents them to be admired (and deplored) as a spectacle of greatness, and a structure inherited from a moral drama that suggests by the nature of its linear progression a relationship of cause and effect. The material of *Cambises* concentrates on the fact rather than its consequences. For that reason we are a little unsure how to interpret the moral implications of Cambises' self-inflicted sword wound.

The same ambiguity runs throughout both parts of *Tamburlaine,* and to a greater extent. The problem is most acute in the last act of the second part. Does Tamburlaine die as a result of his having razed Babylon, shot the Governor in cold blood, and then made a bonfire of some copies of the Koran? It is the order of events that inevitably raises this question in our minds. Does Marlowe mean to suggest that his hero has gone one step too far at this point, and has called down upon himself the final judgment of the gods? We are tempted into such an interpretation because Tamburlaine's mysterious illness climaxes a succession of events, each of which might be construed in a moral context.

The contrary impulse is equally strong, however, to consider Tamburlaine's death as the natural end of a long and busy life, and attributable to physical and temperamental rather than providential causes. Indeed, Marlowe insists on a physiological explanation in the diagnosis of Tamburlaine's first physician:

> I view'd your urine, and the hypostasis,
> Thick and obscure, both make your danger great;
> Your veins are full of accidental heat,
> Whereby the moisture of your blood is dried:
> The humidum and calor, which some hold
> Is not a parcel of the elements,
> But of a substance more divine and pure,
> Is almost clean extinguished and spent;
> Which, being the cause of life, imports your death.
>
> [Part II, V, iii, 82–90]

Marlowe implicitly repudiates the moral implication of the sequence that has led to this moment of death. Whether Tamburlaine is a fortunate warrior who dies triumphantly in his old age, or a choleric man whose astrologically predestined humours bring about the fatal distemper of his fiery temperament,[20] he is in either case unconquered until death arbitrarily puts an end to his glory. Furthermore, as in *Cambises*, the emphasis in the body of the play itself is on the deeds of Tamburlaine rather than the consequences, on his aspiration rather than his overthrow. Ultimately the Fates decree that he must die, as all men must, whether they are good or bad:

> Where death cuts off the progress of his pomp,
> And murderous Fates throws all his triumphs down.
>
> [Prologue to Part II]

Marlowe, like Preston, is involved in the conflict between a structure of inherently moral progression and conclusion, and an impulse toward factual chronicle that glorifies the deed for its own sake. The imperfectly resolved tension between the two aims is revealed in the ambiguity of attitude toward prophesy. For if Tamburlaine's death is attributed to natural causes by his physician, other persons throughout the two plays foresee the necessity of divine retribution:

> What means this devilish shepherd, to aspire
> With such a giantly presumption,
> To cast up hills against the face of heaven,
> And dare the force of angry Jupiter?   [Part I, II, vi, 1–4]

Zenocrate is sorrowfully sure that her lover's persecutions of his rival kings can lead only to a similar fate for himself:

> Ah, Tamburlaine, my love, sweet Tamburlaine,
> That fightst for sceptres and for slippery crowns,
> Behold the Turk and his great emperess!   [Part I, V, ii, 293–295]

At her death, she pronounces a moral comment on their life together that captures perfectly the ambiguity of spiritual and earthly message in both parts of *Tamburlaine*:

> Sweet sons, farewell; in death resemble me,
> And in your lives your father's excellency.   [Part II, II, iv, 75–76]

Tamburlaine's resolve to keep her embalmed body ever with him, even though her soul has departed, dramatizes the ultimate futility of all his endeavors, and introduces a pervasive note of *vanitas vanitatum* in this dominantly secular play. Also, several deaths in *Tamburlaine* are attributed directly to divine vengeance rather than to natural causes. Sigismund's last confession, for example, acknowledges the moral consequence of his acts as unflinchingly as Cambises had done:

> Discomfited is all the Christian host,
> And God hath thundered vengeance from on high,
> For my accursed and hateful perjury.
> O just and dreadful punisher of sin,
> Let the dishonour of the pains I feel
> In this my mortal well-deserved wound
> End all my penance in my sudden death!
> And let this death, wherein to sin I die,
> Conceive a second life in endless mercy!   [Part II, II, iii, 1–9]

In short, the question of causality and its important relation to dramatic structure seems to have been only imperfectly resolved in Marlowe's own mind, and as a result the inherited linear structure is not perfectly adapted to his material. The contradictory impressions of divinity and bestiality are never reconciled, and their interplay creates the basic interest of the drama.[21] An analysis of *Tamburlaine*'s "primitive" structure helps to explain its source and rationale, and at the same time reveals some of the ambiguities resulting from the transitional use of moral structure in a secular context.

XV *The Jew of Malta*

Much of the difficulty in interpreting *The Jew of Malta* stems from the same uneasy juxtaposition of moral structure and secular content already found in *Tamburlaine.* The protagonist, Barabas, is in part a lifelike Jewish merchant caught in a political feud on Malta, and in part an embodiment both of the morality Vice and of the unrepenting protagonist in homiletic "tragedy." In some early scenes of the play he is psychologically complex and briefly pitiable; and yet T. S. Eliot astutely interprets *The Jew* as a savage farce.[1] Spivack traces the farcical nature of Barabas to the stage tradition of the Vice: the way in which Barabas puts himself on show to the audience, the treachery to friend and foe alike, the theatrical laughing and weeping, the expert intrigue for its own sake.[2] The attempt to reconcile these strange opposites of plausibility and farce in Barabas' character leads to a series of moral uncertainties. H. S. Bennett calls *The Jew* "a challenge to our powers of assimilation,"[3] and most of its critics have pointed to the play's unevenness of tone and incongruity of effect.

Some critics and editors have attributed the lack of consistency in *The Jew* to a supposedly unreliable text, containing substantial revisions penned during the long years between the original production of 1589–1591 and the earliest printed version of 1633. Tucker Brooke, for example, believes it "probable that the extant text incorporates the results of at least two separate revisions; the first carried out before the revival in 1601, to which Henslowe alludes, the second that which must have been necessary before so old a work could be presented at Court and at the Cock-pit."[4] These two assumptions are based only on a priori reasoning; Henslowe alludes merely to a performance in 1601, not to a revision. Nevertheless the argument has received widespread support, seemingly because scholars in search of classically "pure" tragedy have not wished to ascribe to Marlowe both the early scenes of tragic conflict and the later scenes of vicious and farcical degeneracy.

Recent studies have suggested, however, that the text of *The Jew* is not unreliable, and that the discrepancies between the 1633 quarto and the original performance are probably not fundamental. Margarete Thimme asserts with conviction that the text is all Marlowe's work.[5] H. S. Bennett, although believing that some drastic changes may have occurred, notes that there was "j cauderm [cauldron] for the Jewe" in the Admiral's inventory of 1598, and concludes that the final scene has not been vitally tampered with in any revision.[6] J. C. Maxwell finds by bibliographical analysis that the deficiencies in the 1633 text are far less the result of changes in manuscript than of an admittedly bad printing. The length of time between composition and publication, he argues, is not so serious as is commonly imagined, since the doctrine of "continuous copy" is an editorial fiction, and since "manuscripts, unlike apples, do not become corrupt simply by lying in a drawer." To class *The Jew* as a text with *The Massacre at Paris*, he concludes, "is to blur the clear distinction between memorial transmission (and, in this case, very poor memorial transmission) and careless printing from a manuscript that may have suffered some minor damage in revision and transcription." [7]

It is not far fetched to suppose that vice comedy may have formed a part of the earliest text of *The Jew*, since Greg has shown vice comedy to have been a part of the basic design of *Faustus*. An examination of structure in *The Jew* confirms the likelihood of basic similarity between the 1633 text and the first performance. The vicious and degenerate comedy in the later scenes is integral to the conception of the whole work as homiletic intrigue. In its original form the play probably contained a sequence of episodic plots corresponding in structure to the plotting phases of such homiletic tragedies as *The Longer Thou Livest* and *Enough Is as Good as a Feast*.

Symmetrical suppression and alternation, although not so sharply demarcated as in *Tamburlaine*, are the essential methods by which *The Jew* is put together. Barabas' partners and victims parade before us in linear sequence, usually in pairs. The two merchants appear only in the first scene, and like homiletic figures serve the limited function of highlighting a characteristic in the protagonist,

colossal wealth and mercenary ingenuity. Similarly, the three Jews
function only in the first two scenes. Possibly they were originally
two in number, for Barabas pointedly bids farewell to only two of
them by name ("Farewell, Zaareth; farewell, Temainte"), and the
third Jew speaks only one inconsequential line ("And very wisely
said; it may be so") in his two appearances on stage. Once the
Jews have served the purpose of evoking pity for Barabas, they are
permanently suppressed. The Abbess and Nun in scene two are
employed only once, as the dupes for Barabas' scheme to remove his
hidden treasure from his confiscated house. Mathias and Lodowick,
the first pair of victims to be slaughtered by Barabas, are introduced late in Act I and disappear in III, ii. They are superseded
by the two Friars, who appear chiefly in the scenes following
the murder of Mathias and Lodowick (III, iii–IV, iii), and then
by the courtesan Bellamira and her accomplice Pilia-Borsa, who
connive with Ithamore to blackmail Barabas after the suppression
of the Friars (IV, iv–V, i). Marlowe's tendency to symmetrical
pairing appears further in the combinations of Barabas and Ithamore,
and of the foreign potentates Calymath and del Bosco. Thus the
episodic nature of the plot is reflected in the series of groupings
surrounding Barabas, as his villainous career moves forward by
intrigue and duplicity.

The episodic succession must end in retribution, according to the
moral formula, and in the final scenes of *The Jew* the action is
dominated by political figures who engineer the retribution: the
Turk Calymath, the Spaniard del Bosco, and Malta's governor
Ferneze. They occupy the structural position of the judges in the
homiletic drama such as Despair, God's Judgment, Correction, and
Perseverance. Throughout the play, moreover, they have occupied
the alternating and separate scenes of moral commentary, previously peopled by homiletic figures of moral purity whose virtuous
conduct contrasted with the depravity of the vicious comedians.
The political world of Malta provides this structural contrast in
the second scene, after Barabas' first solo appearance, and in the
fourth scene (II, ii), after Barabas' success in removing his treasures
from his house. The appearance of del Bosco (III, v) punctuates
the interval between the slaughter of Mathias and Lodowick and
the slaughter of the two Friars. The final grouping of the governors
and princes in Act V corresponds structurally not only to the

avengers in morality drama but to the procession of "reward" personalities whose triumphs offset the defeat and punishment of the protagonist. Of course there is something bizarre in considering Ferneze as a judge or "reward" figure, and it is the contrast between moral justification implicit in the homiletic structure of the play and Marlowe's accurate portrayal of *Realpolitik* that we shall consider in evaluating the play's ambiguity. It is important at present to emphasize the pervasiveness of the homiletic structure in the sequential progression of Barabas' victims and in the alternating and contrasting appearance of his enemies or judges.

A feasible casting for the speaking parts of *The Jew* requires at least seven experienced actors and three boys, and demonstrates the technical advantage of suppression and alternation in pairs: (1) Barabas (2) Machiavel, Ithamore (3) Ferneze (4) Calymath, first Friar (5) first Merchant, first Jew, Lodowick, second Friar (6) second Merchant, second Jew, Mathias, del Bosco (7) Pilia-Borsa, Messenger, Guard, Basso, Slave. The ranks of the boys would have to include two seasoned performers together with one or two beginners: (1) Abigail and Bellamira (2) Abbess and Katherine (3) Nun. It is quite possible that a few more adult actors were available, and that the doubling assignments need not have been this heavy. Even if the actors themselves did little alternating of roles, however, the structural heritage of alternation survives strongly.

No nondramatic source has been discovered for the plot and order of events in *The Jew*, and Bakeless conjectures that "probably none exists."[8] Ethel Seaton has shown that Philip Lonicerus' *Chronicorum Turcicorum tomi duo*, used by Marlowe in assembling materials for *Tamburlaine*, Part II, contains a reference to one Juan Miques or Michesius, a well-known Jewish man of affairs who may have served as a model for Barabas' character.[9] Miques also appears in Belleforest's *Cosmographie Universelle*, and other Jews named David Passi and Alvaro Mendez may similarly have contributed to Marlowe's conception of his hero.[10] With only these few general sources for *The Jew*, scholars have generally agreed that Marlowe (and possibly collaborators) must have improvised a great deal. "Out of a haze of surmise and unreliable report he saw clearly enough the main lines of his character. His reading and general knowledge of recent and current history gave him the rest."[11] As in the case of *Tamburlaine*, Part II, therefore, the structural ordering of events appears to have been the creation of the dramatist and his popular company. It is probably this fact which accounts for the linear arrangement of episodes, and the prominence of homiletic intrigue, in the sequence of the action.

Even if the structure of vice "tragedy" is clearly present in *The Jew*, this element can scarcely account for the play's greatness. As in *Tamburlaine*, Marlowe's genius cannot here be forced into the restrictive mold of the homiletic drama. Marlowe sees in Barabas far more than a maliciously evil Worldly Man. He reaches beyond the type to a particular person, and is seemingly less interested in moral example than in the intricate causality of human behavior. And yet however imperfectly Marlowe may fit into the homiletic formula, that formula does exist in his drama, and it exerts a profound if ambivalent effect. Paradoxically it is Marlowe's search for new themes that places such emphasis upon the older format, by exaggerating its incongruity in a drama of increasingly secular values. This incongruity can best be measured in a scene-by-scene analysis, describing on the one hand the elements of homiletic farce progressing to a "tragic" end for the unrepentant protagonist, and, on the other, the elements of a psychological treatise depicting a persecuted Maltese Jew. The study will necessarily focus upon the protagonist, and will have to examine the delineation of character insofar as Barabas appears to be a person of complex human emotions as well as a purely vicious type. Nevertheless the ultimate interest here lies in the conflict between the intricacy of character portrayal and inherited moral structure.

The prologue, spoken by Machiavel, is a conventional morality device heralding the appearance of the unregenerate protagonist. Machiavel himself poses as the personification of evil. This popular misconception of the Italian writer is in fact only a veneer, a topical label for the Father of Lies.[12] Marlowe prefers to clothe his personifications in historical garb, but the disguise does not conceal the fact that Machiavel's function, like that of Satan in *Conflict of Conscience*, is to serve as the progenitor of evil for his emissary in the world of men. Just as Satan promises to call forth his lieutenants Hypocrisy, Avarice, and Tyranny, Machiavel (who is significantly no longer a living person but a "soul" or spirit of malevolence) bids us prepare for his viceroy, the Jew:

And let him not be entertain'd the worse
Because he favours me.

Machiavel personifies in abstract and absolute form the vices
that are to be found in Barabas: utter lack of conscience ("there
is no sin but ignorance") and inordinate greed:

[He] smiles to see how full his bags are cramm'd,
Which money was not got without my means.

The tone of Machiavel's speech is one of diabolical amusement at
his own villainy. We are to be entertained by a display of extraordinary cunning motivated solely by the love of evil for its own
sake.

The first dramatic vision of Barabas confirms the image of evil.
He is clever, miserly, devoid of conscience. His love for his daughter
Abigail proves to be merely an extension of his self-absorbed greed.
His narrow charity excludes even the three brethren of his race
with whom he discusses the expected arrival of the Turkish fleet:

Why, let 'em come, so they come not to war;
Or let 'em war, so we be conquerors. —
Nay, let 'em combat, conquer, and kill all.
So they spare me, my daughter, and my wealth.   [*Aside.*
                                              [I, i, 148–151]

In fact he deliberately dupes the three Jews in his explanation of
the Turkish visit, and quiets their fears only to ponder after their
departure, "These silly men mistake the matter clean." It would
be an error, then, to sympathize with Barabas as the representative
victim of a downtrodden race, since his ill-will applies equally to
Christian, Turk, and Jew. We can no more expect him to abjure
his native evil than Worldly Man in *Enough Is as Good as a Feast,*
who is guaranteed by his prolocutor to be stout in villainy and
"in any wise wil not bow."

After this traditional exposition of the unredeemable worldling,
the moral formula introduces a confrontation in the second scene
between Barabas and his dramatic counterparts. At this point the
ambiguity commences, for according to the moral pattern Barabas'
enemies and future victims should represent the cause of virtue.
Instead, because Marlowe's interest in his protagonist is too deep
for simple denunciation, we are suddenly faced with the irony

of finding Barabas the sympathetic victim of Christian treachery. Ferneze's method of taxation is patently despotic, and his refusal to allow Barabas to pay the tax after momentary reconsideration, in lieu of total forfeiture, is arbitrary. Barabas' defense becomes, by a curious inversion, the pleading of a wronged, sensitive, and helpless person:

> The man that dealeth righteously shall live:
> And which of you can charge me otherwise?
>
> . . . .
>
> Ay, let me sorrow for this sudden chance;
> 'Tis in the trouble of my spirit I speak:
> Great injuries are not so soon forgot.   [I, ii, 117–118, 207–209]

The second Jew, as he and his fellows depart, expresses a choric reaction to the preceding scene:

> On, then: but, trust me, 'tis a misery
> To see a man in such affliction.   [I, ii, 212–213]

An Elizabethan audience, whatever its attitudes toward Jews in general, would have reacted with some indignation to Barabas' broadly human plight. The dramatist intended his audience to view his "villain," for the moment at least, with genuine sympathy.

When Barabas is left alone on stage, however, he reveals that his noble passion was in fact contrived as a means of deceiving others and winning sympathy from them. He laughs exultingly at his cleverness in duping them, and at the pity he has evoked:

> See the simplicity of these base slaves.
> Who, for the villains have no wit themselves,
> Think me to be a senseless lump of clay,
> That will with every water wash to dirt!
> No, Barabas is born to better chance,
> And fram'd of finer mould than common men,
>
> . . . .
>
> For evils are apt to happen every day.   [I, ii, 215–224]

He informs Abigail that she need not moan "for a little loss," since he has stored away more than has been confiscated. Even the news that he cannot gain access to his house to remove the treasure deters him for only a moment. He has a plan for every emergency.

Clearly Barabas' passionate reaction to the tax was all a pretense, intended to trick the audience as well as the three Jews. The revelation in soliloquy of this hypocrisy is an ironic undercutting of the apparent tragedy for a comic purpose. It shows Barabas as the "Vice," who mockingly and boastfully reveals his strategy to his audience after having cheated them into misplaced sympathy. His hate is not provoked by Ferneze's persecution; Barabas hated the world before, as a matter of policy.

At the same time, the injustice of Ferneze's decree remains a fact, and Barabas has been treated ignominiously. A second purpose of this second scene, then, is to provide an understandable motivation for the Jew's hate and his subsequent deeds of revenge. He is put in a position of having to fight back, so that his misanthropic behavior is made plausible:

> Daughter, I have it: thou perceiv'st the plight
> Wherein these Christians have oppressed me:
> Be rul'd by me, for in extremity
> We ought to make bar of no policy.   [I, ii, 270–273]

The Vice has been secularized in the person of Barabas, a man with dangerous enemies. This aspect of Barabas shows something far more subtle and lifelike than the type of unrepentant Worldly Man. Even Abigail, a sympathetic character, perceives at first the justice of her father's retaliatory tactics. She reluctantly agrees to help in deceiving the nuns, so that Barabas may retrieve the money from his house. The Jew's plan to win back his own property from the Christians, even if by slightly devious means, is only to demand an eye for an eye. In one sense all of Barabas' later acts are acts of vengeance or self-defense, and stem from Ferneze's first pitiless deed. Hence the first two scenes are crucial in justifying Barabas' subsequent treachery. Nevertheless, the need for providing motivation should not obscure the purely Vice-like conception of Barabas' original character.

Critics have often contrasted the degeneracy of Barabas into pure villain in the last three acts of *The Jew* with his moral complexity as a person in the earlier scenes — a contrast usually accounted for by the theory of multiple authorship.[13] As we have seen, however, the Jew was actually a villain when he appeared in the first scene. His later career of viciousness is simply a return to his original nature rather than a new and puzzling development in character. Once Marlowe has established Barabas' motivation for revenge, he turns again to the pattern of vicious and comic intrigue. The structure becomes that of plotting and degeneracy in the homiletic drama, such as Worldly Man's succession of unfair triumphs over his innocent victims Tenant, Servant, and Hireling in *Enough Is as Good as a Feast*.

The shift to a structure of vice intrigue commences in Act II, iii, with the alliance of Barabas and Ithamore, the slave who is to assist in the Jew's acts of "revenge."[14] Ithamore, too, is given a motivation for anti-Christian hatred. Barabas welcomes him as a comrade in hate:

> Why, this is something: make account of me
> As of thy fellow; we are villains both:
> Both circumcised; we hate Christians both.   [II, iii, 214–216]

Yet their alliance for the purpose of revenging themselves upon Christian persecutors is patently a pretext. They not only "hate Christians both" but "are villains both"; the former is the ostensible motivation, the latter the basically vicious fact. Barabas' victims of the past have not all been Christians. He has turned his hatred upon invalids, orphans, and helpless persons without distinction of sect or nationality:

> As for myself, I walk abroad a nights
> And kill sick people groaning under walls:
> Sometimes I go about and poison wells.   [II, iii, 175–177]

In battle he has delighted in playing the villain with both sides:

> And in the wars 'twixt France and Germany,
> Under pretense of helping Charles the Fifth,
> Slew friends and enemy with my stratagems.   [II, iii, 188–190]

The description here does not correspond realistically with what we know of Barabas' life. He has been a merchant, not a warrior. In earlier speeches he has deliberately relinquished temporal power to Christian kings, asking only for peace that he may gain more wealth (I, i, 127–133). The present recital of vicious accomplishments is the record of a universalized genius of evil, not of the specific man. At the same time, Barabas does have particular and valid reasons for hating Christians, especially Ferneze.

Recognizing this dual aspect in the play's exposition, we may follow in successive scenes the resulting divergence of aim between a series of psychologically motivated revenges and a parade of triumphs by the Worldly Man over his innocent victims. Barabas' first deed of "vengeance" is directed against Mathias and Lodowick, two rivals for the love of Abigail. Barabas does not object to their love for his daughter; but Lodowick is the son of Malta's governor, and his blood must pay the price of Ferneze's unjust taxation. Barabas' hatred of Lodowick is therefore understandable:

> As sure as heaven rain'd manna for the Jews,
> So sure shall he and Don Mathias die:
> His father was my chiefest enemy.   [II, iii, 249–251]

The reason for Mathias' death is far less clear, however. It is merely specious logic on the part of Barabas to include Mathias' name with Lodowick's in the speech just quoted. Mathias is guilty of no offense. Moreover, Abigail is genuinely in love with him. She consents, though much against her will, to aid in the plot against Lodowick without realizing that her father plans to destroy her lover as well. Her love for Mathias is not a moral problem for Barabas but an opportunity for intrigue. After both young men have been slain, Abigail broken-heartedly questions the necessity of Mathias' death:

> Admit thou lov'dst not Lodowick for his sire,
> Yet Don Mathias ne'er offended thee.   [III, iii, 43–44]

What delights Barabas in the episode of Lodowick and Mathias is the cleverness of his act. He needs two victims in order to play one against the other. Mathias must die to complete a scheme of ingenious crime. Like Iago, another descendant of the Vice, Barabas operates through false rumor, the jealousies of love, setting friend against friend by means of evil suggestion.

Once Barabas has entered upon his career of revenge, each succeeding act is motivated in part by the need to suppress those who know too much or have revolted against him, or by the desire to further his revenge against Ferneze and the government. The structural result is a sequence of episodes involving a succession of victims, usually in pairs, who are suppressed with the forceful regularity of homiletic drama. Abigail learns the truth of Mathias' death, and turns nun in earnest. Consequently she is a potential enemy to the Jew on two counts, of disloyalty and possession of dangerous knowledge:

> For she that varies from me in belief,
> Gives great presumption that she loves me not;
> Or, loving, doth dislike of something done.   [III, iv, 10-12]

Her death must be the result, as another "vengeance" stemming from Barabas' original hatred for Ferneze. At the same time Barabas' primary concern in dispatching Abigail is less with the motive of his deed than with its execution. The Italian tradition of revenge, introduced by Machiavel, may serve in part as a literary source for Barabas' method in handling poisons, but the emphasis on artistry in evil is also the mark of the Vice and Worldly Man. Barabas gloats over his precious secret poison which cannot be detected upon the victim's body, and chuckles at the ironic appropriateness of a deadly porridge sent as alms to the nunnery.

The slaughter of the nuns leads to yet another situation in which Barabas has to protect himself by further violence. Friar Barnardine receives Abigail's dying confession of her father's villainy, and with Friar Jacomo he confronts Barabas with threatened exposure. Like Abigail, therefore, the Friars have become dangerous enemies to Barabas and must be dispatched with haste and skill:

> Now I have such a plot for both their lives,
> As never Jew nor Christian knew the like:
> One turn'd my daughter, therefore he shall die;
> The other knows enough to have my life,
> Therefore 'tis not requisite he should live.   [IV, i, 120-124]

This soliloquy emphasizes the two elements underlying Barabas' actions. The last three lines present the plausible motivation, although it is curious that the Jew speaks of only one Friar as possessing the knowledge of his crimes. Obviously Barabas realizes that both are partakers of the secret; "I fear they know we sent the poison'd broth," he whispers to Ithamore. The device of attributing a different motive to each of the two Friars is too rhetorical to be sincere. But it is in the two preceding lines that Barabas speaks as the Vice. This plot is to be a masterpiece, and the Jew prepares his audience to admire the beauty of its conception. The execution of his design is everything that he promises. He plays on the rapacity of the Friars, and pits them against each other (as he had done with Mathias and Lodowick) in the manner of the Vice by appealing to their ruling passion, greed.

The next episode, in which Ithamore becomes infatuated with the courtesan Bellamira and conspires with her and Pilia-Borsa to blackmail Barabas, is a business of comic intrigue. The scenes here are more burlesque than in the incident with the Friars: the tavern life and brothel humor, the quarrel over a whore, the grotesque "humors" of Pilia-Borsa's affected manner, and Barabas' ingenious disguise as a French musician in order to spy on the blackmailers. This vice comedy acts as a ludicrous and degenerate parody of the more serious bloody deeds of Barabas and Ithamore.

Even in this late episode, however, the motivation depends plausibly upon the train of events that has preceded this action. Barabas' need to do away with Ithamore and his new companions is identical with that which had brought Abigail and the Friars to their deaths, disloyalty to Barabas combined with knowledge that could expose him to the law:

> Well, I must seek a means to rid 'em all,
> And presently; for in his villainy
> He will tell all he knows, and I shall die for't.   [IV, v, 63–65]

At the same time, we know that Barabas had planned to rid himself of Ithamore sooner or later in any case. He deserves Ithamore's epithet of "bottle-nosed knave" (III, iii, 10) identifying him as a recognizable stage type.[15] It is his nature to hate everyone, even his fellows in vice, and the destruction of Ithamore stems ultimately from this simple hate.

Thematic unity in these scenes of worldly ambition follows that of the mid-century popular play. No hypothesis of later textual emendation is required to explain the connection between these successive episodes. In one sense, Barabas' acts depend upon one another as he seeks to revenge his wrongs or to cover up for his crimes. On the other hand, insofar as each evil deed is the result of Barabas' purely evil nature, there is no development of motivation at all. Each variation on the theme of vice casts additional light on the nature and operation of evil. The process does not logically unfold, but elaborates and intensifies by repeated example. The play moves steadily toward comic decline. Each succeeding incident

becomes more ludicrous and more wildly improbable than the
one before, as the reign of pure vice becomes increasingly separated
from its original motive.

The structure of the final act follows the inevitable conclusion
of all homiletic "tragedy," descending lower and lower into an
insane depravity that can end only in punishment for the protagonist
and restoration of order for those who remain. Barabas' frenzy
in the manipulations of state affairs destroys even the pretense that
he is driven by a desire for vengeance. When the Turks deliver
Ferneze into his power, he is in a position to complete the personal
"revenge" that has supposedly motivated all his previous acts of
violence. Instead of doing so, he plots the destruction of his Turkish
allies. The Vice traditionally knows no sides, and always prefers
to pit one side against the other rather than seek aid against his
supposed enemies. Barabas abandons the cause of revenge for one of
intrigue for its own sake:

> Thus, loving neither, will I live with both.   [V, ii, 111]

He boasts to the audience of his treachery in turning against the
Turks, who would have helped him to destroy the uncircumcised
Christians he professedly hates:

> Why, is not this
> A kingly kind of trade, to purchase towns
> By treachery, and sell 'em by deceit?
> Now tell me, worldlings, underneath the sun
> If greater falsehood ever has bin done?   [V, v, 46-50] [16]

Even when he is dying, having been trapped by Ferneze's counter-
plot, the Jew boasts of his villainy and promises that he had intended
the destruction of both sides:

> And, had I but escap'd this stratagem,
> I would have brought confusion on you all,
> Damn'd Christians, dogs, and Turkish infidels!   [V, v, 84-86]

Barabas' farewell is that of the evil genius in the moral play who
aims at the annihilation of everything decent "underneath the sun."

Barabas' punishment appears to answer for his sins. The formula
of the moral play demands providential justice to end the worldly
success of vice, and we ought to be satisfied with Barabas' fate.
His death is not accidental, like that of Cambises or Tamburlaine.

A boiling cauldron is sufficient atonement even for a lifetime of atrocities. The Jew was evil, and he answered for it; the lesson seems clear and edifying. The difficulty, however, lies in the instrument of that justice. Ferneze lacks the personal virtue to act as agent of God's righteous anger; and yet the moral framework of the play puts him in a position of doing just this. In fact, Ferneze speaks of himself in this role:

> So, march away; and let due praise be given
> Neither to Fate nor Fortune, but to Heaven.   [V, v, 123–124]

Almost in the same breath, Ferneze perpetrates his own last act of duplicity by refusing to free Calymath, whom the Jew's treason has delivered into his hands. The play ends where it began, without the establishment of a moral order on Malta but merely with the restoration of the expediency that has always been Ferneze's method of governing. His appeal to divine justice is a mockery.

This curious dilemma has come about through the transference of a secular story into the structure of moral drama. In order to rationalize the native viciousness of Barabas it is necessary to provide him with enemies and persecutors; and since he is a Jew on the island of Malta, the Christians must play the part of villainy in those crucial first scenes when for a short time our sympathy focuses on Barabas. These Christians on Malta are Roman Catholics, and Catholics frequently appeared on the Elizabethan stage as villains. Nevertheless, the portrayal of them as evil results in moral confusion in the ensuing scenes of the play, since they cannot justly provide a virtuous foil for Barabas' villainy. For example, the two Friars are presented as greedy and unscrupulous in their desire for gold. They are also lecherous, and have mistresses within the walls of the convent. To dupe such unworthy members of a much-feared church in Marlowe's day must have merited applause rather than condemnation. The anti-Papist jokes, often on Barabas' lips, surely evoked appreciation from his original audience:

> And yet I know the prayers of those nuns
> And holy friars, having money for their pains,
> Are wondrous; — *and indeed do no man good.*   [*Aside.*
> [II, iii, 80–82]

The same problem of moral ambiguity occurs in *Faustus* when the protagonist snubs the Prince of Rome and his superstitious Friars.

In *The Jew*, the function of such anti-Catholicism is to provide motivation for Barabas' acts as a Maltese Jew; but because Barabas is also a villain, such factors work against the moral function of the plot, which suggests that all of his acts are wicked and are to be punished.

If the conflict is evident in Barabas' religious enemies and victims, it is even more apparent in his political antagonists. Quite early in the action Ferneze is singled out as the man who must bring the Jew to justice. As Barabas grows more violent and evil, Ferneze comes inevitably to represent his moral opposite. The governor is prompted to revenge by the death of his son and Don Mathias:

> Upon which altar I will offer up
> My daily sacrifice of sighs and tears,
> And with my prayers pierce impartial heavens,
> Till they [reveal] the causers of our smarts,
> Which forc'd their hands divide united hearts.   [III, ii, 31-35]

Ferneze repeatedly refers to himself as the executor of divine law in hunting down Barabas. When the supposedly dead body of the Jew is thrown over the walls of the city, Ferneze remarks:

> Wonder not at it, sir; the heavens are just.   [V, i, 55]

It is in the context of moral drama that such a conclusion is to be expected. The structure of the play demands a relationship between cause and effect in Barabas' career. The difficulty is that in rationalizing Barabas' original plight, Marlowe has created villains out of those very persons who must later become the agents of retribution.

Ultimately, Marlowe's world of chronicle is morally neutral. Ferneze, Calymath, and del Bosco are no better and no worse than Barabas; Ferneze's final victory is merely a fact. The contest for Malta is a struggle for balance of power between leaders who are inspired by a lust for dominion and wealth:

> *Ferneze.* What wind drives you thus into Malta road?
> *Basso.* The wind that bloweth all the world besides,
>   Desire of gold.   [III, v, 2-4]

Abigail sees that the material world does not always proceed according to God's plan, and therefore makes a second and entirely devout conversion to the life of a nun:

> But I perceive there is no love on earth,
> Pity in Jews, nor piety in Turks. [III, iii, 50–51]

Such injustices are never denied or amended, and they fit uneasily into a dramatic plan inherited from a religious tradition. Once again, as in *Tamburlaine*, we find in the combination of secular material and moral structure a key to the play's characteristic ambiguity.

XVI *Edward II*

Edward II, probably first performed in 1592–1593 when Pembroke's company was most active in London, is generally acclaimed as Marlowe's most carefully constructed play, and his most successful in the creation of plausible historical characters. It represents a mature fusion of moral structure with the secular subject matter toward which Marlowe was constantly striving. The play is manifestly more of a chronicle than *The Jew* or *Faustus*, and its personages are historically authentic in a setting more familiar to Marlowe's audiences than the remote and colorful milieu of the Scythian Tamburlaine. Thus *Edward II* is more closely linked to secular reality than any of Marlowe's other plays. Its chief characters contain less generic personification than his other protagonists. Among Marlowe's plays, therefore, it affords least opportunity for a study of indebtedness to the morality drama, and will be discussed least extensively. Nevertheless the moral ambiguity of *Edward II* is not unlike that to be found in Marlowe's other productions, an ambiguity that derives its existence from a pronounced though vestigial moral element within the play.

As is often the case in Marlowe, the ambiguity in *Edward II* arises from the conflict between factual account as it was set down in the playwright's source, and moral causality implied in the structural order of the drama. In this instance Marlowe was guided by Holinshed's chronicle of the reign of Edward II, and the secular element in the play is dominant. Marlowe is often so intent on dramatizing what actually took place in history that many critics have found no moral pattern in his reporting of these facts. Charlton and Waller, for example, argue that "We are not asked to consider whether Edward deserved his fate; we are not led either to be sorry for the Queen or to be repelled by her infamous desertion [of

Edward]. It is merely the essence of what happened." The play "owes something of its grim power to a certain naturalistic quality."[1] Yet it would be more correct to say that our moral reactions are confused, rather than suspended, as we follow the progress of this crowded narrative. Actually we are both "sorry for the Queen" and "repelled by her infamous desertion," and Marlowe's difficulty is in reconciling these converse impulses. His main problem is to compress the events of twenty-three years into the framework of a single drama, and in doing so to motivate the changes of character indicated in his source.[2] His reliance on the structural formulas of the popular theater to solve this problem creates a conflict between the moral tradition and his factual material.

Edward II chronicles a civil conflict between two political forces represented by the King and Young Mortimer, the leader of the Barons' revolt. Each has his counselors and allies, and the enmity between the two camps is so pervasive that virtually every person in the play is obliged to cast his lot with one or the other. The question of allegiance is a profoundly moral one for the King's brother, Kent, and for the others involved, even if the playwright appears to withhold judgment. In outline, therefore, the play is one of epic confrontation between opposing forces, inviting comparison of their rival claims from both participant and spectator.

Furthermore, these forces move simultaneously in the diverging paths of the homiletic tragedy, such as *Enough Is as Good as a Feast*. Mortimer's fortune exalts him, like the Worldly Man, through a series of triumphs until he topples and is punished. Conversely, King Edward suffers the ignominy of unfavorable reputation and persecution at the hands of Mortimer, until finally his cause wins moral justification like that of Christian Faith in *The Tide Tarrieth* or Just in *Like Will to Like*. By the end of *Edward II*, the moral formula clearly intends retribution for Mortimer as a means of terminating his brief worldly success. Mortimer's period of favor with Fortune is no more substantial than that of Moros, whom Lady Fortune exalts for a time in *The Longer Thou Livest* to demonstrate the temporary reign of Folly. King Edward's claim to ultimate redress is vindicated in the action of his son:

> Sweet father, here unto thy murdered ghost
> I offer up this wicked traitor's head;

And let these tears, distilling from mine eyes,
Be witness of my grief and innocency.   [V, vi, 99–102]

In the intermediate morality, this scheme of divided paths for the opposed protagonists invariably separated the godly from the profane, and rewarded each according to his merit. Its structural force in *Edward II* similarly implies a contrast between a meek but worthy king and his depraved persecutor. Marlowe's preoccupation with complexity of character, however, forbids such a plain interpretation of right and wrong. Just as he sought plausible reasons for Barabas' viciousness, here he delves into the reasons for King Edward's unpopularity with the nobles, and is not satisfied with a simple explanation of Mortimer as the Worldly Man. He becomes especially interested in Queen Isabella's motives for transferring her loyalty to Mortimer. At the same time he retains the pattern of dual protagonists as a solution for his casting dilemma. The result is that his characters occupy two spheres, human complexity and moral abstraction. The complexity appears chiefly in the exposition, as in *The Jew of Malta,* in order to set an historical event in motion, whereas moral causality leading to a restoration of order figures increasingly in the play's continuation and denouement.

The technical debt of *Edward II* to popular convention stems from the necessity of assigning a large number of parts to ten or so company members, additional hired actors, and two to four boys.[3] Nearly thirty named adult male roles may feasibly be cast for eleven actors: (1) King Edward (2) Young Mortimer (3) Edmund Earl of Kent (4) Gaveston, Hugh Spencer, Trussel, Gurney (5) Lancaster, Sir John of Hainault, Bishop of Winchester (6) Warwick, Rice ap Howel, Matrevis (7) Pembroke, Mower, Berkeley (8) Bishop of Coventry, Beaumont, Young Spencer (9) Archbishop of Canterbury, Baldock (10) Levune, Mayor of Bristow, Leicester (11) Mortimer Senior, Arundel, Abbot, Lightborn. The feminine and juvenile roles call for two experienced boys, one to play Queen Isabella and the other the King's Niece and Prince Edward. The ladies in attendance on the King's Niece would require only younger boys.

Casting suppression is pronounced. Only four characters are central to the entire play: Edward, Young Mortimer, Isabella, and Kent. All the rest exist, in morality fashion, chiefly to highlight a particular phase in the careers of the protagonists. Mortimer Senior, Lancaster, Warwick, and their peers belong solely to the period of Young Mortimer's baronial protest against Edward's caprice. Matrevis, Gurney, and Lightborn seem part of an almost

	Act I *First quarrel* *and reconciliation*	*Acts II–IV, i* *Second quarrel;* *death of Gaveston;* *defeat of the Barons*	*Act IV, ii–vi* *Invasion of* *England; capture* *of the King*	*Act V* *Murder of the King;* *punishment of* *Mortimer* *and Isabella*
				Lords
			Monks	
			Abbot	
		Prince Edward	Prince Edward	Prince Edward
		Levune		
		Arundel	Arundel	
King's		Hugh Spencer	Hugh Spencer	
Party		Baldock	Baldock	
		Young Spencer	Young Spencer	
		Ladies		
		King's Niece		
	Beaumont			
	Gaveston	Gaveston		
	King Edward	King Edward	King Edward	King Edward
	Kent	Kent	Kent	Kent
	Isabella	Isabella	Isabella	Isabella
	Young Mortimer	Young Mortimer	Young Mortimer	Young Mortimer
	Mortimer Senior			
	Bishop of Coventry			

	Archbishop of
	  Canterbury
				(Archbishop of
				  Canterbury)

	Lancaster	Lancaster		
	Warwick	Warwick		
	Pembroke	Pembroke		
Mortimer's		Horse-boy James		
Party		Soldiers		
		Fife and drum		
			Sir John of Hainault	
			Rice ap Howel	
			Mayor of Bristol	
			Mower	
			Leicester	Leicester
				Bishop of Winchester
				Trussel
				Berkeley
				Matrevis
				Gurney
				Lightborn

entirely different story of suborned murder and duplicity. Similarly, in the King's party Gaveston lives as an embodiment of Edward's extravagance for only ten scenes out of twenty-three, whereas Baldock and the two Spencers occupy the middle portion of the play. Like the authors of hybrid chronicle, Marlowe treats lesser historical figures in sequence. He justifies the procedure by moving from phase to phase in the dual account of contending forces.

Except for an inconsequential appearance of the Archbishop of Canterbury (V, iv), no suppressed figures return in the final scenes. *Edward II*, despite its acclaimed superiority of structure over Marlowe's earlier plays, is still linear in movement. Its sequential plan thematically illustrates vicious decline for Mortimer and simultaneous deliverance for Edward. The focus in cast moves from the barons and their ecclesiastical peers in the early scenes of revolt, to the King's captors, prison-keepers, and murderers in the final action. At the beginning we see Mortimer surrounded by nobles, and his cause is identical with theirs: an understandable grievance against the promotion of sycophants and the neglect of the realm's defense. As the other lords withdraw, however, the concept of revolt is increasingly identified with Mortimer and the Queen. The cause that had previously been the outcry of an entire estate becomes a crude struggle for personal supremacy. Mortimer's relationship with the Queen, uncertain at first, is enhanced by their partnership in ambition. In the final scenes Mortimer is surrounded not by barons but by hirelings and murderers. The few lords remaining, like Leicester, nominally support Mortimer but are plainly distressed by his highhanded treatment of the King.

Edward's changing fortune is also brought about structurally by a shift of the *dramatis personae*. The all-important presence of Gaveston in the first half of the play continually emphasizes Edward's weakness. Once Gaveston is removed, no matter how much we may have disapproved of the corruption before, we are less apt to dwell upon it. Young Spencer and Baldock, who succeed Gaveston as royal favorites, are perhaps no less dangerous, but they are less in evidence. When they in turn disappear, Edward is left in the hands of Mortimer's hirelings rather than of his own sycophants. Mortimer and the Queen remain without dangerous enemies and without noble allies; Edward is finally friendless and a pitiful victim. His son, young Edward, is also at the mercy of Mortimer until he emerges finally as the avenger of his father and the agent of virtuous recovery.

However much a conventional structure of dual protagonists in *Edward II* may suggest moral victory for the King, the historical "facts" of Edward's reign contradict the simple pattern of right and wrong. The Elizabethans evidently viewed Edward's reign with mixed feelings. In Marlowe's source (Holinshed) and later in Michael Drayton's *Mortimeriados* (1596), for example, much of the blame for civil discord rests with the incompetent and effete King. According to Drayton, young Mortimer is at first the leader of a legitimate and glorious cause. Isabella is originally more victim than wrong-doer, a "poor wife-widowed queen."[4] Only when they carry their cause to the point of regicide do Isabella and Mortimer lose favor with the Elizabethan public.

Marlowe's dramatic problem is to reconcile this historical account of complex characters and shifting sympathies with the structural formula of unrepentant vice. The Worldly Man Mortimer and his consort in rebellion, whose reign of earthly domination must lead to overthrow, are seen at first as human beings with understandable and even laudable motives. Conversely, their "virtuous" victim Edward must appear at first to deserve a large measure of their enmity. These considerations work at cross purposes to the underlying emphasis of the moral formula. The result, as in *The Jew*, is that a highly "naturalistic" exposition yields increasingly to the pattern of the moral "tragedy" of vice. Characterization, like that of Barabas, begins with plausibility and moves toward viciousness for Marlowe's worldly protagonists. The action of the play descends from a contest between two political powers into a series of cynical intrigues.

Of the central figures, Isabella is perhaps the most perplexing in her extremes of behavior.[5] On first impression one is tempted to suppose her loyal and sincere. She holds onto the hope of reconciliation in spite of Edward's indifference to her. In soliloquy (II, iv) she protests her adoration for her husband, and is in anguish at the prospect of deserting him. Her indecisiveness in this internal monologue is psychologically perceptive and convincing. Isabella thus seems a good-hearted but weak-willed woman who consents reluctantly to accept Mortimer's drive for power only because she has no other choice. Thereafter the lust for power begins to corrupt her too, until she becomes an adulteress and willing accomplice in murder.

Despite the plausibility of her behavior in the beginning, however, Isabella increasingly conforms to the structural plan of moral decline for the worldly practitioners of vice. A curious suspicion emerges concerning Isabella's supposed relationship with Mortimer. At first she defends her reputation with dignity and seeming candor against Gaveston's charge of adultery. Later, however, this apparently baseless slander turns out to be entirely valid. What is the explanation for this surprising reversal? In retrospect, Marlowe partly suggests that Isabella has been deluding us with her protestations of innocence.

In the later portions of the play Isabella becomes "the subtle queen" (III, iii, 86), an expert intriguer and a hypocrite. The honest Kent laments the dissembling by which Isabella furthers her fortunes:

> But Edmund, calm this rage,
> Dissemble, or thou diest; for Mortimer
> And Isabel do kiss, while they conspire:
> And yet she bears a face of love forsooth.
> Fie on that love that hatcheth death and hate.   [IV, v, 20–24]

Isabella's continuing protests of concern for Edward, and her lamentations that circumstances have forced her into reluctant opposition to him ("I rue my lord's ill-fortune; but alas, / Care of my country call'd me to this war," IV, v, 73–74), are exposed as patent hypocrisy when we learn that she not only acquiesces in Edward's death, but actually proposes it:

> But, Mortimer, as long as he survives,
> What safety rests for us, or for my son?
> *Mortimer junior*. Speak, shall he presently be dispatch'd and die?
> *Queen Isabella*. I would he were, so it were not by my means.
>   [V, ii, 42–45]

She compounds this duplicity by asking Edward's jailers to convey to him a message of her love and loyalty; Mortimer's delighted comment is "Finely dissembled. Do so still, sweet queen" (V, ii, 74). To Kent she protests her wish to have Edward set at liberty; Kent's aside is "Ah, they do dissemble" (V, ii, 86).

Dissembling is of course one of the stocks-in-trade of the Vice, and although it would be misleading to label Isabella as a vice character, we can see by comparing her with Barabas that Marlowe relies on the moral tradition in his depiction of the Queen's personality. As in the case of *The Jew*, Marlowe suggests that Isabella's piety, loyalty, and humility have been and still are weapons of intrigue, intended to deceive her enemies and her audience at the same time. It must be emphasized that this vice-like quality can explain only a part of her character. After all, Isabella does reveal in soliloquy (II, iv) a convincing display of divided loyalty, and because she is debating with herself the monologue seems perfectly sincere. However, because her critics have found in her later behavior a change too great to be accounted for by Marlowe's psychological analysis of motive,[6] we are left with the impression that Marlowe approaches Isabella from the viewpoint of two dramatic traditions. Insofar as her function is derived from the moral tradition, therefore, Isabella's character is primarily static rather than dynamic.[7] Marlowe proceeds through the revelation of her natural depravity rather than through development of her human weakness. He uncovers a quality of absolute evil in her nature, and accounts for her apparent change by a gradual unmasking of her true identity.

Mortimer's character undergoes much the same sort of revelation in place of development, and the same transition from rationally motivated behavior to pure viciousness. Marlowe is careful at first to give him plausible motives, as he had done with the Jew. Mortimer professes to hate Gaveston for the ill effects of his corrupt presence on the public weal. As champion of "the murmuring commons" he wins our respect. His subsequent villainy, like that of Macbeth, might be explained in terms of the corrupting effect of power upon a naturally ambitious man. But Marlowe portrays him as representing something more basically evil than ambition. Mortimer becomes a cunning manipulator, a master of duplicity. Although his goal is still personal power, he becomes, like Barabas, more and more concerned with the cleverness of the means of his success. Plotting the death of the King, Mortimer devises in Latin a warrant for Edward's execution, ambiguously worded in such a way that the sender cannot be held accountable. He reads it to the audience for their approval of his diabolical skill, adding:

And therefore will I do it cunningly.   [V, iv, 5]

As an added touch of intrigue, Mortimer arranges the death of the man who is to bear the warrant and commit the assassination, by means of a secret token that will be recognized by Edward's prison-keepers, Matrevis and Gurney.

Having informed the audience of this ingenious plot, Mortimer calls forth the man chosen to do his murder, Lightborn. Their short scene together is appropriately comic in the grim vein of the Vice and his henchmen. Lightborn boasts of his skillful atrocities of the past in a manner that suggests Ithamore's first conversation with Barabas:

> 'Tis not the first time I have killed a man.
> I learn'd in Naples how to poison flowers;
> To strangle with a lawn thrust through the throat;
> To pierce the windpipe with a needle's point;
>
> . . . .
>
> But yet I have a braver way than these.   [V, iv, 30–37]

His career in crime is generic, like those of Barabas and Ithamore. Mortimer and Lightborn chuckle appreciatively in admiration of their own cleverness, ignoring all moral consideration. The Baron then sends Lightborn on his way, with a slip of the tongue that almost gives away his own plan for the assassin's subsequent death:

> Take this; away, and never see me more.
> *Lightborn.* No[?]
> *Mort. jun.* No,
> Unless thou bring me news of Edward's death.   [V, iv, 43–46]

Left to himself, Mortimer continues in a jocular vein to unveil his own machinations by which he has cajoled the peers into naming him protector. His bag of tricks includes a show of mock humility and unwillingness to assume so great a task:

> They thrust upon me the protectorship,
> And sue to me for that that I desire.
> While at the council-table, grave enough,
> And not unlike a bashful puritan,
> First I complain of imbecility,
> Saying it is *onus quam gravissimum;*
> Till, being interrupted by my friends,
> *Suscepi* that *provinciam* as they term it;
> And to conclude, I am Protector now.   [V, iv, 56–64]

Mortimer's pretended reluctance calls to mind the artistry of another "Vice," Richard III, who so aptly cajoles the London citizens into offering him the crown by following Buckingham's advice: "Play the maid's part, still answer nay, and take it." [8] Mortimer stands revealed as the Worldly Man at the height of his success before inevitable catastrophe, and his last scenes are accordingly a series of comic boasts and triumphs over his victims. Of course there is a great deal more to Mortimer than the type of Worldly Man. Marlowe is concerned, as in his other creations, less with moral example than with human personality. At the same time the moral pattern is undeniably present, and contributes to the restless power of Marlowe's characterization.

The change in King Edward is opposite to that in Mortimer and Isabella. He himself is never regarded as vicious, but only misguided, inexperienced, and pleasure-seeking. Nevertheless Marlowe imputes evil to his rule in the persons of his sycophants, who embody many vice-like qualities. Gaveston repeatedly identifies himself as a flatterer and hypocrite. When he encounters three poor men who hope to find service at court, he promises to aid them but confides to the audience his insincerity in doing so:

> But yet it is no pain to speak men fair;
> I'll flatter these and make them live in hope.   [*Aside.*
>
> [I, i, 42–43]

In a similar manner he boasts of his power over the pliant King.

Young Spencer and Baldock, the parasites who next win their way into royal favor, are also accomplished in the methods of villainy:

> *Spencer jun.* Then, Baldock, you must cast the scholar off,
>   And learn to court it like a gentleman.
>   'Tis not a black coat and a little band,
>
>   .   .   .   .
>
>   And saying, 'Truly, an't may please your honour,'
>   Can get you any favour with great men;
>   You must be proud, bold, pleasant, resolute,
>   And now and then stab, as occasion serves.
> *Bald.* Spencer, thou knowest I hate such formal toys,
>   And use them but of mere hypocrisy.
>
>   .   .   .   .

> Though inwardly licentious enough,
> And apt for any kind of villainy. [II, i, 31–51]

The death of these sycophants satisfies the requirement in a moral play for an intelligible relationship between cause and effect. Once Edward has been separated from his evil counselors, he becomes the innocent victim whose suffering must be avenged. Mortimer and Isabella, who behave increasingly like the unrepentant protagonists in vice "tragedy," must receive punishment for their crimes. In meting out these retributions, *Edward II* is more in accord with the moral formula than is *Tamburlaine* or *The Jew*. Mortimer's death is not, like Tamburlaine's, the natural end to a busy and successful life. The young prince Edward is a fit instrument for restoring virtuous rule in a way that Ferneze was not. Queen Isabella perceives the justice in the disclosure of her crimes:

> I fear'd as much; murther cannot be hid. [*Aside*. [V, vi, 46]

Although it is always an oversimplification to suppose that Marlowe is chiefly concerned with moral statement, that statement is still present in the inherited structure of the play.

The ending of *Edward II* thus appears to be morally unambiguous. Ultimately the virtuous are separated from the depraved, and each group receives merited justification or destruction. Ambiguity occurs only when we compare this traditional conclusion with the earlier scenes of political conflict, when Edward was the dissolute and prodigal King, Mortimer the forthright defender of English freedoms, and Isabella the deserted wife. Marlowe's use of the homiletic formula, especially in the concluding scenes of this play, engenders a dichotomy in the characters between moral absolutes and psychological complexities. Even in his most secular play, the homiletic tradition contributes an important part. This aspect of *Edward II* necessarily ignores much of what is new in Marlowe, and is critically significant only so long as it is seen as a residual force operating through the playwright's theatrical environment. The moral tradition, although much changed in its outward appearance, provides in *Edward II*, as in Marlowe's other works, a clue to the relationship between structural organization and moral statement.

XVII The Conflict of Conscience and *Doctor Faustus*

Recent studies have concluded that *Doctor Faustus* is one of Marlowe's latest plays, and perhaps the last.[1] It is in any case his masterpiece in the moral tradition, and will serve admirably to summarize Marlowe's use of homiletic methods and materials. The debt of *Faustus* to the morality has long been acknowledged — the spiritual conflict, the Good and Evil Angels, the seven Deadly Sins — but these borrowings still require systematic exploration in order to determine the position of *Faustus* in the historical development of the form, and the structural logic in this crowning achievement of Psychomachia drama. To arrive at this historical understanding, it is necessary first to examine a hybrid morality on a strikingly similar subject, Nathaniel Woodes's *The Conflict of Conscience* (printed in 1581).

The question of Marlowe's direct indebtedness to Woodes's play is controversial. Lily B. Campbell finds little evidence of Marlowe's having known the earlier play.[2] Spivack, on the other hand, cites "general and specific" similarities. For example, the protagonists in both plays receive counsel from good and evil angels, and they suffer torments of despair even though they are intellectually aware of heavenly forgiveness.[3] With or without direct connection, *Conflict of Conscience* deserves study as an important link in the dramatic tradition between *The Longer Thou Livest* and *Faustus*. I have reserved it for discussion now rather than with the hybrid moralities, because of its amateurish quality which suggests that the play was not written for production on the public stage.[4] Yet by drawing its essential elements from that stage, and introducing into the moral framework a new aspect of secularism, *Conflict of Conscience* helped point the way in which Marlowe could adapt the moral play to his genius.

Conflict of Conscience is a remarkable hybrid in two ways. It embodies a transition from allegorical representation to specific chronicle, and from a moral Psychomachia of happy ending to one of tragic ending. Its sources, for example, are both historically specific and morally representative. Woodes drew his material for the play largely from the historical account of Francesco Spira, an Italian Protestant turned recusant.[5] Yet the author also borrowed from Foxe's *Acts and Monuments*; the central trial scene, in particular, is a composite of many such trials or "examinations" in Foxe.[6] The biography of Spira is historically remote, whereas Foxe's representative stories of martyrdom bring the play closer to home for all English Protestants.

This dual tendency, to describe both a particular man and a universal spiritual problem, is apparent in the play's two texts. *Conflict of Conscience* happens to exist in two issues of a single edition.[7] The second of these is identical with the first except for the title page, prologue, and final scene. In one, the historical name appears in the title, "The most lamentable Hystorie, of the desperation of Frauncis Spira." In the other, Spira's name gives way to: "A most lamentable example, of the dolefull desperation of a miserable worldlinge, termed, by the name of PHILOLOGVS." One is a "Hystorie," the other an "example." The prologue of the second version enlarges upon the author's motives for the substitution:

> And here, our Author, thought it meete, the true name to omit,
> And at this time, imagine him PHILOLOGVS to be,
> First, for because, a Comedie, will hardly him permit,
> The vices of one priuate man, to touch particulerly,
> Againe, nowe shall it stirre them more, who shall it heare or see,
> For if this worldling had ben namde, we wold straight deeme in minde,
> That all by him then spoken were, our selues we would not finde.
>
> [ll. 36–42]

Philologus means the love of talk, to the detriment of God's word. Every man may see himself in this Philologus, and must take this "example" to heart rather than observe from a distance the tragic career of a specific historical personage.

Stressing the universality of his protagonist, Woodes idealizes the unfortunate end of Spira into the last-minute salvation which must rescue Everyman, even in the hour of death, from the wiles of

Satan. In the first version the *Nuntius* of the final scene announces a conclusion of unrelieved tragedy:

> Oh dolefull newes, which I report, and bring into your eares,
> Philologus by deepe dispaire hath hanged himselfe with coard.
>
> [ll. 2411–2412]

By the alteration of a few key words, the second version brings about an extraordinary change:

> Oh joyfull newes, which I report, and bring into your eares,
> Philologus, that would haue hangde himselfe with coard,
> Is nowe conuerted unto God, with manie bitter teares.
>
> [second issue, ll. 2411–2413]

As Spivack comments, "Rarely in the history of the drama has the issue between tragedy and comedy been decided so economically."[8] The important fact, however, is not that Woodes could produce the difference by changing so few words, but that his alteration is symbolic of the manner in which the entire body of Psychomachia drama was able to adapt itself to a tragic pattern, simply by terminating its usual progression of spiritual downfall and recovery before the final phase. The earliest of Psychomachia drama contained in its phases of comic and grotesque degeneracy the materials for a tragic resolution. The phenomenon developed in plays like *The Longer Thou Livest* and *Conflict of Conscience*, and reached its fullest maturity in the comic degeneracy of Doctor Faustus' own decline.

Woodes, then, is able to portray the life of an historical personage who is also a universal type, and whose career is potentially either tragic or glorious. Woodes employs the conventional framework of the late intermediate morality, since it too combines topical content with allegory, and comic elements with tragic. The result is an easy transition to the spiritual biography of a man. Spira's (or Philologus') career follows a predictable course of original innocence, plotting and temptation by the forces of evil, transgression, warnings, remorse, and finally retribution or recovery. The *dramatis personae* are sharply divided between good and evil, and they rule the stage in alternating scenes of moral uplift and satiric comedy. At first Satan appears (I, i) to praise his darling son, the Pope, and to promise the arrival of Avarice, Tyranny, and Hypocrisy to overthrow Christ's ministry on earth (for the resemblance to Machiavel in *The Jew,* see Chapter XV above). In the ensuing scene (I, ii) Philologus and Mathetes resolve to suffer martyrdom patiently in the cause of truth. In Act II the plotters appear, as predicted by Satan, and engage in the usual comic routine of quarrel, fight for mastery, and eventual agreement, followed by plotting, invention of disguise names, and the like. Act III, i, returns to Philologus, now suffering from personal fear at the prospect of Romish tyranny. The climactic scene of the play (III, ii, through IV, i) is the inquisition in which Philologus answers bravely and intelligently the questioning of the Cardinal, Cacon (a Scots Papist), Tyranny, and the rest, only to break down at last under the worldly enticement of Sensual Suggestion. Cacon provides the burlesque humor of dialect, allusions to drinking, and other staples of comic villainy. The ensuing scene (IV, iv) is one of spiritual struggle between Suggestion and his opponents, Spirit and Conscience. These alternating conversations resemble those of Faustus' Good and Evil Angels. By way of contrast (V, iii), the Vice Hypocrisy exults in his success, and bids a comic farewell to the audience. The final scenes return to the serious question of Philologus' salvation, as he is visited by "Confusion and Horror of the Mind," by his pious friends Theologus and Eusebius, and by his sons Gisbertus and Paphinitius. Their counsel ends in a spiritual stalemate, and it is only in the brief sixth act, really an epilogue, that a Nuntius declares the ending to be victory or defeat.

The almost rhythmic alternation of the Psychomachia plot from good to evil and from serious to comic, as indicated in the accompanying scheme, demonstrates the extent to which this immediate predecessor of *Faustus* is a part of the structural tradition of the morality. Alternation remains as a convention in this play, even though Woodes probably did not write for an actual troupe. Evidently the phenomenon of alternation had become a hallmark of the morality, even for a writer who could not employ it in a practical manner for the stage.

Woodes's clumsy casting chart, intended for any who might wish "to show this Comedie in priuate houses, or otherwise," reveals in its ineptness the author's misunderstanding of the convention. Instead of doubling opposites he doubles similar types,

	I, i	I, ii	II, i–ii	III, i	III, ii–IV, i	IV, iv–v	V, iii	V, iv–v	VI
								Eusebius	Nun-
								Theologus	tius
								Gisbertus	
Forces								Paphini-	
of								tius	
Good						Con-			
						science			
						Spirit			
		Mathetes							
Hero		Philo-		Philo-	Philo-	Philo-	Philo-	Philo-	
		logus		logus	logus	logus	logus	logus	
	Satan								
			Tyranny		Tyranny				
Forces			Avarice		Avarice				
of			Hypoc-		Hypoc-		Hypoc-		
Evil			risy		risy		risy		
					Cacon				
					Cardinal				
					Sugges-	Sugges-			[Nun-
					tion	tion			tius]

and the result is both awkward and inefficient. Player one, for example, portrays only the Prologue, Mathetes, Conscience, and Paphinitius; he has no role in any comic scene, and in fact is idle during the whole middle portion of the play (II through IV, i). At the same time player five acts only Cardinal and Cacon, two characters who appear almost simultaneously, and in only one scene. The player has only seven lines in which to change from one role to the other. Although this is technically possible, it is wholly unnecessary here. Since Woodes is not working under actual theatrical conditions he is unaware of the mechanical advantages of his alternating pattern; notwithstanding, he retains it as a convention:

> Yet to refresh the myndes of them that be the Auditors,
> Our Author intermixed hath, in places fitt and meete,
> Some honest mirth, yet alwaies ware, DECORVM, to exceede.
>
> [Prologue of second issue, ll. 66–68]

Similarly, the principle of ordered suppression persists in *Conflict of Conscience* as a practice of homiletic method rather than of theatrical expediency. It persists in this play because the author — aware, like Marlowe, of the five-act structure — found a satisfactory sense of unity in the progression of episodic actions which lead to a conclusion. Many of Woodes's characters appear only in one scene

or in one phase, because they are superseded by their homiletic
successors. The mode of Philologus' temptation is sequential. Satan
himself can act on earth only through the mediation of his lieutenant vices. They act upon Philologus in turn, for it is only after
Hypocrisy and Avarice have failed that Tyranny (the inquisition)
unveils his more violent weapons:

> Firstly to inuegle the people relygious:
> For greedinesse of gaine, who will be soone prezed:
> And for feare least heereafter they should be dispised:
> Of their owne freewill, will maintaine Hypocrisie
> So that Auarice alone, shall conquere the Cleargie.
>
> . . . .
>
> If not, then to threaten them with open Tyranny.   [ll. 699–708]

Other Protestant allegories of the Catholic counter-Reformation
follow a similar order of events. In Book I of the *Faerie Queene*,
for example, Spenser depicts a progression from Catholic hypocrisy
(Archimago, Duessa) and Avarice (Kirkrapine and others) to the
proud tyranny of Orgoglio. Tyranny is commonly a late arrival in
the sequential progression of allegorical drama.

The progression of the serious message in *Conflict of Conscience*
is anticipated by the speeches of its protagonists. The theme of the
play, enunciated in I, ii, is that God sends affliction to men in order
to bring them to patience and a sounder faith in His wisdom:

> For trouble bring forth pacience, from pacience dooth insue
> Experience, from experience Hope, of health the ankor true.
>
> [ll. 221–222]

The individual events of plotting, temptation, and recovery are
construed as episodes in the trial of Mankind. Accordingly Spirit,
Conscience, Horror, and others appear when needed and disappear
when their functions have been superseded by the movement of
the plot. Thus, both alternation and suppression are vital means of
homiletic statement in this immediate predecessor of *Doctor Faustus*.

In *Conflict of Conscience*, it is the struggle between the impulse
toward biography and the impulse toward generic representation
that produces the two endings. One may imagine that Woodes
originally conceived of his work as an edifying spiritual biography;
but in adapting his historical source to a moral structure he perceived that the organization of events, and the whole weight of

tradition behind that organization, impelled him to an idealized ending in place of the historical one. It is this tension between what is or was, and what ought to be, that produces a very real excitement in the play (despite its mediocre style) up to the final scene. It is inescapably true that Philologus could be saved or damned until the last moment. The author's final decision in favor of a happy ending is not one of caprice or arbitrary use of *deus ex machina,* but stems from the central conflict in transitional drama between secular fact and religious ideal.

In *Doctor Faustus* one finds a remarkably similar ambivalence of artistic aims: the "facts" of Faustus' life as they had been set down in various accounts and legends, and the generic predicament of a blasphemer. The idealized moral situation is suggested by the structural convention in which the play was written. The tension between what could be and what actually takes place is the primary source of conflict in Faustus' spiritual biography, and owes its power to the morality heritage.

Marlowe — and perhaps a collaborator or collaborators — took the story of Doctor Faustus chiefly from an English translation of the German "Faust-Book," which may not have been published until 1592.[9] The structural method of borrowing from this source was an inherited one. Just as Preston and his company had found Taverner's order of events a suitable basis of construction for the hybrid, *Cambises,* Marlowe and his company adopted the structural outline of the "Faust-Book" as a primary guide for a popular stage version. Havelock Ellis comments, "In the incidents of the drama, *and their sequence,* he followed his authority. The wearisome comic passages, which Marlowe may or may not have written, are copied with special fidelity."[10] F. P. Wilson also notes that the writer of the comic scenes was able to borrow wholesale from the "Faust-Book" the trivialities of practical humor in Faustus' decline. "Marlowe's collaborator invented almost nothing except the dialogue. There in the pamphlet he found the jests about the Pope's buffet, the courtier's horns, the horse-corser who pulled Faustus' leg from his body, the forty-dollar horse that vanished when ridden into the water, the consumption of the load of hay."[11]

The question of multiple authorship is fortunately not vital to this inquiry. We are concerned not primarily with the power of Marlowe's "mighty line" nor with the personal quality of his tragic vision, but with the structure of a popular drama and its debt to the shaping forces of a competitive commercial theater. Whether or not Marlowe wrote the comic scenes,[12] they were certainly demanded by his company; for it was unthinkable that a popular homiletic drama, at least partly in the tradition of *The Longer Thou Livest* and *Conflict of Conscience,* should fail to portray evil as comic and depraved villainy. As Greg has demonstrated, the play in its original form contained a mixture of high seriousness and debased practical joking,[13] and was an integral product of the Elizabethan popular stage.

A persistent disregard for the popular tradition has led to the charge that the "wearisome comic passages" in *Faustus* are a grotesque artistic blemish in the design of the whole, and that "the middle of the play always was disfigured by comic and clownish scenes not only feeble in invention but grossly out of harmony with the tragic theme."[14] To dismiss the comedy either as textually extraneous or as unworthy of the play is a mistaken attempt, at least in historical terms. To ask that the play be written as a "pure" tragedy, building up the force of its terror without digressive interruption, is to ask for that which Elizabethan popular audiences had never imagined or desired. The history of the morality points above all else to the fact that the Psychomachia was composed of a mixture of the serious and the grotesque. It would be far more surprising to find *Faustus* free of comedy than to find it as it is. The presence of such traditional comedy, in fact, tends to confirm Greg's demonstration that the extant texts of 1604 and 1616 are reasonably true to the original performance. The comic material should be read not as an excrescence that interferes with enjoyment of the "pure Marlowe," but as an integral expression of the Psychomachia. The prose source, with its alternating pattern of comic and serious, indicates that comic depravity and tragic decline were united in the initial artistic interpretation of Faustus' character. Most misunderstanding of the comedy in this play has arisen from an inadequate appreciation of the function of burlesque humor in Christian homiletic tragedy.

From this perspective, it appears that the comic scenes are not placed haphazardly at odd intervals throughout the play.[15] *Faustus* employs the established pattern of alternation between edification and amusement, serious message and satiric inversion of normality.

Faustus' first revelation of his fatal ambition, and his conversation with the necromancers Valdes and Cornelius, are followed in the second scene by a comic dialogue between Wagner and two Scholars, in which the servant makes a humorous application of the sophistry and syllogistic arguments of his learned master. In scene three Faustus tries his art of conjuring and bargains to meet Mephistophilis again in his study at midnight — a meeting which takes place in scene five. In the interim, scene four, we are treated to a burlesque conjuration involving Wagner and two devils with "vild long nails." These first five scenes closely correspond in the two texts of 1604 and 1616. The method of regular and symmetrical alternation appears to have been a characteristic of the original performance.[16]

The comic scenes are not merely diversion to hold the attention of the "groundlings." They treat Faustus' heinous sins satirically, by exposing them to grotesque exaggeration and caricature. Things terrible in themselves are made absurdly funny, and by such means the audience is given a defense against the evil. Perhaps it is because the detachment thus created interferes with our complete identification with Faustus, that many critics find the tragic catharsis to be confused and incomplete. Nonetheless, the comic method has its value in the moral drama of example. We are meant to laugh at evil as well as fear it. Like the heroes of all vice "comedy," Faustus is intended to be admirable and yet depraved.

It is noteworthy that although Wagner is Faustus' servant, the two scarcely cross paths in the play. In the first scene Faustus commands Wagner to carry a message to Valdes and Cornelius; Wagner is on stage only long enough to receive this order (ll. 63–66). Again, in scene twelve, Wagner steps in for the last eight lines of the scene to inform his master that the Duke of Vanholt earnestly entreats his company. Apart from these trivial conversations, master and servant never meet. Instead, Wagner appears in the "digressive" comic scenes of the play. His essential relationship to Faustus is one of personified contrast between satire and tragedy. Like Huf, Ruf, and Snuf in *Cambises*, he fulfills the functions of vice comedy in scenes that are related only thematically to the main action. And like Huf, Ruf, and Snuf, his purely comic presence needs to be rationalized in a play dealing with historical persons. Consequently this "Vice" is provided with an apprentice-

ship, just as his predecessors in hybrid chronicle had been transformed into soldiers or rustics.

Other "digressive" characters are similarly justified. The Clown
in scene four is introduced as a prospective servant for Wagner, in
order that the comic resemblance of Wagner to Faustus may be
complete. Robin the Ostler (scenes viii and ix) is evidently connected with Faustus' household in some way, for he is able to steal
one of Faustus' conjuring books from his library. Through him,
his fellows, Rafe and the Vintner, find topical excuse for their
presence in the play, although the functional relationship of all of
them to Faustus' story is indirect.

The dramatic source of this comic material is immediately discernible in the intermediate moral drama, as well as in the "Faust-
Book"; hence the ease with which the writer of the comic scenes was
able to incorporate so much "Faust-Book" material into the play
with a minimum of alteration. The familiar and beloved routines
are all present, just as they later appear in *1 Henry IV*: the quarrels
between the "Vice" and his cohorts, the struggle for supremacy
(Wagner and the Clown), the comic physical violence on stage, the
suggestive or indecent jests about wenches' plackets or cuckolds'
horns, the obscene punning on "raw mutton" and the like, the
tavern humor (involving the Vintner), and the jokes about thievery
(Robin and Rafe steal the Vintner's silver goblet). In the manner
of the hybrid play, this humor is no longer concerned with the
temptation of a mankind hero, but dwells apart in scenes of degenerate viciousness bearing only thematic relationship to the career
of the protagonist. The comic villains dramatize in ludicrous fashion
the besetting sins of Faustus himself: ambition, covetousness, and
the sins of the flesh. These failings in Faustus are overshadowed
somewhat by his nobility of mind, but the failings nevertheless
exist. The "vice figures" illustrate the debased aspects of Faustus'
nature by indirection and analogy. They personify the purely degenerate side of Faustus and so allow the loftiness of his tragedy to
exist more coherently in its own right. Their function is like that
of the Vice in *Horestes*, who portrays the quality of unnatural revenge in the hero and thereby absolves Horestes of the responsibility
of matricide.

The division of these functions in *Faustus* between vicious and
tragic character is not complete, however, and it is the bifurcation

of Faustus' own personality between base physical desires and Promethean aspiration that arouses dispute concerning the message of the play. If one dismisses as unworthy and irrelevant the comic material involving both Faustus and the "digressive" characters, it is natural to dwell upon the noble mind here overthrown. Even though his quest for unlimited knowledge is blasphemous, it is a quest of impressive daring and intellect; and insofar as Faustus aims at this enlargement of human power his overthrow may be interpreted as a martyrdom for a great cause. Such a view is squarely at odds with the orthodox morality of the final chorus:

> Faustus is gone; regard his hellish fall,
> Whose fiendful fortune may exhort the wise
> Only to wonder at unlawful things,
> Whose deepness doth entice such forward wits
> To practice more than heavenly power permits.

If the comic material is considered as integral, and is read with as much emphasis as the serious portions of the play, the moral balance is restored. Not only do the "digressive" vice characters comment satirically on Faustus' acts, but his own behavior is also infused with the tradition of mixed seriousness and debased humor. Once again, the comic scenes alternate with the moments of high passion in the play, and serve as a commentary upon them. One of the great scenes, for example, is that in which Faustus signs his pledge with the devil (scene v), and then immediately suffers his first pangs of conscience (scene vi). Mephistophilis calls in Lucifer and Belzebub to reconcile Faustus to his damnation, and in order to soothe his restless soul they bring on the pageant of the seven Deadly Sins. The action suddenly descends from sublimity to a humorous cataloguing of the various forms of evil. Faustus' quest for knowledge gives way to a rapt involvement in the petty and ridiculous consequences of his act. The contrast has psychological value as relief from the tensions of the previous scene; and its moral is clear in the context of moral mixed drama. Throughout the morality, the seven Deadly Sins have epitomized the comically evil side of the Psychomachia. In *Faustus* the sins are relegated to one sequence only, but the sequence fulfills its time-honored function as a satiric portrayal of the wages of evil. The presence of the Deadly Sins suggests that Faustus himself generically incorporates their several qualities in his ambition, covetousness, and fleshly lust.

There is a trace of the Vice in his universalized acquaintance with evil and his penchant for practical humor.

Continuing the pattern of alternation, Faustus' sojourn in Rome (scene vii) registers the same juxtaposition of exalted quest and absurd practical joking. The account of the voyage to Rome, which begins the scene, is an inspiring adventure in cosmography. Faustus recounts his visits to "Maro's golden tomb" and hears a description of the seven hills of Rome. After this ennobling dialogue we view the ultimate purpose of the journey in the discomfiting of the Pope. The coarse anti-Papist humor is typical of vice comedy in the Protestant moralities. We are let down, as we are intended to be let down, by the sequence of the events. Again, Faustus' exploits in the court of the German Emperor degenerate from a commendable interest in great figures of the past, such as Alexander,

> Chief spectacle of the world's preeminence,
> The bright shining of whose glorious acts
> Lightens the world with his reflecting beams,   [x, 36–38]

to the reproof of a knight who has dared to defy the great magician. Similarly, the burlesque episode of the Horse-corser interrupts Faustus' solemn meditation on

> the restless course
> That Time doth run with calm and silent foot,
> Short'ning my days and thread of vital life.   [xi, 1–3]

In every pair of alternations the transition is from sublimity to triviality, and the concluding phase of each alternation serves as a satiric moral commentary on the vanity of what has gone before.

Faustus' own comic sequences, therefore, like the "digressive" comic sequences of Wagner and his fellows, exploit popular "vice" routines: the suggestive jokes about paramours and cuckoldry, the coarse physical violence in the Pope's chambers, and the like. The dualism of emphasis between noble aspiration and petty achievement is everywhere evident in Faustus' speeches. His first desire, after signing his compact with the devil, is to learn more of the nature of heaven and hell (scene v). Soon tiring of this, however, he begins to demand the fleshly comforts of lust, vast personal riches, and a private army to yield him immense worldly power; or, lechery, covetousness, and worldly pride:

But, leaving off this, let me have a wife, the fairest maid in Germany, for I am wanton and lascivious, and cannot live without a wife.

[v, 144–147]

The structure of this alternation from serious to comic is reinforced in *Faustus* by a symmetry in casting. The configuration of two, as in *The Jew of Malta*, appears again and again. The forces of good find their counterparts in evil, as in Bale's *Three Laws* or many similar plays. The Good Angel and the Evil Angel are obvious examples; the contrast is hardly less marked between Valdes and Cornelius on the one hand and the two virtuous Scholars on the other. In the final scenes of the play, Mephistophilis finds his opposite in the mysterious Old Man. Lucifer and Belzebub come as a duo to quiet Faustus' mind. The "digressive" comic characters appear in pairs: Wagner and the Clown, Robin Ostler and Rafe, Wagner and the Horse-corser. Two actors could easily fill these five roles, for their appearances are staggered in sequence. Similarly, the audiences or victims of Faustus' magic parade in a series of twos, together with extras: the Pope and the Cardinal (with Friars), the Emperor of Germany and the Knight (with attendants), the Duke of Vanholt and his Duchess (probably with attendants). The demand for extras is so arranged that one group of hired actors could appear sequentially as Friars, attendants on the German Emperor and the Duke of Vanholt, devils (in several appearances), and the seven Deadly Sins. The tradition of versatility in acting "straight" and "character" parts doubtless had an important place in the production of the play. The *Faustus* of the 1604 edition could be performed by nine actors, one or two boys (the lesser of the two perhaps taking such mute parts as Alexander's Paramour, Helen of Troy, and the female devil) and seven extras. Since this version was perhaps intended for provincial acting,[17] the original cast may have been slightly larger.

The structure of *Faustus*, then, grows from the elements of alternation, symmetry, and orderly suppression; and it is particularly in connection with the last of these factors that we return to the moral implications of structure upon the message of the play. For in its pattern of linear episodes and sequence of homiletic characters, *Faustus* is squarely in the tradition of the dramatic Psychomachia. In fact, its scope — encompassing the whole of a man's life and the general question of damnation and salvation — looks back past the narrower intermediate moralities to the early moral plays like *Per-severance* and *Mundus et Infans*. The over-all plan of the play is nothing less than the spiritual biography of its protagonist from birth until death and from innocence to damnation:

> Only this, gentlemen: we must perform
> The form of Faustus' fortunes, good or bad.   [Chorus, ll. 7–8]

By "form" the poet means the course, the progression of event. In the usual manner of moral mixed drama, the events portrayed are to be both good and bad. The chorus carries us in a few lines over the period of Faustus' youth and rise to fame, bringing us immediately to the point at which the Psychomachia normally commences: the crisis of innocence corrupted, of virtue brought into conflict with its diabolical opposite. Valdes and Cornelius are the plotters of this first phase, and once their devices have achieved fruition in Faustus' blasphemy, they are no longer needed and accordingly are suppressed. Lucifer and Belzebub, with their wondrous magic shows, figure briefly in the spiritual struggle resulting from the downfall, and thereafter leave the rest to Mephistophilis, the central "Vice." The Scholars, who appear only at the beginning and end of the play, represent the virtuous norm of moral behavior (like Mathetes and Theologus in *Conflict of Conscience*) by which the extent of Faustus' depravity can be measured.

The journey to Rome, in scene seven, begins the phase of comic depravity which, in the Psychomachia, invariably follows temptation and downfall. As a descendant of such dissolute wastrels as Worldly Man and Moros, Faustus passes quickly through one vicious incident after another, variously exhibiting the theme of vice's tawdry reward. Worldly Man had lorded it over his Tenant, Servant, and Hireling, exulting in worldly success until God's Plagues brought catastrophe. Similarly, Faustus prankishly discomfits the Pope, the Cardinal, the Knight, and the rest, all of whom appear only once to illustrate the nature of Faustus' temporal might. Inevitably retribution ends Faustus' brief span of mastery. The most important figure of the last phase is the Old Man, a personage like Heavenly Man in *Enough Is as Good as a Feast*, who reestablishes the moral order by the contrast of his spiritual triumph with the protagonist's terrifying defeat.

Omitting for the moment the alternating comic "digressive"

material, the "form of Faustus' fortunes, good or bad" proceeds as in the diagram, introducing new characters with each phase. Despite

Phase 1 (*i–ii*) *Plotting and temptation*	*Phase 2* (*iii–vi*) *Downfall and spiritual struggle*	*Phase 3* (*vii–xiii*) *Degeneracy*	*Phase 4* (*xiv–xv*) *Damnation*
Faustus	Faustus Mephistophilis	Faustus Mephistophilis	Faustus Mephistophilis
Good Angel	Good Angel		
Evil Angel	Evil Angel		
Cornelius			
Valdes			
	Lucifer		
	Belzebub		
	Devils		Devils
	7 Deadly Sins		
		(a) Pope Cardinal Friars	
		(b) Emperor Knight Attendants	
		(c) Duke of Vanholt Duchess (others?)	
			Scholars Helen of Troy Old Man

its sequential presentation of incident, therefore, *Faustus* achieves a unity of structure found in all Psychomachia drama, based upon the conflict between good and evil for the soul of a man. *Faustus* has dramatic integrity, even though it violates the classical "unities" in encompassing an entire lifetime of activity, in traversing the geographical bounds of Christendom, and in mixing comic and serious treatment. All the events in Faustus' spiritual life are relevant to the single question of salvation or damnation.[18]

In this analysis we have been looking at Faustus as a type of moral protagonist; his story follows the pattern of generic figures like Worldly Man or Moros. We must account, however, for the

fact that Faustus is also a semihistorical personage, a specific individual as well as moral abstraction. Marlowe's play embodies the
sort of opposition found in *Conflict of Conscience*, between the
"facts," as they had been imaginatively created in the "Faust-Book"
material, and the moral lesson implied by the traditional structure
of homiletic drama. The "Faust-Book" was of course legend rather
than reliable chronicle. Nevertheless its hero was a person to whom
Marlowe felt himself strongly attracted, perhaps as a mythic prototype of Marlowe's own aspiration. Insofar as the author directed his
imagination to the presentation of a remarkable personality, admirable in the scope of his endeavor even though motivated by evil
intent, the artistic focus is on tragic failure and on the pitiable
spectacle of perverted genius:

> Cut is the branch that might have grown full straight,
> And burnéd is Apollo's laurel bough
> That sometime grew within this learned man.   [Final Chorus]

Insofar as the author employs the moral convention, however, the
emphasis is on inherent depravity and the inevitable consequences
of "devilish exercise." The moral structure, leading inexorably from
cause to effect, prompts us to look on Faustus as a man to be con-
demned. We are to learn from his evil example, and excessive sympathy on our part would betray in us a questioning of God's
retribution for a "hellish fall." [19] The shift in tone of the last chorus
from tragic sympathy ("Cut is the branch that might have grown
full straight") to explicit moral denunciation ("regard his hellish
fall, / Whose fiendful fortune may exhort the wise / Only to wonder
at unlawful things") reveals the imperfect union of the two impulses. Marlowe, and perhaps his collaborator, have attempted to
achieve tragic stature for the protagonist in a tradition of mixed
drama.

Nevertheless, it is from the inherited structure of the morality
that *Faustus* receives much of its compelling strength as a drama
of spiritual conflict. The force of the story stems from the weight
of the issue — the fate of a man's immortal soul — and from its
application to the condition of all mankind. The tension of the
drama, as in *Conflict of Conscience*, lies in the apparent uncertainty
of the outcome.[20] Although Faustus is in fact irrecoverably damned,
like Moros the fool, we find ourselves pleading with him throughout

the play to accept God's mercy. Even though he, as an actual person, cannot repent, his representative human predicament accentuates the necessity of his recovery as a sign of hope to all Christians in similar torment. The intermediate morality provided the pattern for both negative and positive conclusion. The dichotomy in *Faustus*, as in *Conflict of Conscience*, is between the Christian ideal and the secular reality. Faustus as Everyman ought to be saved, even in his final hour; yet as a specific person, he is damned. Woodes felt the influence of the moral tradition sufficiently to alter his "facts" and underplay the individuality of his protagonist. Marlowe clings to tragedy, but the representational quality of his central personage adds a poignancy which would be lacking in a more objectively historical biography. It is the interplay between moral structure and secular content that relates *Faustus* to *Tamburlaine*, *The Jew*, and *Edward II*, and defines in all of them the fascination and yet the ambiguity of the dramatic message.

Doctor Faustus represents a remarkable advance over the Tudor moralities, and the improvement owes much to the various strands of Renaissance learning which have perforce been taken for granted in this study. Nevertheless the lines of structural development in a constantly expanding national and popular theater are clear in outline and important in consequence. It was in the early morality that the organization of the troupes first left its unmistakable and pervasive imprint upon the sequential, progressive, and alternating form of the Psychomachia plot. It was in the constant reworking of this essential pattern that the Tudor morality evolved its own formulas for comic subplot and for a homiletic tragedy of vice. In its hybrid union with the secular materials of chronicle, biography, and romance the morality tended to endow those subjects with its own dramatic conventions of progressive incident and character.

The diversity of aim between realistic expression of factual occurrence and the traditional rendition of a moral pattern inevitably produced an irresolution in the English popular theater at a time when Marlowe was its leader. The paradoxes of Tamburlaine's glorious wickedness and his ambiguous death, and of Barabas' human plight and inhuman villainy, owe much to this transition in the drama. So indeed do Isabella's seeming virtue and cunning hypocrisy, Mortimer's righteous patriotism and Machiavellian intrigue, and King Edward's languid irresolution and honorable death.

Above all, the paradox is present in *Faustus,* in its moving tragedy of noble character and its explicit denunciation of moral failure, in its hero's sympathetic aspiration and deplorable degeneracy. This paradox was central to the process by which the English moral drama made its contribution to the late Elizabethan theater. In his plays written for public audiences, Marlowe achieved a vital fusion of secular subject and traditional form, and began an era of incomparable drama that was, at the height of its achievement, both secular and moral.

Appendix: Plays "Offered for Acting"
The Texts of the Plays

A List of Works Frequently Cited
Notes · Index

Appendix:
Plays "Offered for Acting"

For the sake of completeness, the following transcriptions include all extant indications of plays "offered for acting" before 1603.

CAMBISES. THOMAS PRESTON. A lamentable tragedy mixed ful of pleasant mirth, conteyning the life of CAMBISES king of PERCIA, from the beginning of his kingdome unto his death, his one good deed of execution, after that many wicked deeds and tirannous murders, committed by and through him, and last of all, his odious death by Gods Justice appointed. Doon in such order as foloweth. By Thomas Preston.

The diuision of the partes.

Councel. Huf. Praxaspes. Murder. Lob, the 3. Lord.	} For one man.	
Lord. Ruf, Commons cry, Commons complaint Lord smirdis. Venus.	} For one man.	
Knight, Snuf. Small habilitie. Proof. Execution. Attendance. second Lord.	} For one man.	
Cambises. Epilogus.	} For one man.	

Prologue. Sisamnes Diligence. Crueltie. Hob. Preparation The I. Lord.	} For one man.
Ambidexter Triall.	} For one man.
Meretrix. Shame. Otian. Mother. Lady. Queene.	} For one man.
Yung childe Cupid.	} For one man

COMMON CONDITIONS. An excellent and pleasant Comedie, termed after the name of the Vice, Common Condicions, drawne out of the most famous historie of Galiarbus Duke of Arabia, and of the good and éeuill successe of him and his two children, Sedmond his sun, and Clarisia his daughter: Set foorth with delectable mirth, and pleasant shewes.

The players names.

. . . . . .

Six may play this Comedie.

CONFLICT OF CONSCIENCE. NATHANIEL WOODES. An excellent new Commedie, Intituled: The Conflict of Conscience. CONTAYNINGE, The most lamentable Hystorie, of the desperation of Frauncis Spera, who forsooke the trueth of Gods Gospell, for feare of the losse of life and worldly goodes. Compiled, by Nathaniell Woodes. Minister, in Norwich.

[issue (b):] An excellent new Commedie, Intituled: The Conflict of Conscience. CONTAYNINGE, A most lamentable example, of the dolefull desperation of a miserable worldlinge, termed, by the name of PHILOLOGVS, who forsooke the trueth of Gods Gospel, for feare of the losse of lyfe, & worldly goods. Compiled, by Nathaniell Woodes. Minister, in Norwich.

The Actors names, deuided into six partes, most conuenient for such as be disposed, either to shew this Comedie in priuate houses, or otherwise.

Prologue.		Sathan.		Auarice.	
Mathetes.		Tyrannye.		Suggestion.	
Conscience.	for one.	Spirit.	for one.	Gisbertus.	for one.
Paphinitius.		Horror.		Nuntius.	
		Eusebius.			
Hypocrisie.		Cardinal.			
Theologus.	for one.	Cacon.	for one.	Philologus	for one.

ENOUGH IS AS GOOD AS A FEAST. WILLIAM WAGER. A Comedy or Enterlude intituled, Inough is as good as a feast, very fruteful godly and ful of pleasant mirth. Compiled by W. Wager.

Seuen may easely play this Enterlude.

The names of the Players.

Worldly man. for one.

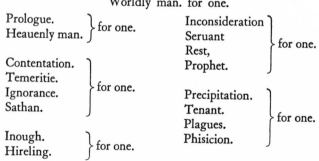

Prologue.	} for one.	Inconsideration	
Heauenly man.		Seruant	} for one.
		Rest,	
Contentation.		Prophet.	
Temeritie.	} for one.		
Ignorance.		Precipitation.	
Sathan.		Tenant.	} for one.
		Plagues.	
Inough.	} for one.	Phisicion.	
Hireling.			

Couetousnes the Uice for an other.

FAIR MAID OF THE EXCHANGE. THOMAS HEYWOOD (?) The Fayre Mayde of the Exchange: With the Pleasaunt Humours of the Cripple of Fanchurch. Very delectable, and full of mirth.

Eleauen may easily acte this Comedie. [A₂]

Berry, *an old man,* Bobbington, Gardiner, Officers, } for one.	Anthony Golding, *Gentleman,* } for one.	
Mall Berry, } for one.	Ferdin. Gold., gent., *and* Wood, } for one.	
Flower, *an humourous old* Bennet, (*man,* Scarlet, Ralph, } for one.	Franke Golding, *Gentleman,* } for one.	
	Bowdler, an *humourous gallant,* } for one.	
Cripple, } for one.	Phillis, *the faire Maide,* } for one.	
Barnard, Flower's *wife,* Vrsula, Boy, } for one.	Fiddle, *the clowne,* } for one.	

HORESTES, AN INTERLUDE OF VICE. JOHN PICKERING. A NEWE Enterlude of Uice Contenyinge, the Historye of Horestes with the cruell reuengment of his Fathers death, vpon his one naturtll Mother. by John Pikeryng.

The players names.

·   ·   ·   ·   ·   ·   ·

The names deuided for vi. to playe.

The fyrst the Uice and Nature. and Dewtey. 3.

2. Rusticus. Idumeus. 2. Sodyer. Menelauus. & Nobulles. 5.

3. Hodge. Counsell. Messenger. Nestor. & Commones. 5.

4. Horestes. a woman. & Prologue. 3,

5. Haulltersicke. Sodyer. Egistus. Harrauld. Fame. Truth and Idumeus. 7.

6. Hempstrynge. Clytemnestra. Prouisyon. & Hermione. 4.

IMPATIENT POVERTY. A Newe Interlude of Impacyente pouerte newlye Imprynted. M.C.L.X.

Foure men may well and easelye playe thys Interlude.

Peace and Coll hassarde and Conscyence, for one man.
Haboundaunce and mysrule for another man.
Impaciente pouerte, Prosperyte, and pouerte, for one man.
Enuye and the sommer for another man.

King Darius. A Pretie new Enterlude both pithie & pleasaunt of the Story of Kyng Daryus, Beinge taken out of the third and fourth Chapter of the thyrd booke of Esdras.

The names of the Players.

.   .   .   .

Syxe persons may easely play it.

King John (ms). John Bale. [Sporadic stage directions constitute a partial indication of the way in which the play was "offered for acting":]

l. 155. Go owt Ynglond, and drese for Clargy.
l. 313. Her go owt Sedwsion and drese for Syvyll Order.
l. 555. Here Kyng Johan and Sivile Order go owt, and Syvile Order drese hym for Sedwsyon.
l. 982. Here go owt Usurpid Power and Privat Welth and Sedycyon: Usurpyd Power shall drese for the Pope; Privat Welth for a Cardynall; and Sedycyon for a Monke. The Cardynall shall bryng in the crose, and Stevyn Launton the booke, bell, and candell.
l. 1060. Here go owt [Private Wealth] and drese for Nobylyte.
l. 1396. Go owt [Private Wealth] and drese for Nobylyte.
l. 1489. Here go owt Clargy and dresse for Ynglond, and Cyvyll Order for Commynalte.
l. 1533. Here Nobelyte go owt and dresse for the Cardynall. Here enter Ynglond and Commynalte.

Life and Repentance of Mary Magdalen. Lewis Wager. A new Enterlude, neuer before this tyme imprinted, entreating of the Life and Repentaunce of Marie Magdalene: not only godlie, learned and fruitefull, but also well furnished with pleasaunt myrth and pastime, very delectable for those which shall heare or reade the same. Made by the learned clarke Lewis Wager.

The names of the Players.

.   .   .   .

Foure may easely play this Enterlude.

Like Will to Like. Ulpian Fulwell. An Enterlude Intituled Like wil to like quod the Deuel to the Colier, very godly and ful of plesant mirth. Wherin is declared not onely what punishement followeth those that wil rather followe licentious liuing, then to esteeme & followe good councel: and what great benefits and commodities they receiue that apply them vnto vertuous liuing and good exercises. Made by Vlpian Fulwel.

Fiue may easely play this enterlude.

The names of the players.

The Prologue			Hance,	
Tom Tospot	for		Uertuous life	for
Hankin hangman	one		Gods promises	one
Tom Colier			Cutbert cutpurs	

Lucifer			Philip Fleming	
Ralfe Roister	for		Pierce Pickpurs	for
Good fame	one		Honour	another
Seueritie				

Nichol newfangle the vice.

THE LONGER THOU LIVEST THE MORE FOOL THOU ART. W. WAGER. A very mery and Pythie Commedie, called The longer thou liuest, the more foole thou art. A Myrrour very necessarie for youth, and specially for such as are like to come to dignitie and promotion: As it maye well appeare in the Matter folowynge. Newly compiled by W. Wager.

The Players names. [A₁ *verso*]

.   .   .   .

Foure may playe it easely.

{ The Prologue. Exercitacion. Wrath.
{ Cruel[t]ie. Goddes Iudgement. } for one.

{ Moros.
{ Fortune. } for another.

{ Disciplyne. Incontinencie.
{ Impietie. Confusion. } for another.

{ Pietie. Idlenes.
{ Ignorance. People. } for another.

LUSTY JUVENTUS. R. WEVER. An Enterlude called lusty Iuuentus, Lyuely discribing the frailtye of youth: of nature, prone to vice: by grace and good counsayll, trayneable to vertue.

The names of the players.

.   .   .   .

Foure may play it easely, taking such partes as they thinke best: so that any one take of those partes that be not in place at once.

MARRIAGE OF WIT AND WISDOM (MS). FRANCIS MERBURY (?) The [Contract] of a Marige betweene wit and wisdome very frutefull and mixed full of pleasant mirth as well for The beholders as the Readers or hearers neuer before imprinted.

The diuision of the partes for six to playe this interlude.

The Prologue		Wantonis	
Idelnes	} for	Fancy	} for
Epilouge	one.	Dolle	one.

Seueritie		Witt	
Ircksomnes	for	Serch	} for
Snatch	one.	Inquisition	one.
Honest Recreat:			

		Good Nurture	
Indulgence		Catch	} for
Wisdome	} for	Lob	one.
Mother bee	one.		

MISOGONUS (MS). LAURENTIUS BARIONA (?) A mery and p[leasaunt comedie called?] Misogonus.

The names of the speakers.

Prologus.	Ph[ilogonus	1.]
Philogonus, pater.	Eupel[as	2.]
Eupelas, fidelis patris vicinus.	Misogonus	[3.]
Cacurgus, morio.	Cacurgus	
Misogonus, filius domesticus.	Prologus	} [4.]
Orgelus, servus misogoni.	Eugonus	
Oenophilus, conservus eius.	Codrus	
Liturgus, servus philogoni.	Sir John	} 5.
Melissa, meretrix.	Epilogus	
Sir Johne, sacerdos.	Orgelus	
Jacke, Clarke.	Isbell	} 6.
Ceister Codrus, rusticus.	Oenophilus	
Alisone, eius vxor, obstitrix.	Madge	} [7.]
Isbell Busbey Testes	Melissa	
Madge Caro vetulae.	Crito	} [8.]
Eugonus, filius peregrinus.	Alison	
Crito, peregrinus.	Jake	} 9.
Epilogus.	Liturgus	10.

MUCEDORUS. A Most pleasant Comedie of Mucedorus the kings sonne of Valentia and Amadine the Kings daughter of Arragon, with the merie conceites of Mouse. Newly set foorth, as it hath bin sundrie times plaide in the honorable Cittie of London. Very delectable and full of mirth [1598].

Eight persons may easily play it.   [A₁ verso]

The King and Rombelo. } { for one.

Mucedorus the prince of Valentia. } { for one.

Amadine the Kinges daughter of Arragon. } { for one.

Segasto a Noble man. } { for one.

Enuie: Tremelio a Captaine, Bremo a wilde man. } { for one.

Comedy, a boy, an ould woman, Ariena Amadines maide. } { for one.

Collen a Counsellor, A messenger. } { for one.

Mouse the Clowne. } { for one.

[1610 edition:]   Ten persons may esily play it.   [A₂ verso]
[adds separate roles for King Valencia and Anselmo]

NEW CUSTOM. A new Enterlude No lesse wittie: then pleasant, entituled new Custome, deuised of late, and for diuerse causes nowe set forthe, neuer before this tyme Imprinted. 1573.

The players names in this Enterlude bée these.

·   ·   ·   ·   ·   ·   ·   ·   ·   ·

Fower may Play this Enterlude.

1 { Peruersedoctrine.

3 { Newe Custome.
    { Auarice.
    { Assurance.

2 { Ignoraunce
    { Hypocrisie.
    { and Edification.

4 { Light of the Gospell.
    { Creweltie.
    { Goddes felicitie.
    { The Prologue.

PATIENT AND MEEK GRISSELL. JOHN PHILLIP. THE COMMODYE OF pacient and meeke Grissill, Whearin is declared, the good example, of her pacience towardes her Husband: and lykewise, the due obedience of Children, toward their Parentes. Newly. Compiled by Iohn Phillip.

Eight persons maye easely play this Commody.

1. Polliticke Perswasion the Uice. the Epiloge. For one.
2. Preface. Marquis. For another.
3. Fidence. Indigence. The second Paidge or Seruing man, The Sonne of Grissill. For another.
4. Reason. Dilligence. Countis Mayd. Pacience. and the Daughter of Grissill. For another.
5. Sobrietie. Countis of Pango. Common people. Constancy.
6. Rumor. Jannickle.
7. Janickells Wife. The first of the Pages. The Nursse.
8. Grissill. The Midwife.

SACRAMENT, PLAY OF THE (CROXSTON MS.).

IX may play yt at ease.   [colophon]

THREE LAWS. JOHN BALE. A Comedy concernynge thre lawes, of nature Moses, & Christ, corrupted by the Sodomytes. Pharysees and Papystes. Compyled by Iohan Bale. Anno M. D. XXXVIII.

Into fyue personages maye the partes of thys Comedy be deuyded.

[G₁ *verso*]

The Prolocutour.	The lawe of Nature.
Cristen fayth.	Couetousnesse.
Infydelyte.	False doctryne.
The first.	The seconde.
The lawe of Moses.	The lawe of Christ.
Idolatrye.	Ambycyon.
Hypocresye.	Sodomye.
The third.	The fourt.

Deus pater.
Vindicta Dei.
The fift.

TIDE TARRIETH NO MAN. GEORGE WAPULL. THE Tyde taryeth no Man. A MOSTE PLEASant and merry commody, right pythie and full of delight. Compiled by George Wapull.

Fowre persons may easily play it.

1. The Prologue, Hurtfull help, the Tenaunt, Faithfull few for one.
2. Paynted profyte, No good Neighbourhood, the Courtyer, Wastefulnesse, Christianitye, Correction for another.
3. Corage the Uice, Debtor, for another.
4. Fayned furtheraunce, Gréedinesse the Marchaunt, Wantonnesse the Woman, the Seriaunt, Authority and Dispayre, for another.

TRIAL OF TREASURE. A new and mery Enterlude, called the Triall of Treasure, newly set foorth, and neuer before this tyme imprinted.

The names of the plaiers,

First, Sturdines, Contentation, Uisitation, Time.
The second, Lust Sapience, Consolation.
The thirde, the Preface, Iust, Pleasure, Gredy gutte.
The fourth, Elation, Trust, a woman, and Treasure, a woman.
The fifth, Inclination the Uice.

VIRTUOUS AND GODLY SUSANNA. THOMAS GARTER. THE COMMODY OF the moste vertuous and Godlye Susanna, neuer before this tyme Printed. Compiled by Thomas Garter.

Eyght persons may easly play it.

1. The Prologue and the Gaylour for one.
2. Ioachim and Iuder for another,
3. Sathan and Uoluptas another,
4. Sensualitas alone.
5. Susanna alone.
6. Helchia, True Report, Ancilla, another,
7. Ill Reporte the Uyce, and Cryer, another.
8. Helchias wyfe, Danyell, Seruus, Serua, for another.

WEALTH AND HEALTH. An enterlude of Welth, and Helth, very mery and full of Pastyme, newly at this tyme Imprinted.

The Names of the players.

. . . .

Foure may easely play this Playe.

The Texts of the Plays

The following list of editions is not intended as a complete bibliography. It enumerates only those editions referred to by line, scene, or page number in the preceding chapters. For a fuller check list of editions see Bernard Spivack, *Shakespeare and the Allegory of Evil* (New York, 1958), and T. W. Craik, *The Tudor Interlude* (Leicester, 1958).

COLLECTIONS CITED

Adams — Joseph Q. Adams. *Chief Pre-Shakespearean Dramas.* Boston, 1924.

Methuen Marlowe — R. H. Case, gen. ed. *The Works and Life of Christopher Marlowe.* Methuen Series. 6 vols. London, 1930–1933.

Baskervill — Charles R. Baskervill, Virgil B. Heltzel, and Arthur H. Nethercot. *Elizabethan and Stuart Plays.* New York, 1934.

Brandl — Alois Brandl. *Quellen des weltlichen Dramas in England vor Shakespeare.* Strassburg, 1898.

Dodsley — Robert Dodsley. *A Select Collection of Old English Plays.* Originally published by Robert Dodsley in the year 1744. 4th edition by W. Carew Hazlitt. 15 vols. London, 1874–1876.

E.E.T.S. — Early English Text Society. London, 1864–.

Jahrbuch — *Jahrbuch der Deutschen Shakespeare-Gesellschaft.* Berlin, 1864–.

M.S.R. — Malone Society Reprints. London, 1907–.

Manly — John M. Manly. *Specimens of the Pre-Shaksperean Drama.* 2 vols. Boston, 1897.

Materialien — Materialien zur Kunde des älteren Englischen Dramas. W. Bang, gen. ed. Louvain, 1902–1914.

T.F.T. — Tudor Facsimile Texts, issued by John S. Farmer. 1907–1914.

PLAYS LISTED ALPHABETICALLY

All for Money, by Thomas Lupton. Roger Warde and Richard Mundee, 1578.
——— Ernst Vogel. *Jahrbuch,* 40 (1904).
Appius and Virginia, "By R. B." William How for Richard Jones, 1575.

—— Ronald B. McKerrow and W. W. Greg. M.S.R., 1911.

The Battle of Alcazar, by George Peele. Edward Allde for Richard Bank-
worth, 1594.

—— A. H. Bullen. *The Works of George Peele.* 2 vols. London, 1888.

Calisto and Melibea, anonymous: J. Rastell? printed by J. Rastell, n.d.

—— W. W. Greg and Frank Sidgwick. M.S.R., 1908.

Cambises, by Thomas Preston. John Allde, n.d.

—— Baskervill.

The Castle of Perseverance, anonymous. Macro MS., n.d.

—— Frederick J. Furnivall and Alfred W. Pollard. *The Macro Plays.*
E.E.T.S., Extra Series, 91 (1904).

The Christmas Prince, anonymous. MS., 1607–1608.

—— Frederick S. Boas and W. W. Greg. M.S.R., 1923.

Clyomon and Clamydes, anonymous. Thomas Creede, 1599.

—— W. W. Greg. M.S.R., 1913.

The Cobbler's Prophesy, by Robert Wilson. John Danter, 1594.

—— A. C. Wood and W. W. Greg. M.S.R., 1914.

Common Conditions, anonymous. William How for John Hunter, n.d.

—— C. F. Tucker Brooke. Elizabethan Club Reprints. New Haven,
Conn., 1915.

The Conflict of Conscience, by Nathaniel Woodes. Richard Bradocke, 1581.
(The early edition exists in two issues, both of the same year.)

—— Herbert Davis and F. P. Wilson. M.S.R., 1952.

The Disobedient Child, by Thomas Ingelend. Thomas Colwell, n.d.

—— Dodsley, II.

Doctor Faustus, by Christopher Marlowe. "Printed by V.S. for Thomas
Bushell," 1604; "Printed for John Wright," 1616.

—— Baskervill.

Edward II, by Christopher Marlowe. William Jones, 1594.

—— H. B. Charlton and R. D. Waller. Methuen Marlowe.

Enough Is as Good as a Feast, by W. Wager. John Allde, n.d.

—— S. de Ricci. Huntington Facsimile Reprints. New York, 1920.

Everyman, anonymous. John Skot, n.d. (Four early editions exist, two
entire and two fragmentary; none is dated.)

—— Adams.

The Fair Maid of the Exchange, anonymous: Thomas Heywood? Henry
Rockit, 1607.

—— Barron Field. The Shakespeare Society, 30. London, 1845.

The Four Elements, by John Rastell. Printed by J. Rastell, n.d.

—— Dodsley, I.

The Four PP, by John Heywood. W. Myddylton, n.d.

—— Adams.

Fulgens and Lucrece, by Henry Medwall. J. Rastell, n.d.

—— Frederick S. Boas and Arthur W. Reed. London, 1926.

Gammer Gurton's Needle, by "Mr. S." Thomas Colwell, 1575.

—— Baskervill.

Gentleness and Nobility, anonymous: John Rastell? printed by J. Rastell, n.d.

―――― John S. Farmer, *The Spider and the Fly, together with an Attributed Interlude entitled Gentleness and Nobility.* Early English Dramatists. London, 1908.

Gismond of Salerne, by Rob. Wilmot and others. MS., 1567–1568.

―――― John W. Cunliffe. *Early English Classical Tragedies.* Oxford, 1912.

Godly Queen Hester, anonymous. William Pickering and Thomas Hacket, 1561.

―――― W. W. Greg. Materialien, 5 (1904).

God's Promises, by John Bale. D. van der Straten? Wesel, 1547?

―――― Dodsley, I.

Gorboduc, by Thomas Norton and Thomas Sackville. John Day, 1570.

―――― Baskervill.

Hickescorner, anonymous. Wynken de Worde, n.d.

―――― Manly, I.

Horestes, by John Pickering. William Griffith, 1567.

―――― Brandl.

Impatient Poverty, anonymous. John Kind, 1560.

―――― Ronald B. McKerrow. Materialien, 33 (1911).

Jack Juggler, anonymous. William Copland, n.d.

―――― Dodsley, II.

Jacob and Esau, anonymous. H. Bynneman, 1568.

―――― Dodsley, II.

The Jew of Malta, by Christopher Marlowe. "Printed by I.B. for Nicholas Vavasour," 1633.

―――― H. S. Bennett. Methuen Marlowe.

Jocasta, by George Gascoigne and Francis Kinwelmarsh. In collection, 1573.

―――― John W. Cunliffe. *Early English Classical Tragedies.* Oxford, 1912.

John Baptist, by John Bale. Edition now lost, without printer's name or date.

―――― John S. Farmer. *The Dramatic Writings of John Bale, Bishop of Ossory.* London, 1907.

John the Evangelist, anonymous. John Waley, n.d.

―――― W. W. Greg. M.S.R., 1907.

John John the Husband, Tib his Wife, and Sir John the Priest, by John Heywood. W. Rastell, 1533.

―――― Brandl.

King Darius, anonymous. Thomas Colwell, 1565.

―――― Brandl.

King John, by John Bale. MS., n.d.

―――― Manly, I.

Liberality and Prodigality, anonymous. Simon Stafford for George Vincent, 1602.

―――― Dodsley, VIII.

The Life and Repentance of Mary Magdalen, by Lewis Wager. John Charlwood, 1566.

——— Frederick I. Carpenter. Chicago, 1902.

Like Will to Like, by Ulpian Fulwell. John Allde, 1568.

——— Dodsley, III.

The Longer Thou Livest the More Fool Thou Art, by W. Wager. William Howe for Richard Jones, n.d.

——— Alois Brandl. *Jahrbuch,* 36 (1900).

Love, The Play of, by John Heywood. William Rastell, 1534.

——— Brandl.

Lusty Juventus, by R. Wever. William Copland and Abraham Veale, n.d.

——— Dodsley, II.

Magnificence, by John Skelton. John Rastell, n.d.

——— Robert L. Ramsay. E.E.T.S., Extra Series, 98 (1906).

Mankind, anonymous. Macro MS., n.d.

——— Manly, I.

The Marriage of Wit and Science, anonymous. Thomas Marshe, n.d.

——— Dodsley, II.

The Marriage of Wit and Wisdom, anonymous: Francis Merbury? MS., 1579.

——— James Halliwell. The Shakespeare Society, 31. London, 1846.

The Misfortunes of Arthur, by Thomas Hughes and others. Robert Robinson, 1587.

——— Dodsley, IV.

Misogonus, anonymous: Laurentius Bariona? MS., 1577.

——— Brandl.

Mucedorus, anonymous. William Jones, 1598 and 1610.

——— Baskervill (1610 edition).

——— T.F.T. (1598 edition).

Mundus et Infans, anonymous. Wynken de Worde, 1522.

——— Manly, I.

Nature, by Henry Medwall. John Rastell? n.d.

——— Brandl.

New Custom, anonymous. William How for Abraham Veale, 1573.

——— Dodsley, III.

Nice Wanton, anonymous. John King, 1560.

——— Manly, I.

The Pardoner and the Friar, by John Heywood. William Rastell, 1533.

——— Francis J. Child. *Four Old Plays.* Cambridge, Mass., 1848.

Patient and Meek Grissell, by John Phillip. Thomas Colwell, n.d.

——— W. W. Greg and Ronald B. McKerrow. M.S.R., 1909.

Philosophaster, by Robert Burton. MS., 1617.

——— Paul Jordan-Smith, trans. Stanford, Calif., 1931.

Ralph Roister Doister, by Nicholas Udall. H. Denham for T. Hackett? 1566–1567?

——— Baskervill.

Respublica, anonymous. MS., 1553.

——— Leonard A. Magnus. E.E.T.S., Extra Series, 94 (1905).

Richardus Tertius, by Thomas Legge. MS., n.d.

———— Barron Field. The Shakespeare Society, 21. London, 1844.

Sacrament, Play of the, anonymous. Croxston MS., n.d.
———— Manly, I.

An Satire of the Three Estates, by Sir David Lindsay. Robert Charteris, 1602.
———— David Hamer. *The Works of Sir David Lindsay,* vol. 2. Scottish Text Society. Edinburgh, 1931–1936.

Sir Thomas More, anonymous. MS., n.d.
———— W. W. Greg. M.S.R., 1911.

Spanish Tragedy, by Thomas Kyd. Edward Allde for Edward White, n.d.
———— Baskervill.

Supposes, by George Gascoigne. In collection, 1573.
———— Baskervill.

Tamburlaine the Great, by Christopher Marlowe. Richard Jones, 1590.
———— Una M. Ellis-Fermor. Methuen Marlowe.

The Temptation of Our Lord, by John Bale. D. van der Straten? Wesel? n.d.
———— T.F.T., 1909.

Thersites, anonymous. J. Tysdale, n.d.
———— Francis J. Child. *Four Old Plays.* Cambridge, Mass., 1848.

Three Ladies of London, by Robert Wilson? Roger Warde, 1584.
———— Dodsley, VI.

Three Laws, by John Bale. Nicolaus Bamburgensis, 1538.
———— M. M. Arnold Schroeer. Halle, 1882.

Three Lords and Three Ladies of London, by Robert Wilson? R. Jones, 1590.
———— Dodsley, VI.

The Tide Tarrieth No Man, by George Wapull. Hugh Jackson, 1576.
———— Ernst Rühl. *Jahrbuch,* 43 (1907).

Tom Tyler and His Wife, anonymous. Second impression, 1661.
———— G. C. Moore Smith and W. W. Greg. M.S.R., 1910.

The Trial of Treasure, anonymous. Thomas Purfoot, 1567.
———— Dodsley, III.

Virtuous and Godly Susanna, by Thomas Garter. Hugh Jackson, 1578.
———— B. Ifor Evans and W. W. Greg. M.S.R., 1937.

Wealth and Health, anonymous. No printer's name or date.
———— W. W. Greg and Percy Simpson. M.S.R., 1907.

Weather, Play of the, by John Heywood. William Rastell, 1533.
———— Brandl.

Wisdom Who Is Christ, anonymous. Macro MS., n.d.
———— F. J. Furnivall and Alfred W. Pollard. *The Macro Plays.* E.E.T.S., Extra Series, 91 (1904).

Wit and Science, by John Redford. MS., n.d.
———— Manly, I.

Witty and Witless, by John Heywood. M.S., n.d.
———— T.F.T., 1909.

Youth, anonymous. John Waley, n.d.
———— W. Bang and R. B. McKerrow. Materialien, 12 (1905).

A List of Works
Frequently Cited

ABBREVIATIONS USED

CL   Comparative Literature
ELH   Journal of English Literary History
HLQ   Huntington Library Quarterly
JEGP   Journal of English and Germanic Philology
JHI   Journal of the History of Ideas
LTLS   London Times Literary Supplement
MLN   Modern Language Notes
MLR   Modern Language Review
MP   Modern Philology
N & Q   Notes and Queries
PMLA   Publications of the Modern Language Association of America
PQ   Philological Quarterly
RES   Review of English Studies
SAQ   South Atlantic Quarterly
SP   Studies in Philology

Armstrong, William A. "The Authorship and Political Meaning of *Cambises*,"
    English Studies, 36: 289–299 (1955).
Bakeless, John. *The Tragicall History of Christopher Marlowe*. 2 vols.
    Cambridge, Mass., 1942.
Baldwin, Thomas W. *The Organization and Personnel of the Shakespearean
    Company*. Princeton, 1927.
———— *Shakspere's Five-Act Structure*. Urbana, Ill., 1947.
Baskervill, C. R. *The Elizabethan Jig*. Chicago, 1929.
Baskervill, C. R., V. B. Heltzel, and A. H. Nethercot, eds. *Elizabethan and
    Stuart Plays*. New York, 1934.
Bennett, H. S., ed. *The Jew of Malta*. (Methuen series *The Works and Life
    of Christopher Marlowe*, gen. ed. R. H. Case.) London, 1931.
Boas, Frederick S. *An Introduction to Tudor Drama*. Oxford, 1933.
———— *Christopher Marlowe: A Biographical and Critical Study*. Oxford, 1940.
Boughner, D. C. "Vice, Braggart, and Falstaff," *Anglia*, 72:35–61 (1954–1955).
Bradbrook, M. C. *The Growth and Structure of Elizabethan Comedy*. London,
    1955.
Bradner, Leicester. "A Test for Udall's Authorship," *MLN*, 42: 378–380
    (1927).

Brandl, Alois, ed. *Quellen des weltlichen Dramas in England vor Shakespeare.* Strassburg, 1898.

Brooke, C. F. Tucker. *The Tudor Drama.* Boston, 1911.

Bullen, A. H., ed. *The Works of Christopher Marlowe.* 3 vols. Boston, 1885.

Calderhead, Iris G. "Morality Fragments from Norfolk," *MP,* 14: 1–9 (1916–1917).

Cameron, Kenneth W. *Authorship and Sources of "Gentleness and Nobility."* Raleigh, N. C., 1941.

Campbell, Lily B. *Divine Poetry and Drama in Sixteenth-Century England.* Cambridge, Eng., 1959.

—— "*Doctor Faustus:* A Case of Conscience," *PMLA,* 67: 219–239 (1952).

Carpenter, Frederick I., ed. *The Life and Repentaunce of Marie Magdalene.* Chicago, 1902.

Chambers, E. K. *The Elizabethan Stage.* 4 vols. Oxford, 1923.

—— *English Literature at the Close of the Middle Ages.* (The Oxford History of English Literature.) Oxford, 1945.

—— *The Mediaeval Stage.* 2 vols. Oxford, 1903.

Charlton, H. B. and R. D. Waller, eds. *Edward II.* (Methuen series *The Works and Life of Christopher Marlowe.*) London, 1933.

Coogan, Sister Mary Philippa. *An Interpretation of the Moral Play, Mankind.* Washington, D. C., 1947.

Craig, Hardin. *English Religious Drama of the Middle Ages.* Oxford, 1955.

Craik, T. W. *The Tudor Interlude.* Leicester, 1958.

Creizenach, W. "Miracle-Plays and Moralities," *Cambridge History of English Literature,* V, 36–60.

Cunliffe, John W., ed. *Early English Classical Tragedies.* Oxford, 1912.

Farnham, Willard. *The Medieval Heritage of Elizabethan Tragedy.* Berkeley, Calif., 1936.

Furnivall, F. J. and Alfred W. Pollard, eds. *The Macro Plays.* (Early English Text Society, Extra Series, 91.) London, 1904.

Gayley, Charles M. *Plays of Our Forefathers.* New York, 1907.

Greg, W. W., ed. *Marlowe's Doctor Faustus: 1604–1616: Parallel Texts.* Oxford, 1950.

—— *Dramatic Documents from the Elizabethan Playhouses.* 2 vols. Oxford, 1931.

Harbage, Alfred B. *Annals of English Drama, 975–1700.* Philadelphia, 1940.

Hillebrand, Harold N. *The Child Actors.* Urbana, Ill., 1926.

Hogrefe, Pearl. *The Sir Thomas More Circle.* Urbana, Ill., 1959.

Kocher, Paul H. *Christopher Marlowe: A Study of His Thought, Learning, and Character.* Chapel Hill, N. C., 1946.

Lawrence, William J. "The Practice of Doubling and Its Influence on Early Dramaturgy," in *Pre-Restoration Stage Studies.* Cambridge, Mass., 1927.

Levin, Harry. *The Overreacher: A Study of Christopher Marlowe.* Cambridge, Mass., 1952.

MacKenzie, W. Roy. *The English Moralities from the Point of View of Allegory.* Boston, 1914.

McCusker, Honor. *John Bale, Dramatist and Antiquary.* Bryn Mawr, Pa., 1942.

McKerrow, R. B., ed. *A Newe Interlude of Impacyente Pouerte.* (Materialien zur Kunde des älteren Englischen Dramas, 33.) Louvain, 1911.

Molloy, Rev. John J. *A Theological Interpretation of the Moral Play, Wisdom, Who Is Christ.* Washington, D. C., 1952.

Murray, John T. *English Dramatic Companies, 1558–1642.* 2 vols. London, 1910.

Nichols, J. G., ed. *The Diary of Henry Machyn.* London, 1848.

Nicoll, Allardyce. *Masks Mimes and Miracles.* London, 1931.

Northbrook, John. *A Treatise Against Dicing, Dancing, Plays, and Interludes,* ed. J. P. Collier. London, 1843.

Ramsay, Robert L., ed. *Magnificence.* (Early English Text Society, Extra Series, 98.) London, 1906.

Reed, A. W. *Early Tudor Drama.* London, 1926.

Ribner, Irving. *The English History Play in the Age of Shakespeare.* Princeton, 1957.

Robinson, F. N., ed. *The Works of Geoffrey Chaucer.* 2nd. ed. Cambridge, Mass., 1957.

Rossiter, A. P. *English Drama from Early Times to the Elizabethans.* London, 1950.

Salter, F. M. *Mediaeval Drama at Chester.* Toronto, 1955.

Sharp, Thomas. *A Dissertation on the Pageants or Dramatic Mysteries Anciently Performed at Coventry.* Coventry, 1825.

Smart, Walter K. *Some English and Latin Sources and Parallels for the Morality of Wisdom.* Menasha, Wis., 1912.

—— "Some Notes on *Mankind*," *MP,* 14: 45–58, 293–313 (1916–1917).

Southern, Richard. *The Medieval Theatre in the Round.* London, 1957.

Spivack, Bernard. *Shakespeare and the Allegory of Evil.* New York, 1958.

Stopes, C. C. *William Hunnis and the Revels of the Chapel Royal.* (Materialien zur Kunde des älteren Englischen Dramas, 29.) Louvain, 1910.

Symonds, John A. *Shakspere's Predecessors in the English Drama.* London, 1884.

Tannenbaum, Samuel A. "Comments on *The Marriage of Wit and Wisdom*," *PQ,* 9: 321–340 (1930).

Thompson, E. N. S. "The English Moral Plays," *Transactions of the Connecticut Academy of Arts and Sciences,* 14: 291–414 (1910).

Wallace, Charles W. *The Evolution of the English Drama up to Shakespeare.* Berlin, 1912.

Wickham, Glynne. *Early English Stages 1300 to 1660.* Vol. 1 of 2 volumes. London, 1959.

Wilson, F. P. *Marlowe and the Early Shakespeare.* Oxford, 1953.

Wine, Celesta. "Nathaniel Wood's *Conflict of Conscience*," *PMLA,* 50: 661–678 (1935).

Wright, Louis B. "Social Aspects of Some Belated Moralities," *Anglia,* 54: 107–148 (1930).

Notes

CHAPTER I: INTRODUCTION: FROM *Mankind* TO MARLOWE

1. John A. Symonds, *Shakspere's Predecessors in the English Drama* (London, 1884), p. 149.

2. C. F. Tucker Brooke, *The Tudor Drama* (Boston, 1911), pp. 110–111. For further expressions of this idea of historic unimportance in the morality, see Charles W. Wallace, *The Evolution of the English Drama up to Shakespeare* (Berlin, 1912), p. 86; and C. E. Vaughan, *Types of Tragic Drama* (London, 1908), p. 103.

3. Frederick S. Boas, *An Introduction to Tudor Drama* (Oxford, 1933), p. 28.

4. Charles M. Gayley, ed., *Representative English Comedies*, 4 vols. (New York, 1903–1914).

5. See in particular Glynne Wickham, *Early English Stages 1300 to 1660* (London, 1959), vol. 1; F. M. Salter, *Mediaeval Drama at Chester* (Toronto, 1955); Richard Southern, *The Medieval Theatre in the Round* (London, 1957); T. W. Craik, *The Tudor Interlude* (Leicester, 1958); and Bernard Spivack, *Shakespeare and the Allegory of Evil* (New York, 1958).

6. John W. Cunliffe, ed., *Early English Classical Tragedies* (Oxford, 1912), p. ix; see also p. xix.

7. See especially Thomas W. Baldwin, *Shakspere's Five-Act Structure* (Urbana, Ill., 1947). Baldwin gives an authoritative account of the process by which Renaissance humanists evolved a theory and practice of classical five-act structure, but he asserts too flatly that the process was basic to all sixteenth-century drama. His thesis is that "the Renaissance wanted to imitate the structure of the old plays" (p. 97), in England as on the Continent. He speaks without sufficient distinction of the "characteristic habit of the age" in relation to a highly specialized list of plays such as *Gorboduc, Warres of Cyrus, Richardus Tertius, Meleager, Herodes,* and *Solymannidae* (p. 364).

8. See Irving Ribner, *The English History Play in the Age of Shakespeare* (Princeton, 1957), p. 42.

9. Madeleine Doran, *Endeavors of Art* (Madison, Wis., 1954), pp. 3f; with acknowledged indebtedness for ideas on "multiple unity" to Heinrich Wölfflin, *Principles of Art History*, trans. M. D. Hottinger (New York, 1932), pp. 159, 166.

10. E. M. W. Tillyard, *Shakespeare's History Plays* (London, 1944), p. 208.

11. See William J. Lawrence, "The Practice of Doubling and Its Influence on Early Dramaturgy," in *Pre-Restoration Stage Studies* (Cambridge, Mass., 1927), pp. 43–78.

12. Alfred B. Harbage, *Annals of English Drama, 975–1700* (Philadelphia, 1940), p. 5.

13. See E. N. S. Thompson, "The English Moral Plays," *Transactions of the Connecticut Academy of Arts and Sciences,* 14: 291–414 (1910).

CHAPTER II: CRITERIA FOR A POPULAR REPERTORY

1. E. K. Chambers, *The Mediaeval Stage* (Oxford, 1903), I, 182.

2. See Cunliffe, ed., *Early English Tragedies*, p. lxv.

3. Thomas M. Parrott and Robert H. Ball, *A Short View of Elizabethan Drama* (New York, 1943), p. 23.

4. Chambers, *Mediaeval Stage*, II, 181–184; and Charles M. Gayley, *Plays of Our Forefathers* (New York, 1907), pp. 285–289.

5. Chambers, *Mediaeval Stage*, II, 183.

6. See Craik, *Tudor Interlude*, p. 1, who uses the term "interlude" in an elastic sense and emphasizes that it should not be limited to "farces or amusing disputations like Heywood's."

7. Gayley, *Forefathers*, p. 280.

8. For a definition of the morality, see W. Roy MacKenzie, *The English Moralities from the Point of View of Allegory* (Boston, 1914), p. 9.

9. Spivack, *Allegory of Evil*, pp. 251–303.

10. For the most recent and complete analysis of the origins of the morality, see Spivack, *Allegory of Evil*, pp. 60–95. Other useful accounts are to be found in Thompson, "English Moral Plays," pp. 293f; Salter, *Mediaeval Drama*, pp. 10–11; Hardin Craig, *English Religious Drama of the Middle Ages* (Oxford, 1955), pp. 338f; and G. R. Owst, *Literature and Pulpit in Medieval England* (Cambridge, Eng., 1933), pp. 471–547.

11. John T. Murray, *English Dramatic Companies, 1558–1642* (London, 1910), vol. 2.

12. Lawrence, *Stage Studies*, p. 44; and Wallace, *Evolution of English Drama*, pp. 58–59, 66, 119.

13. For the background of the minstrel bands, and the question of their descent from the Roman *mimus,* see W. Beare, *The Roman Stage* (London, 1950); Allardyce Nicoll, *Masks Mimes and Miracles* (London, 1931); and E. K. Chambers, *English Literature at the Close of the Middle Ages* (Oxford, 1945), pp. 1–2; cf. Philip S. Allen, "The Mediaeval Mimus," *MP,* 7: 329–344 (1909–1910), and 8: 1–44 (1910–1911).

14. Harold J. Child, "Secular Influences on the Early English Drama," *Cambridge History of English Literature* (Cambridge, Eng., 1907–), V, Chap. II; and Nicoll, *Masks Mimes and Miracles*, pp. 164–175.

15. John E. Wells, *A Manual of the Writings in Middle English, 1050–1400* (New Haven, 1926–), pp. 178–179, 546; and Gayley, *Forefathers*, p. 285.

16. Wickham, *Early English Stages,* pp. 187, 268–269.

17. John Northbrook, *A Treatise Against Dicing, Dancing, Plays, and Interludes,* ed. J. P. Collier (London, 1843), p. 98; and William J. Griffin, "Notes on Early Tudor Control of the Stage," *MLN,* 58: 50–54 (1943).

18. Louis B. Wright, "Notes on *Fulgens and Lucres*: New Light on the Interlude," *MLN,* 41: 97–100 (1926).

19. Iris G. Calderhead, "Morality Fragments from Norfolk," *MP,* 14: 1–9 (1916–1917); and E. K. Chambers, *The Elizabethan Stage* (Oxford, 1923), II, 356.

20. C. Walter Hodges, *The Globe Restored* (London, 1953), pp. 34f.

21. Wickham, *Early English Stages,* pp. 243–244.

22. Chambers, *Mediaeval Stage,* I, 69, and *Elizabethan Stage,* II, 78–83.

23. See Wilhelm Creizenach, *The English Drama in the Age of Shakespeare,* trans. from *Geschichte des Neueren Dramas* (London, 1916), p. 16.

24. Chambers, *Elizabethan Stage*, II, 78.

25. R. Willis, *Mount Tabor, or Private Exercises of a Penitent Sinner* (London, 1639), pp. 110–114.

26. W. K. Smart, "Some Notes on *Mankind*," *MP*, 14: 45–58, 293–313 (1916–1917).

27. Anon., *Mankind*, ed. John M. Manly in *Specimens of the Pre-Shaksperean Drama* (Boston, 1897), I, 315–352. The editions of the plays to which all subsequent scene, line, or page numbers refer may be found listed in "The Texts of the Plays." Throughout, in quoting from texts of early plays I have transliterated all letters, such as the thorn, that do not appear in the modern alphabet. As a further convenience for printing I have expanded some routine contractions of Tudor typography. Otherwise the texts are transcribed as they appear in the editions I have used. Accordingly, some quotations appear in original spelling and some in modern, and styles of punctuation vary with different editors.

28. Smart, "Notes on *Mankind*," *MP*, 14: 306–308; and F. J. Furnivall and Alfred W. Pollard, eds., *The Macro Plays* (London, 1904), pp. xi–xii.

29. For another epilogue addressed to "wursheppful souereyns" in a Norfolk morality, see Calderhead, "Morality Fragments," *MP*, 14: 7.

30. Sister Mary Philippa Coogan, *An Interpretation of the Moral Play, Mankind* (Washington, D. C., 1947), pp. 95–96.

31. Alois Brandl, ed., *Quellen des weltlichen Dramas in England vor Shakespeare* (Strassburg, 1898), p. xxxi.

32. Coogan, *Interpretation of Mankind*, pp. 111 and *passim;* and A. W. Reed, Review of Sister Mary Philippa Coogan's *An Interpretation of the Moral Play, Mankind, RES*, 24: 246–248 (1948).

33. Craig, *English Religious Drama*, pp. 350–351.

34. See, for example, Joseph Quincy Adams, ed., *Chief Pre-Shakespearean Dramas* (Boston, 1924), p. 304, note; cf. Furnivall and Pollard, eds., *Macro Plays*, p. xiii, who conjecture that the parts of Tityvillus and Mischief were doubled.

35. Smart, "Notes on *Mankind*," *MP*, 14: 308–309.

36. Walter K. Smart, "*Mankind* and the Mumming Plays," *MLN*, 32: 21–25 (1917).

37. Mabel M. Keiller, "Influence of *Piers Plowman* on the Macro Play of *Mankind*," *PMLA*, 26: 339–355 (1911); and W. Roy MacKenzie, "A New Source for *Mankind*," *PMLA*, 27: 98–105 (1912).

38. See M. C. Bradbrook, *The Growth and Structure of Elizabethan Comedy* (London, 1955), pp. 16–17.

39. Harbage, *Annals of English Drama*, p. 38; and Gertrude M. Sibley, *The Lost Plays and Masques: 1500–1642* (Ithaca, N. Y., 1933), pp. 44, 75.

40. For an acrid but inconclusive debate on the dating of this play, see Samuel A. Tannenbaum, "Comments on *The Marriage of Wit and Wisdom*," *PQ*, 9: 321–340 (1930); W. W. Greg, "The Date of *Wit and Wisdom*," *PQ*, 11: 410 (1932); and "Dr. Tannenbaum Replies," *PQ*, 12: 88–90 (1933).

41. Arthur Brown, "Two Notes on John Redford," *MLR*, 43: 508–510 (1948). For the connection of this play with the humanist program of education, see Pearl Hogrefe, *The Sir Thomas More Circle* (Urbana, Ill., 1959), pp. 314–322.

42. Robert Withington, "Experience, the Mother of Science," *PMLA*, 57: 592 (1942).

43. Craik, *Tudor Interlude*, pp. 15–16.

44. W. Carew Hazlitt, ed., *A Select Collection of Old English Plays*, 4th ed. (London, 1874–1876), II, 322.

45. For a conjecture that the play would have consisted of three acts, see Tannenbaum, *"The Marriage of Wit and Wisdom," PQ,* 9: 324, n. 4.

46. MacKenzie, *The English Moralities,* p. 173. Sidney Race has argued that the vulgarities and profanity of *The Marriage of Wit and Wisdom,* and also those of Redford's play, are the forgeries of John Payne Collier; an argument of no merit. " 'The Marriage of Wit and Wisdom,' " *N & Q,* 198: 18–20 (1953); and "The Moral Play of Wit and Science," *N & Q,* 198: 96–99 (1953).

47. For the similarity of this practical joking to Feste's treatment of Malvolio in *Twelfth Night,* see D. C. Boughner, "Vice, Braggart, and Falstaff," *Anglia,* 72: 35–61 (1954–1955).

48. Tannenbaum, *"The Marriage of Wit and Wisdom," PQ,* 9: 323.

49. *Ibid.,* p. 325.

CHAPTER III: AUSPICES FOR THE ÉLITE DRAMA

1. See Bradbrook, *Growth and Structure of Comedy,* p. 5; and Cunliffe, ed., *Early English Tragedies,* pp. lix–lxiii.

2. Wallace, *Evolution of English Drama,* p. 35.

3. Wickham, *Early English Stages,* pp. xliii, 179–253.

4. Leicester Bradner, "Stages and Stage Scenery in Court Drama before 1558," *RES,* 1: 447–448 (1925); and Craik, *Tudor Interlude,* pp. 13–14, 46–47.

5. Leicester Bradner, "A Test for Udall's Authorship," *MLN,* 42: 378–380 (1927); Wallace, *Evolution of English Drama,* p. 93; and Lily B. Campbell, *Divine Poetry and Drama in Sixteenth-Century England* (Cambridge, Eng., 1959), p. 189.

6. Leonard A. Magnus, ed., *Respublica* (London, 1905), pp. xiv–xvi. Baldwin, *Five-Act Structure,* p. 412, praises the structure of *Respublica* and of *Liberality and Prodigality* as being the most classically correct of the English morality plays.

7. See Craik, *Tudor Interlude,* pp. 27–28; and Lawrence, *Stage Studies,* pp. 45–46.

8. Harold N. Hillebrand, *The Child Actors* (Urbana, Ill., 1926), p. 59; and Chambers, *Elizabethan Stage,* II, 25.

9. Wallace, *Evolution of English Drama,* pp. 11, 37–40; J. G. Nichols, ed., *The Diary of Henry Machyn* (London, 1848), p. 206; and Hillebrand, *Child Actors,* pp. 47, 117.

10. C. C. Stopes, *William Hunnis and the Revels of the Chapel Royal* (Louvain, 1910), p. 14.

11. Chambers, *Elizabethan Stage,* II, 13, n. 2; and Hillebrand, *Child Actors,* pp. 16–17.

12. Harold N. Hillebrand, "Sebastian Westcote, Dramatist and Master of the Children of Paul's," *JEGP,* 14: 568–584 (1915); and Albert Feuillerat, *Documents Relating to the Office of Revels in the Time of Queen Elizabeth* (Louvain, 1908), p. 119.

13. Louis B. Wright, "Social Aspects of Some Belated Moralities," *Anglia,* 54: 107–148 (1930).

14. Campbell, *Divine Poetry and Drama,* pp. 198–201.

15. Cf. Craik, *Tudor Interlude,* pp. 30–31, who argues that because there are five verses in the epilogue the play may have been performed by the Perorator and five actors. Such doubling would be feasible; but it is equally possible that some of the lesser boy actors appeared on stage in the epilogue without speaking a verse.

16. Bradner, "Test for Udall's Authorship," *MLN,* 42: 378–380.

17. Craik, *Tudor Interlude,* p. 30; it seems highly conjectural to assume that this doubling would have taken place, as Craik has done.

18. Craik, *Tudor Interlude*, pp. 122–123, n. 24.

19. Stopes, *William Hunnis*, p. 268. Baldwin, *Five-Act Structure*, pp. 418–419, finds the structure somewhat more sequential and narrative than in the perfectly constructed classical play, but allows that "in a way" the structure reaches the epitasis in the third act.

20. Chambers, *Elizabethan Stage*, III, 25–27.

21. Campbell, *Divine Poetry and Drama*, pp. 207–210.

22. W. H. Williams, "The Date and Authorship of 'Jacke Jugeler,'" *MLR*, 7: 289–295 (1912).

23. Felix E. Schelling, *Elizabethan Drama, 1558–1642* (Boston, 1908), I, 85–87; and Wallace, *Evolution of English Drama*, pp. 96–97.

24. Chambers, *Mediaeval Stage*, I, 336–371. For examples of comically unpointed letters, in Latin, from the fifteenth and sixteenth centuries, see James R. Kreuzer, "Some Earlier Examples of the Rhetorical Device in *Ralph Roister Doister* (III. iv. 33f)," *RES*, 14: 321–323 (1938).

25. Thomas Legge, *Richardus Tertius*, ed. Barron Field (London, 1844), pp. 73–75.

26. Robert Burton, *Philosophaster*, trans. Paul Jordan-Smith (Stanford, Calif., 1931), p. 16.

27. Cunliffe, ed., *Early English Tragedies*, pp. lxxvi–lxxviii.

28. F. S. Boas and W. W. Greg, eds., *The Christmas Prince* (Oxford, 1923), pp. 104–106 and 132–134.

29. Campbell, *Divine Poetry and Drama*, pp. 167–168.

30. Hillebrand, *Child Actors*, pp. 18–19.

31. A. Wigfall Green, *The Inns of Court and Early English Drama* (New Haven, 1931), pp. 8–21.

32. The sustained decorum of *Gorboduc* was sufficient to win rare praise from Alexander Pope for a "propriety in sentiments, a dignity in the sentences, an unaffected perspicuity of style . . . in a word, that chastity, correctness, and gravity of style which are so essential to tragedy." Quoted in Cunliffe, ed., *Early English Tragedies*, p. lxxxi.

33. Nichols, ed., *Diary of Henry Machyn*, p. 275; quoted in Chambers, *Elizabethan Stage*, III, 457.

34. Chambers, *Elizabethan Stage*, IV, 273, document xxxi.

35. Cunliffe, ed., *Early English Tragedies*, pp. lxxxiii–lxxxvi.

36. Evangelia H. Waller, "A Possible Interpretation of *The Misfortunes of Arthur*," *JEGP*, 24: 219–245 (1925); Gertrude Reese, "Political Import of *The Misfortunes of Arthur*," *RES*, 21: 81–91 (1945); William A. Armstrong, "The Topicality of 'The Misfortunes of Arthur,'" *N & Q*, n.s., 2: 371–373 (1955), and "Elizabethan Themes in *The Misfortunes of Arthur*," *RES*, n.s., 7: 238–249 (1956).

37. T. W. Craik, "The True Source of John Heywood's 'Johan Johan,'" *MLR*, 45: 289–295 (1950); cf. Ian C. Maxwell, *French Farce and John Heywood* (Melbourne, 1946), pp. 56–69.

38. A. W. Reed, *Early Tudor Drama* (London, 1926), p. 124.

39. F. S. Boas, "Early English Comedy," *Cambridge History of English Literature*, V, 94.

40. Southern, *Medieval Theatre*, p. 98; and Wickham, *Early English Stages*, p. 154, figure 10.

41. Joseph Quincy Adams, Jr., "John Heywood's *The Play of the Weather*," *MLN*, 22: 262 (1907); and Kenneth W. Cameron, *John Heywood's "Play of the Weather"* (Raleigh, N. C., 1941), pp. 36–59.

42. Wickham, *Early English Stages,* pp. 204–205.

43. Hillebrand, *Child Actors,* pp. 56–57, 62–63.

44. Harbage, *Annals of English Drama,* pp. 26–27.

45. R. J. Schoeck, "Satire of Wolsey in Heywood's 'Play of Love,'" *N & Q,* 196: 112–114 (1951); Kenneth W. Cameron, *The Background of John Heywood's "Witty and Witless"* (Raleigh, N. C., 1941); and Karl Young, "The Influence of French Farce upon the Plays of John Heywood," *MP,* 2: 109–116 (1904–1905).

46. Reed, *Early Tudor Drama,* pp. 106–112; and Esther C. Dunn, "John Rastell and 'Gentleness and Nobility,'" *MLR,* 12: 266–278 (1917). Cf. C. F. Tucker Brooke, "'Gentleness and Nobility'; The Authorship and Source," *MLR,* 6: 458–461 (1911); and Kenneth W. Cameron, *Authorship and Sources of "Gentleness and Nobility"* (Raleigh, N. C., 1941), pp. 59–89.

47. F. N. Robinson, ed., *The Works of Geoffrey Chaucer,* 2nd ed. (Cambridge, Mass., 1957), pp. 704, 861–862.

48. Robinson, ed., *Chaucer,* "Wife of Bath's Tale," l. 1162.

49. Cameron, *Gentleness and Nobility,* p. 30.

50. F. S. Boas and A. W. Reed, eds., *Fulgens & Lucres* (London, 1926), pp. xix–xx.

51. Eugene M. Waith, *"Controversia* in the English Drama: Medwall and Massinger," *PMLA,* 68: 286–303 (1953).

52. Claude E. Jones, "Notes on *Fulgens and Lucres," MLN,* 50: 508–509 (1935); cf. A. W. Reed, "Sixt Birck and Henry Medwall, *De Vera Nobilitate," RES,* 2: 411–415 (1926), who assumes that boys took the parts of "A" and "B."

53. Reed, *Early Tudor Drama,* pp. 100–101; W. Roy MacKenzie, "A Source for Medwall's *Nature," PMLA,* 29: 189–199 (1914); and Hogrefe, *The More Circle,* pp. 259–260.

54. Harbage, *Annals of English Drama,* pp. 24–25. For what is known of the stage, see Reed, *Early Tudor Drama,* pp. 230–233.

55. Sir Thomas More, *Utopia,* trans. Ralph Robinson, Everyman's Library (London, 1951), pp. 23–24.

56. M. E. Borish, "Source and Intention of *The Four Elements," SP,* 35: 149–163 (1938); Elizabeth M. Nugent, "Sources of John Rastell's *The Nature of the Four Elements," PMLA,* 57: 74–88 (1942); George B. Parks, "Rastell and Waldseemüller's Map," *PMLA,* 58: 572–574 (1943); Johnstone Parr, "More Sources of Rastell's *Interlude of the Four Elements," PMLA,* 60: 48–58 (1945); and Hogrefe, *The More Circle,* pp. 268–274.

57. Reed, *Early Tudor Drama,* pp. 11f and 187–201.

58. See Wallace, *Evolution of English Drama,* p. 55.

59. See C. R. Baskervill, "John Rastell's Dramatic Activities," *MP,* 13: 557–560 (1915–1916).

Chapter IV: The Popular Canon

1. Brooke, *Tudor Drama,* p. 57.

2. Furnivall and Pollard, eds., *Macro Plays,* p. 76.

3. Southern, *Medieval Theatre,* pp. 20–21; and W. K. Smart, *"The Castle of Perseverance:* Place, Date, and a Source," *Manly Anniversary Studies* (Chicago, 1923), pp. 42–53.

4. Southern, *Medieval Theatre,* pp. 28–30.

5. Wickham, *Early English Stages,* pp. 302–305.

6. Chambers, *Close of the Middle Ages,* p. 45.

7. Thomas Sharp, *A Dissertation on the Pageants or Dramatic Mysteries Anciently Performed at Coventry* (Coventry, 1825), p. 38. Although the performance here described took place in 1584, its traditional character suggests long-established method.

8. Wickham, *Early English Stages,* pp. 154–155.

9. Walter K. Smart, *Some English and Latin Sources and Parallels for the Morality of Wisdom* (Menasha, Wis., 1912), pp. 78–79, 87–89; Willard Farnham, *The Medieval Heritage of Elizabethan Tragedy* (Berkeley, Calif., 1936), pp. 196–197; and Rev. John J. Molloy, *A Theological Interpretation of the Moral Play, Wisdom, Who Is Christ* (Washington, D. C., 1952), p. xiii and App. II, pp. 198–215.

10. See below, Chapter VIII.

11. Both Bale and Skelton may actually have had close contact with a member of the humanist circle: Bale was perhaps arrested on the same heresy charge in 1536 as was Rastell, and Skelton's *Magnificence* is assigned to Rastell's press. See Honor McCusker, *John Bale, Dramatist and Antiquary* (Bryn Mawr, Pa., 1942), pp. 5–6; and Reed, *Early Tudor Drama,* p. 106; cf. Ian A. Gordon, *John Skelton, Poet Laureate* (Melbourne, 1943), p. 136.

12. J. H. P. Pafford and W. W. Greg, eds., *King Johan* (London, 1931), p. xxii; and Jesse W. Harris, *John Bale* (Urbana, Ill., 1940), pp. 100–105.

13. McCusker, *John Bale,* pp. 14, 75–76; Murray, *English Dramatic Companies,* II, 36; and W. Creizenach, "Miracle-Plays and Moralities," *Cambridge History of English Literature,* V, 36–60.

14. Edwin S. Miller, "The Roman Rite in Bale's *King John,*" *PMLA,* 64: 802–822 (1949).

15. Robert L. Ramsay, ed., *Magnificence* (London, 1906), pp. xlviii–l.

16. Craik, *Tudor Interlude,* p. 128, n. 45.

17. Ramsay, ed., *Magnificence,* pp. xlv–xlvi.

18. See Lawrence, *Stage Studies,* pp. 47–48.

19. Cf. T. W. Craik, "The Political Interpretation of Two Tudor Interludes: *Temperance and Humility* and *Wealth and Health,*" *RES,* n.s., 4: 98–108 (1953), who concludes from the complimentary address to Mary that the play was written for acting at court. Although this play may have been performed for the court as well as for other audiences, such a compliment for the monarch was conventional in popular performances of the time.

20. W. W. Greg, ed., *Henslowe's Diary* (London, 1904–1908), I, 131 and II, 228 reveals that a "Like unto Like" was performed by Pembroke's Men at the Rose on October 28, 1600, as an old play. Greg thinks it may be identified with Fulwell's play.

21. Wright, "Social Aspects of Moralities," *Anglia,* 54: 124–127.

22. Louis B. Wright, "Juggling Tricks and Conjury on the English Stage before 1642," *MP,* 24: 269–284 (1926–1927); and Craik, *Tudor Interlude,* p. 120, n. 14.

23. Brooke, *Tudor Drama,* pp. 110–111.

24. McCusker, *John Bale,* pp. 77–78; and Southern, *Medieval Theatre,* p. 100.

25. Wright, "Social Aspects of Moralities," *Anglia,* 54: 114, n. 1; and Spivack, *Allegory of Evil,* p. 236, and p. 474, n. 9.

26. Celesta Wine, "Nathaniel Woodes, Author of the Morality Play *The Conflict of Conscience,*" *RES,* 15: 458–463 (1939).

27. See above under discussion of *New Custom.* On the structure of *Conflict of Conscience* see Baldwin, *Five-Act Structure,* pp. 419–423, who concludes that classical structure is only clumsily approximated in Woodes's play, and conjectures therefore that the act divisions are the addition of the publisher.

28. Frederick I. Carpenter, ed., *The Life and Repentaunce of Marie Magdalene* (Chicago, 1902), pp. xiv–xv.

29. Craik, *Tudor Interlude*, p. 30; cf. Campbell, *Divine Poetry and Drama,* pp. 215–216, who conjectures that the play was intended primarily for the university community although she allows that it may have been acted before paying audiences elsewhere.

30. See Craik, *Tudor Interlude,* p. 35.

31. Thompson, "English Moral Plays," p. 346; and Campbell, *Divine Poetry and Drama,* pp. 210–211.

32. Of the thirty-eight roles thus distributed, two are actually identical: Lady and Queen, assigned to the first boy. However, the Queen's waiting-maid and Marian-May-be-Good, who appear in the play, do not figure into the casting chart. Hence it seems likely that the six men and two boys actually presented thirty-nine roles.

33. Chambers, *Elizabethan Stage,* II, 85–89; and Murray, *English Dramatic Companies,* I, 26–42.

34. William A. Armstrong, "The Authorship and Political Meaning of *Cambises,*" *English Studies,* 36: 289–299 (1955).

35. Cf. Cunliffe, ed., *Early English Tragedies,* p. lxx, who follows Feuillerat and Collier in supposing that "such a crude production could never have been performed before any audience but one of the lowest description."

36. James E. Phillips, "A Revaluation of *Horestes* (1567)," *HLQ,* 18: 227–244 (1954–1955).

37. Chambers, *Elizabethan Stage,* II, 91–92; and Murray, *English Dramatic Companies,* I, 297–298.

38. W. W. Greg, "John Phillip — Notes for a Bibliography," *The Library,* 3rd ser., 1: 302–328, 396–423 (1910).

39. R. B. McKerrow and W. W. Greg, eds., *Patient Grissell* (London, 1909), pp. xiii–xiv.

40. Craik, *Tudor Interlude,* p. 125, n. 24 (vii).

41. Louis B. Wright, "A Political Reflection in Phillip's *Patient Grissell,*" *RES,* 4: 424–428 (1928).

42. Craik, *Tudor Interlude,* p. 17.

43. Campbell, *Divine Poetry and Drama,* p. 221.

44. Marvin T. Herrick, "Susanna and the Elders in Sixteenth-Century Drama," *Studies in Honor of T. W. Baldwin,* ed. Don Cameron Allen (Urbana, Ill., 1958), pp. 131–132; and Campbell, *Divine Poetry and Drama,* pp. 219–222.

45. R. Warwick Bond, *Early Plays from the Italian* (Oxford, 1911), pp. xci f; and Campbell, *Divine Poetry and Drama,* p. 202.

46. G. L. Kittredge, "The 'Misogonus' and Laurence Johnson," *JEGP,* 3: 335–341 (1900–1901). G. C. Moore-Smith, "Misogonus," *London Times Literary Supplement* (July 10, 1930), p. 576, calls *Misogonus* a Cambridge play but ascribes it to Anthony Rudd. See also Samuel A. Tannenbaum, "A Note on *Misogonus,*" *MLN,* 45: 308–310 (1930).

CHAPTER V: "FOUR MEN AND A BOY"

1. See, for example, Symonds, *Shakspere's Predecessors,* pp. 177–181; Cunliffe, ed., *Early English Tragedies,* p. lxv.

2. Gayley, *Forefathers,* pp. 289–290.

3. These figures are derived from a variety of sources, and hence are not per-

fectly consistent. Different editions employ differing policies as to the inclusion of stage directions in the line numberings. Fortunately this drama contains little prose, which always constitutes a problem for line counting. All too many editions, including Dodsley's *Old English Plays*, are unnumbered, in which case the totals are my own. Nevertheless the margin of error is reasonably small. The figures have been checked against those of B. J. Whiting, *Proverbs in the Earlier English Drama* (Cambridge, Mass., 1938), and correspond with reasonable closeness throughout. A comparison with the figures in J. E. Bernard, Jr., *The Prosody of the Tudor Interlude* (New Haven, 1939), indicates more variation, owing chiefly to the fact that Bernard is concerned with numbers of metrical lines. In the notable differences his totals are as follows: *Juventus* 1234, *Three Estates* 4570, *Respublica* 936, *Jacob and Esau* 1702, *Wit and Wisdom* 783, *Mary Magdalen* 2116, *Darius* 1567, *Like Will to Like* 1169, *Tide Tarrieth* 1811, *Trial of Treasure* 1011, *Horestes* 1073, and *Common Conditions* 1872.

4. From evidence external to the plays themselves, C. R. Baskervill, *The Elizabethan Jig* (Chicago, 1929), p. 44, cites a company of six or seven players, "Sir Francis Lake's Men," who were touring in the north of England in 1556.

5. Symonds, *Shakspere's Predecessors*, p. 177. See also Brooke, *Tudor Drama*, p. 58: "The later moralities were usually performed by companies of four or five men and a boy,— the boy, of course, taking women's parts."

6. McCusker, *John Bale*, p. 76.

7. Craik, *Tudor Interlude*, pp. 34–35.

8. Cf. Lawrence, *Stage Studies*, p. 73, who concludes (erroneously, I believe) that doubling involving a mixing of the sexes was rare in Elizabethan drama, and was usually done only by adult actors taking on elderly female roles. He cites as a rare exception the late play *The Wild Goose Chase*, performed at Blackfriars in 1631, in which John Honeyman doubled the parts of Mariana the courtesan and the Young Factor. In the plays here cited, Wantonness and Abominable Living are obviously courtesans doubled by adult actors.

9. Coogan, *Interpretation of Mankind*, p. 1, n. 4.

10. See W. W. Greg, Review of *The Elizabethan Stage*, by E. K. Chambers, *RES*, 1: 101–102, (1925), and Lawrence, *Stage Studies*, pp. 73–74, concerning the unreliable casting list by "Dramaticus" for *The Shoemakers' Holiday*, which assigns four female parts to grown men.

11. Salter, *Mediaeval Drama*, p. 48; Wickham, *Early English Stages*, pp. 271–272; and Nicoll, *Masks Mimes and Miracles*, p. 192.

12. Lawrence, *Stage Studies*, p. 54.

13. For a discussion of the "ruffler," see Boughner, "Vice, Braggart, and Falstaff," *Anglia*, 72: 50–51.

Chapter VI: The Tradition of Versatility

1. T. W. Baldwin, *The Organization and Personnel of the Shakespearean Company* (Princeton, 1927).

2. For a discussion of this phenomenon in *Enough Is as Good as a Feast*, see Craik, *Tudor Interlude*, pp. 40–41.

3. Sharp, *Dissertation on the Pageants at Coventry*, p. 38. Cited in Craik, *Tudor Interlude*, p. 131, n. 24.

4. Lawrence, *Stage Studies*, pp. 61–62.

5. Cf. Craik, *Tudor Interlude*, p. 36, who conjectures that the part of Idumeus did not need to be halved, and that accordingly the division of the parts was the work of the publisher.

6. See Craik, *Tudor Interlude*, pp. 41–42.

7. C. J. Sisson, "Bibliographical Aspects of Some Stuart Dramatic Manuscripts," *RES*, 1:427–429 (1925); and Lawrence, *Stage Studies*, pp. 61–62.

8. Since the subject of stage dress has been discussed recently by Craik, *Tudor Interlude*, pp. 49–92, this investigation will attempt simply to relate costuming to the problems of interval and versatility of costume change.

9. See also Bottom's speech to the mechanics in *Midsummer Night's Dream*, IV, ii: "Get your apparel together, good strings to your beards, new ribbands to your pumps."

10. Lawrence, *Stage Studies*, pp. 55–56.

11. Craik, *Tudor Interlude*, p. 49.

12. Wickham, *Early English Stages*, pp. 103–111; and Stopes, *William Hunnis*, pp. 38–39.

13. Albert Feuillerat, "An Unknown Protestant Morality Play," *MLR*, 9: 94–96 (1914).

14. Lawrence, *Stage Studies*, p. 55.

15. See Craik, *Tudor Interlude*, pp. 33–34.

16. See Baskervill, *Elizabethan Jig*, pp. 79–80.

17. C. R. Baskervill, V. B. Heltzel, and A. H. Nethercot, eds., *Elizabethan and Stuart Plays* (New York, 1934), p. 168, n. 5.

18. Brooke, *Tudor Drama*, p. 57.

CHAPTER VII: DOUBLING PATTERNS IN THE 1580'S AND 1590'S

1. W. W. Greg, "The Evidence of Theatrical Plots for the History of the Elizabethan Stage," *RES*, 1: 257–274 (1925).

2. W. W. Greg, ed., *Dramatic Documents from the Elizabethan Playhouses* (Oxford, 1931). Volume I contains commentary, volume II reproductions and transcripts.

3. W. W. Greg, *Two Elizabethan Stage Abridgements: The Battle of Alcazar & Orlando Furioso* (London, 1922).

4. These figures are based upon Greg's tabulations of the plots, to be found on the charts provided with his *Dramatic Documents*, volume II (loose-leaf, in an envelope flap attached to the inside back cover); and on the section entitled "Actor Lists" in volume I, 43–69, a collection of relevant facts concerning the actors whose names appear in the plots. I have relied on Greg's authority in deciding which actors were sharers, which hired men, and which boys (spellings and abbreviations are as they appear on the charts).

In *2 Seven Deadly Sins* the following actors appear to be sharers: Brian, Phillipps, Pope, R. Burbadg, Harry [Condell?], W. Sly, and the two actors portraying Henry VI and Lydgate. Hired men include R. Cowley, John Duke, Ro. Pallant, John Sincler, Kit, Tho. Goodale, J. Holland, and Vincent. The seven Deadly Sins and Mercury are unassigned and may have been played by unnamed "supers." Boys: T. Belt, Saunder, Nick, Ro. Go., Ned, and Will.

In *Frederick and Basilia* the sharers include [Edward] Allen, [Edward] Jubie, Dunstann, Martyn [Slaughter], and Tho. Towne. Hired men: Richard Allen, Rob. Ledbeter, Ed. Sutton, Charles [Massey], Sam [Rowley], Tho. Hunt, and black Dick. Boys: Pigg, Dick (Dutton's boy), Will, and Griffin. Additional attendants and gatherers are called for.

In *Battle of Alcazar* the following appear to be sharers: Ed. Allen, Doughton, Towne, [Edward] Jubie, Shaa, Jones, Charles [Massey], and Sam [Rowley]. Massey and Rowley appear on the sharer list of Mar. 1598 but not that of Oct. 1597; hence they are referred to as sharers for this play, but hired men in *Frederick and Basilia*. The important role of Sebastian is unassigned and would probably require another sharer, perhaps John Singer or William Birde. In addition, H. Jeffes and Anthony Jeffes were sharers evidently from 1597 to 1602, although neither has the prefix "Mr." in the plots. Hired men: Rich. Allen and Hunt (both referred to as "Mr." but without other evidence of their having been sharers), W. Kendall, W. Cartwright, Robin Taylor, George Somersett, Tho. Drom. Boys: Dick Jubie, James, Tom (?) Parsons, Dab, Harry, Allen's boy, Towne's boy, and the actor of Calipolis.

In *1 Tamar Cam* the sharers are Allen, Denygten, Bourne [Birde], Towne, Singer, Sam [Rowley], Charles [Massey], [Edward] Jubie, H. Jeffes, A. Jeffes. Hired men: Dick Jubie, W. Cartwright, Thom. Marbeck, W. Parr, George, and Tho. Parsons. Boys: Jack Grigorie, Deyngten's Will, James, Gils his boy, and the actors of Palmeda and Tarmia. A final procession calls for eight "supers."

5. The gatherers were often numerous, and had a reputation for dishonesty. Some were women. See Greg, ed., *Dramatic Documents*, I, 55.

6. Cf. Lawrence, *Stage Studies*, p. 60, who postulates a more ironclad distinction between the principal players and the hired men, allowing for no doubling of primary roles. Although he correctly points out that such doubling in *2 Seven Deadly Sins* takes place only in separate portions of a composite play (actually three plays in one), his estimate does not apply as well to *1 Tamar Cam* or *Alcazar*.

7. Baldwin, *Organization and Personnel*, p. 184.

8. *Ibid.*, p. 197.

9. *Ibid.*, pp. 178–179.

10. *Ibid.*, p. 246 and charts facing p. 229.

11. *Ibid.*, p. 199.

12. *Ibid.*, p. 204.

13. More than one book will be required to correct the misunderstandings brought about by Baldwin's zealous but indiscreet surmises. The effort will be Herculean, because of the erudition and hard work that he gave to his scholarship. Only when his errors have been clarified will his real contributions earn proper acknowledgment.

14. The versatility of the actor was proverbial in the early seventeenth century. Donald Lupton, in *London and the Countrey carbonadoed* (1632), observes that "a player often changes: now he acts a monarch, to-morrow a beggar; now a soldier, next a tailor." Sir Thomas Overbury in his *Characters* (1614-1616) similarly employs the familiar metaphor: "What [the actor] doth feignedly, that do others essentially: this day one plays a monarch, the next a private person. Here one acts a tyrant, on the morrow an exile: a parasite this man to-night, to-morrow a precisian, and so of divers others." Both quoted in John Dover Wilson, ed., *Life in Shakespeare's England*, 2nd ed. (Cambridge, Eng., 1913), pp. 163 and 174.

15. Edwin Nungezer, *A Dictionary of Actors* (New Haven, 1929); and Chambers, *Elizabethan Stage*, II, 306–310.

16. Cf. Baldwin, *Organization and Personnel,* p. 203, who concludes of Burbage, "Of pure comedy he had almost none." Baldwin is not consistent on the question of the actors' ability to shift from comic to serious roles. At times he segregates these functions categorically: "Cowley then evidently belongs to the comic crew, and consequently does not appear in all the plays" (p. 254). Again, he says that Shakespeare as an actor must have avoided comic parts since his "known" (*sic*) roles are all serious (p. 266). On the other hand, as quoted earlier, he gives to Thomas Pope the roles of Sir Toby Belch and Aaron, Falstaff and Shylock.

17. Even the clown was free to play other roles: in 2 *Seven Deadly Sins,* for example, the comedian Pope plays Arbactus and leaves Will Fool to John Duke. There is no reason to suppose Arbactus a comic part. See Greg, ed., *Dramatic Documents,* I, 63.

18. For exceptions see previous chapter, note 7.

19. Lawrence, *Stage Studies,* p. 76.

20. W. W. Greg, ed., *Antonio and Mellida & Antonio's Revenge* (London, 1921), Induction, ll. 26–29; discussed in Lawrence, *Stage Studies,* p. 63.

CHAPTER VIII: THE ORIGINS OF POPULAR DRAMATIC STRUCTURE

1. See Lawrence, *Stage Studies,* p. 46.

2. Harold C. Gardiner, S.J., *Mysteries' End* (New Haven, 1946).

3. Wickham, *Early English Stages, passim;* George R. Kernodle, *From Art to Theatre* (Chicago, 1944), pp. 52–108; Alice S. Venezky, *Pageantry on the Shakespearean Stage* (New York, 1951); and Nicoll, *Masks Mimes and Miracles,* pp. 175–213.

4. Ramsay, ed., *Magnificence,* p. cxxxii.

5. Cf. Lawrence, *Stage Studies,* p. 52, who feels that the authors of these early plays with limited casts were wise to confine themselves to a feasible scope. He gives them too much credit for what was historically a mere expediency.

6. See Thompson, "English Moral Plays," p. 393.

7. For an account of the origins of the Psychomachia, and its development in the medieval cycle plays, the most recent and thorough treatment is to be found in Spivack, *Allegory of Evil,* pp. 71–95.

8. See A. P. Rossiter, *English Drama from Early Times to the Elizabethans* (London, 1950), p. 95.

9. Johan Huizinga, *The Waning of the Middle Ages* (London, 1924), pp. 1–45.

10. Southern, *Medieval Theatre,* pp. 149–151.

11. See Morris L. Arnold, *The Soliloquies of Shakespeare* (New York, 1911), pp. 97–100.

12. Spivack, *Allegory of Evil,* has shown the metaphoric significance of the Vice's generic nature. "The metaphorical plot of intrigue required a significant single intriguer, and its homiletic aim required that he should be conspicuous as the *root* of all the evils represented" (p. 147). Whereas Spivack's study emphasizes the growth of an idea, the concern here is with the progress of a theatrical organization and its resulting structure. The two are compatible; organization and idea continually reinforced one another in moral drama.

13. Henry N. MacCracken, "A Source of *Mundus et Infans,*" *PMLA,* 23: 486–496 (1908); and F. J. Furnivall, ed., *Hymns to the Virgin and Christ* (London, 1867), pp. 58–78.

14. Smart, *Sources and Parallels for Wisdom*, p. 6; see also Rossiter, *English Drama*, p. 99.

15. Molloy, *Theological Interpretation of Wisdom*, p. x and Appendix I, pp. 193–197; Smart, *Sources and Parallels for Wisdom*, pp. 7–8; and Joseph C. Green, *The Medieval Morality of Wisdom Who Is Christ: A Study in Origins* (Nashville, Tenn., 1938), p. ix. Cf. Chambers, *Close of the Middle Ages*, p. 61, whose charge of imprecision of thought in *Wisdom* led to Molloy's convincing defense.

16. Craig, *English Religious Drama*, pp. 334–335, 338.

CHAPTER IX: THE PIONEERING CONTRIBUTIONS OF BALE AND SKELTON

1. Anna J. Mill, "The Influence of the Continental Drama on Lyndsay's 'Satyre of the Thrie Estaitis,'" *MLR*, 25: 425–442 (1930); Anna J. Mill, "Representations of Lyndsay's *Satyre of the Thrie Estaitis*," *PMLA*, 47: 636–651 (1932); and Edwin S. Miller, "The Christening in *The Three Estates*," *MLN*, 60: 42–44 (1945).

2. See Reed, *Early Tudor Drama*, p. 100.

3. Cf. McCusker, *John Bale*, p. 96, who minimizes the significance of Bale's influence on the later moralities. Her appraisal does not take structural development into account.

4. Cf. Lawrence, *Stage Studies*, p. 52, who doubts erroneously that the play could be performed by five actors. Craik, *Tudor Interlude*, p. 32, demonstrates that it could be easily accomplished, allowing for a short break before Act V while the player of Vindicta Dei changes for Deus Pater. Even Craik misses the point that Deus Pater and Vindicta Dei are really the same divine Person. There is no indication that He leaves the stage between Acts IV and V; on the contrary, He opens Act V by referring to His own prior action as Vindicta Dei: "As ye haue seane here, how I haue strycken with fyre / The pestylent vyce, of Infydelyte" (ll. 1894–1895).

5. Baldwin, *Five-Act Structure*, notes that Bale's play does not conform to the classical ideal. In dismissing the play's form as "simply the structure of the sermon" (p. 347), however, Baldwin betrays his indifference to a native conception of structure. Elsewhere he comments of the popular drama, "Since these plays were not written properly as either comedies or tragedies, but as early moral plays, we ought not to expect too much of them structurally" (p. 356).

6. Ramsay, ed., *Magnificence*, p. xlviii.

7. *Ibid.,* p. xlviii.

8. *Ibid.,* pp. xxvi-xxviii.

9. *Ibid.,* p. xlviii.

10. *Ibid.,* p. l.

11. Smart, "Notes on *Mankind*," *MP*, 14: 119–120.

CHAPTER X: THE INTERMEDIATE MORALITY: REPETITION, EXPANSION, AND ELABORATION

1. See, for example, Alfred W. Pollard, ed., *English Miracle Plays, Moralities and Interludes*, 8th ed. (Oxford, 1927), p. liii.

2. R. B. McKerrow, ed., *A Newe Interlude of Impacyente Pouerte* (Louvain, 1911), pp. x-xiv.

3. McKerrow, ed., *Impacyente Pouerte*, pp. x-xiv; and Wright, "Social Aspects of Moralities," *Anglia*, 54: 111.

Chapter XI: Dual Protagonists and a Formula for Homiletic Tragedy

1. See W. Creizenach, "Miracle-Plays and Moralities," *Cambridge History of English Literature*, V, 60; and Craik, *Tudor Interlude*, p. 40. For date of the play see E. Beatrice Daw, "Two Notes on *The Trial of Treasure*," *MP*, 15: 53–55 (1917–1918). On authorship see Leslie M. Oliver, "William Wager and *The Trial of Treasure*," *HLQ*, 9: 419–429 (1945–1946).

2. See Craik, *Tudor Interlude*, p. 38.

3. See H. H. Adams, *English Domestic or Homiletic Tragedy, 1575 to 1642* (New York, 1943), pp. 1–5.

4. Robinson, ed., *Chaucer*, "Prologue to the Monk's Tale," ll. 1973–1977.

5. Farnham, *Medieval Heritage*, pp. 173–178, 193–194.

6. This debate on the proper uses of money seemingly owes much to John Heywood's *Play of Love*; see Thompson, "English Moral Plays," p. 346.

7. See Craik, *Tudor Interlude*, pp. 36–37.

Chapter XII: The Transition to Chronicle

1. Many lost plays surviving only in title may also have been hybrid plays; see Spivack, *Allegory of Evil*, pp. 253–254.

2. See Northbrook, *Treatise against Plays*, p. 92.

3. Campbell, *Divine Poetry and Drama, passim,* argues that the new form of Biblical play at this time was intended to rival and counteract the pagan influence of the classics.

4. The actual casting is not worked out for *Mary Magdalen*. The title page states merely that "Foure may easely play this Enterlude." Carpenter, ed., *Marie Magdalene*, pp. xiv-xv, has demonstrated that "foure" is probably a misprint for five.

5. Cf. Campbell, *Divine Poetry and Drama*, pp. 217–218, who finds this stage direction ambiguous.

6. See Brandl, ed., *Quellen*, pp. lxvi-lxviii; and Ola Winslow, *Low Comedy as a Structural Element in English Drama from the Beginnings to 1642* (Menasha, Wis., 1926), p. 62.

7. The advanced degree of secularization in *Darius* may be partly owing to the fact that the play was probably favored with a reception at court in addition to its popular audience (see Chapter IV, above). Its element of debate and reflections on governmental policy would be of interest to the monarchy, despite the play's manifest lack of literary polish. Most of the hybrid chronicles here discussed — notably *Horestes* and *Cambises* — were intended for London and courtly performances as well as the provinces. It was in this vital center of intellectual activity that advances in structure moved most swiftly.

8. Spivack, *Allegory of Evil*, pp. 259–262. For a discussion of Equity as a secular development from ideas of divine and civil justice in older plays like *Perseverance* and *Respublica*, see J. Wilson McCutchan, "Justice and Equity in the English Morality Play," *JHI*, 19: 405–410 (1958).

9. A third Biblical chronicle, *Godly Queen Hester*, reveals hybrid secularization at work in the boys' courtly drama at a considerably earlier date (1525-1529). The moral personifications Pride, Adulation, and Ambition appear in a dramatically separate action, as in *King Darius*. They never meet the concrete Biblical per-

sonages nor further the action of the Biblical plot; instead, they serve as choric figures to comment upon Chancellor Aman's alarming rise to power. Since Aman is probably a satiric portrait of Wolsey, their function closely parallels that of the personifications in *King Darius*, bringing home to a Reformation audience the political significance of Scriptural incident. *Hester* is nevertheless a boys' play, and its doubling pattern is so unlike that of troupe drama that its segregation of Biblical episode and allegory does not mark a contribution to structural formula for the popular theater. Concerning the satire of Wolsey, see Madeleine H. Dodds, "Early Political Plays," *The Library*, 3rd ser., 4: 393–408 (1913). For a much earlier political use of the Book of Esther in the drama, see Wickham, *Early English Stages*, pp. 70–71. In the pageant of 1392 commemorating Richard II's reconciliation with the City of London, Esther's story was allegorized into a pointed moral for Richard and his Queen.

10. Farnham, *Medieval Heritage*, p. 259.

11. Cunliffe, ed., *Early English Tragedies*, p. lxx.

12. On the justification of Horestes' revenge, see E. B. de Chickera, "Horestes' Revenge — Another Interpretation," *N & Q*, n.s., 6: 190 (1959).

13. Spivack, *Allegory of Evil*, pp. 273–274.

14. Spivack, *Allegory of Evil*, pp. 264, 278.

15. See Wright, "Social Aspects of Moralities," *Anglia*, 54: 113.

16. Farnham, *Medieval Heritage*, p. 267. Taverner, a Cambridge M. A., translated and adapted the materials of the Cambises story from Herodotus in a collection of incidents concerning several famous men of the classical past. The work was popular in the 1550's and 1560's.

17. Ribner, *English History Play*, pp. 58–59.

18. Armstrong, "Political Meaning of *Cambises*," *English Studies*, 36: 289–299.

19. See for example MacKenzie, *English Moralities*, p. 249, who underestimates the importance of the homiletic debts in *Cambises*.

20. Spivack, *Allegory of Evil*, pp. 309–310.

21. See Ribner, *English History Play*, p. 58.

Chapter XIII: The Transition to Romance

1. See C. R. Baskervill, "Some Evidence for Early Romantic Plays in England," *MP*, 14: 229–251, 467–512 (1916–1917); and C. F. Tucker Brooke, "On the Source of *Common Conditions*," *MLN*, 31: 474–478 (1916).

2. Stephen Gosson, *Plays Confuted in Five Actions* (London, n.d. [1582], imprinted for Thomas Gosson), "The 2. Action," sig. C₆ *recto;* available in W. Carew Hazlitt, ed., *The English Drama and Stage under the Tudor and Stuart Princes, 1543–1664* (London, 1869), p. 181.

3. Harbage, *Annals of English Drama*, pp. 40–45.

4. G. L. Kittredge, "Notes on Elizabethan Plays," *JEGP*, 2: 8–9 (1898–1899).

5. Spivack, *Allegory of Evil*, pp. 291–292.

Chapter XIV: *Tamburlaine the Great*

1. F. P. Wilson, *Marlowe and the Early Shakespeare* (Oxford, 1953), p. 26.

2. Wilson, *Marlowe and Shakespeare*, p. 28.

3. Wilson, *Marlowe and Shakespeare*, pp. 70–75; and W. W. Greg, ed., *Marlowe's Doctor Faustus: 1604–1616: Parallel Texts* (Oxford, 1950), pp. 15f.

4. John Bakeless, *The Tragicall History of Christopher Marlowe* (Cambridge, Mass., 1942), I, 190.

5. Bakeless, *Tragicall History*, I, 204–205.

6. C. H. Herford and A. Wagner, "The Sources of Marlowe's 'Tamburlaine,'" *The Academy: A Weekly Review of Literature, Science, and Art*, 24: 265–266 (1883).

7. Bakeless, *Tragicall History*, I, 214–238.

8. The tripartite construction of Part I has been noted by Harry Levin, *The Overreacher: A Study of Christopher Marlowe* (Cambridge, Mass., 1952), pp. 34–35. The Persian victory is "a little drama in itself, the substance of the first and second acts," followed by the history of Bajazeth in Act III and of the Arabian campaign in Acts IV and V.

9. Lawrence, *Stage Studies*, pp. 67–68, estimates a company strength of eighteen players, four of whom are boys, for the entire production of *Tamburlaine* Part I.

10. Una M. Ellis-Fermor, ed., *Tamburlaine the Great*, in the Methuen series *The Works and Life of Christopher Marlowe*, gen. ed. R. H. Case (London, 1930), p. 41.

11. Frederick S. Boas, *Christopher Marlowe: A Biographical and Critical Study* (Oxford, 1940), pp. 88, 100.

12. Levin, *Overreacher*, p. 35.

13. Shakespeare, *Henry V*, Prologue to Act I.

14. Lecture by Alfred Harbage, English 125a, "Tudor Drama," Harvard University, 1957–1958.

15. Wilson, *Marlowe and Shakespeare*, pp. 20–24.

16. Some studies which emphasize the subjective element in Marlowe's creation of his power-seeking Scythian are Paul H. Kocher, *Christopher Marlowe: A Study of His Thought, Learning, and Character* (Chapel Hill, N. C., 1946); Una M. Ellis-Fermor, *Christopher Marlowe* (London, 1927), pp. 24–60; John H. Ingram, *Christopher Marlowe and His Associates* (London, 1904), pp. 110–112; Ingram, *Marlowe and His Poetry* (London, 1926), pp. 42f; and Levin, *Overreacher*, pp. 30–54.

17. Roy W. Battenhouse, *Marlowe's Tamburlaine: A Study in Renaissance Moral Philosophy* (Nashville, Tenn., 1941), pp. 248–253; see also Leslie Spence, "Tamburlaine and Marlowe," *PMLA*, 42: 604–622 (1927).

18. Wilson, *Marlowe and Shakespeare*, pp. 18–19; see also Kocher, *Marlowe*, pp. 69–70.

19. Farnham, *Medieval Heritage*, p. 269.

20. Don Cameron Allen, "Renaissance Remedies for Fortune: Marlowe and the *Fortunati*," *SP*, 38: 188–197 (1941); Carroll Camden, Jr., "Tamburlaine: The Choleric Man," *MLN*, 44: 430–435 (1929); and Johnstone Parr, *Tamburlaine's Malady and Other Essays on Astrology in Elizabethan Drama* (University, Ala., 1953), pp. 3–23.

21. Katherine Lever, "The Image of Man in *Tamburlaine*, Part I," *PQ*, 35: 421–427 (1956).

CHAPTER XV: *The Jew of Malta*

1. T. S. Eliot, "Marlowe," *Selected Essays, 1917–1932* (New York, 1932), pp. 104–105; also available in *Elizabethan Essays* (London, 1934) and *The Sacred Wood*, 6th ed. (London, 1948).

2. Spivack, *Allegory of Evil*, pp. 346–353. My discussion of *The Jew* inevitably

owes much to Spivack's brief but incisive analysis of Barabas' position in the history of the Vice.

3. H. S. Bennett, ed., *The Jew of Malta*, in the Methuen *Works of Marlowe* (London, 1931), p. 19.

4. C. F. Tucker Brooke, ed., *The Works of Christopher Marlowe* (Oxford, 1910), pp. 231–232.

5. Margarete Thimme, *Marlowes "Jew of Malta"* (Halle, 1921), pp. 8–17.

6. Bennett, ed., *The Jew*, pp. 6–9. In the diction of the play, Bennett finds little evidence to support Fleay's view that Thomas Heywood contributed some scenes.

7. J. C. Maxwell, "How Bad is the Text of 'The Jew of Malta'?" *MLR*, 48: 435–438 (1953).

8. Bakeless, *Tragicall History*, I, 334.

9. Ethel Seaton, "Fresh Sources for Marlowe," *RES*, 5: 385–401 (1929).

10. Boas, *Marlowe*, pp. 131–132. Passi was first suggested by C. F. Tucker Brooke, "The Prototype of Marlowe's Jew of Malta," *London Times Literary Supplement* (June 8, 1922), p. 380.

11. Bennett, ed., *The Jew*, p. 12.

12. See Irving Ribner, "Marlowe and Machiavelli," *CL*, 6: 348–356 (1954).

13. See, for example, A. H. Bullen, ed., *The Works of Christopher Marlowe* (Boston, 1885), I, xl–xli; and Wilson, *Marlowe and Shakespeare*, pp. 64–66. See also Bennett, ed., *The Jew*, pp. 15–19.

14. Spivack, *Allegory of Evil*, p. 349.

15. See Craik, *Tudor Interlude*, p. 51.

16. Quoted to much the same effect in Spivack, *Allegory of Evil*, p. 351.

Chapter XVI: *Edward II*

1. H. B. Charlton and R. D. Waller, eds., *Edward II*, in the Methuen *Works of Marlowe* (London, 1933), p. 55.

2. Charlton and Waller, eds., *Edward II*, pp. 32–36.

3. See Lawrence, *Stage Studies*, pp. 68–70.

4. Michael Drayton, *Mortimeriados. The Lamentable ciuell warres of Edward the Second and the Barrons*; in *The Works of Michael Drayton*, ed. J. William Hebel (Oxford, 1931), I, 305–392.

5. Charlton and Waller, eds., *Edward II*, p. 47.

6. See Charlton and Waller, eds., *Edward II*, p. 47: "So much devotion and so cruel a desertion, so much gentleness at the beginning and such callous hypocrisy at the end, go badly together; and critics have often complained with some reason of Marlowe's handling of the character."

7. See Wilson, *Marlowe and Shakespeare*, pp. 95–98.

8. *Richard III*, III, vii, 50.

Chapter XVII: *The Conflict of Conscience* and *Doctor Faustus*

1. Greg, ed., *Doctor Faustus*, pp. 1–14.

2. Lily B. Campbell, "*Doctor Faustus*: A Case of Conscience," *PMLA*, 67: 219–239 (1952).

3. Spivack, *Allegory of Evil*, p. 474, n. 9. These similarities between Philologus and Faustus may suggest only that Marlowe was familiar with Woodes's source,

the autobiographical narrative of Francesco Spira, rather than with Woodes's play.

4. See Chapter IV, above, and Celesta Wine, "Nathaniel Wood's [*sic*] *Conflict of Conscience*," *PMLA*, 50: 661–678 (1935).

5. Spira is perhaps best known because of John Bunyan. Spira's spiritual sufferings brought Bunyan to the verge of despair. See John Bunyan, *Grace Abounding to the Chief of Sinners,* ed. John Brown (Boston, 1888), para. 163.

6. Leslie M. Oliver, "John Foxe and *The Conflict of Conscience*," *RES*, 25: 1–9 (1949).

7. William A. Jackson, "Woodes's *Conflict of Conscience*," *London Times Literary Supplement* (September 7, 1933), p. 592; corrected on a bibliographical error by W. W. Greg in a later issue of *LTLS* (October 26, 1933), p. 732. See also Wine, *"Conflict of Conscience,"* *PMLA*, 50: 661; *The Conflict of Conscience,* ed. Herbert Davis and F. P. Wilson (London, 1952), introduction; and Spivack, *Allegory of Evil,* pp. 238–239.

8. Spivack, *Allegory of Evil,* p. 239.

9. F. S. Boas, ed., *Doctor Faustus,* in the Methuen *Works of Marlowe* (London, 1932), pp. 6–15; and Greg, ed., *Doctor Faustus,* pp. 1–14.

10. Havelock Ellis, ed., *Christopher Marlowe,* Mermaid Series (London, 1887), p. xxxvii. Italics mine.

11. Wilson, *Marlowe and Shakespeare,* pp. 69–70.

12. See Bullen, ed., *Works,* I, xxviii-xxix, for the view that "Marlowe never attempted to write a comic scene."

13. Greg, ed., *Doctor Faustus,* pp. 15f; and Wilson, *Marlowe and Shakespeare,* pp. 70–74. Cf. Albert Feuillerat, *The Composition of Shakespeare's Plays* (New Haven, 1953), pp. 13–17.

14. Wilson, *Marlowe and Shakespeare,* p. 74.

15. See Robert Ornstein, "The Comic Synthesis in *Doctor Faustus,*" *ELH,* 22: 165–172 (1955). Cf. Percy Simpson, *Studies in Elizabethan Drama* (Oxford, 1955), pp. 107f.

16. See Greg, ed., *Doctor Faustus,* for parallel texts. The scene numbers refer to the A-text; the B-text is printed in acts and scenes. Quotations and references in this chapter are to Baskervill and others, eds., *Elizabethan and Stuart Plays,* pp. 349–373.

17. Greg, ed., *Doctor Faustus,* pp. 29–62.

18. Roland M. Frye, "Marlowe's *Doctor Faustus*: The Repudiation of Humanity," *SAQ,* 55: 322–328 (1956).

19. On *Faustus* as an ethical play, see Joseph T. McCullen, "Dr Faustus and Renaissance Learning," *MLR,* 51: 6–16 (1956).

20. Campbell, "A Case of Conscience," *PMLA,* 67: 219f.

Index